CRISIS IN BLANC AND WHITE

CRISIS IN BLANC AND WHITE

URBANIZATION AND ETHNIC IDENTITY IN FRENCH CANADA

Richard Dalton Basham

G.K.HALL&CO.
70 LINCOLN STREET, BOSTON, MASS.

SCHENKMAN PUBLISHING COMPANY
Cambridge, Mass.

Library of Congress Cataloging in Publication Data
Basham, Richard Dalton.
  Crisis in blanc and white.

  Bibliography: p.
  Includes index.
  1. French-Canadians — History. 2. Québec (Province) —
History — Autonomy and independence movements.
3. Canada — English-French relations. 4. Urbanization —
Québec (Province). 5. Biculturalism — Québec (Province).
I. Title.
F1053.B29   1978   971'.004'41   78-16950
ISBN 0-8161-8251-5

This publication is printed on permanent/durable acid-free paper
MANUFACTURED IN THE UNITED STATES OF AMERICA

To Jean-Paul Desbiens, André Laurendeau, René Lévesque, Claude Ryan, Pierre Trudeau, and Pierre Vallières, who may not all desire independence but who should provide ample proof to French and English Canadians alike that there is little reason to fear the consequences of separation should it ever become a reality.

CONTENTS

PREFACE

Events move quickly when a people regains a sense of destiny. Such is the state of Québec today. Long isolated in a corner of the North American continent, the essentially rural society of French Canada only truly began to urbanize and industrialize in the first half of the twentieth century. When industrialization and the movement to cities came it was directed not by an indigenous French Canadian middle class but by Britains, English Canadians, and Americans.

Drawn rudely from the security of an isolation which had insulated them from the rest of the continent, French Canadians found themselves incorporated at the lowest level of North American industrial society. Foreign economic domination produced in essence an ethnic proletariat under constant pressure to assimilate to the dominant English-language culture of North America. Wrenched from isolation and faced with powerful assimilative pressures, French Canadians have been forced to search within themselves for individual and collective solutions to their inescapable dilemmas: Can an acceptable French identity be forged in North America today? If so, can it be achieved within Canada or must French Canadians dissolve the Canadian bond and create a separate, independent French state?

On November 15, 1976, the citizens of Québec flocked to the

polls to elect a new government. As the results trickled in, English Canada shuddered. From 30 percent of the vote and 6 seats in the 1973 election, René Lévesque's separatist *Parti Québécois* had managed to poll 41 percent of Québec's votes and gain 69 of the 110 seats in Québec's National Assembly. In contrast, the ruling Liberals' share of Québec's electorate declined from 55 percent and 102 legislative seats in 1973 to 34 percent of the vote and 28 seats. Even liberal Premier Robert Bourassa lost his seat in the *Parti Québécois* landslide.

After the initial shock of the election many English Canadians have sought comfort in what may soon seem only technicalities: that the majority of Québec voters do not appear to favor separation, that the *Parti Québécois* victory represented a rejection of the Liberals, not an endorsement of its separatist goals, and that in any event Québec could not separate without approval from Ottawa or even from London. Most seem to feel that a bit of tinkering, or at most a reworking, of the British North America Act is all that is needed to resolve Canada's latest crisis. Such is not the case. While most *québécois* probably do not yet favor independence and would reject it in a referendum held today, they will have several years to adjust to separatist government before the *Parti Québécois* places the matter before the electorate. For many, English and French alike who have followed the growth of Québec's sense of self and the frustrations faced by *québécois* within Canada, separation seems a logical and reasonable culmination to events set in motion long, long ago. For others, separation of Québec from Canada conjures up nightmares of the absorption of what will remain of Canada into the United States, of a revolutionary or fascist Québec, or, even, of the communal wars of Ireland or Lebanon. Whatever the outcome, now is not the time for threats of economic, political, or military retaliation to thwart the will of Québec's people. It is a time for long-delayed understanding which I hope this book will help to provide.

ACKNOWLEDGMENTS

I would like to express my deepest gratitude to Professors George DeVos and Alan Dundes for their brilliant, stimulating seminars, to Professor James N. Anderson for his guidance and willingness to sponsor my independent study, to Professor Neil J. Smelser for taking me on as an additional burden to a very heavy schedule and providing an incisive critique to the first draft of this book, and to the Ford Foundation for providing support for my graduate study and the research which underlies this book.

FRENCH CANADA IN CRISIS

1

Fàce [sic] à l'arrogance du gv. fédéral et de son valet Bourassa, fàce [sic] à leur mauvaise foie évidente, le FLQ a donc décidé de passer aux actes.

Pierre Laporte, Ministre du Chômage et d l'Assimilation a été execute [sic] a 6.18 ce soir par la cellule Dieppe (Royal 22^{iem}) [sic].

Vous trouverez le corps dans le coffre du Chevrolet vert (9J2420) à la base de St-Hubert.

Nous vaincrons
FLQ

PS Les exploiteurs du peuple Québecois n'ont qu'a [sic] bien se tenir" (La Presse; 26 Fevrier 1971:A1).

Faced with the arrogance of the Federal Government and its lackey Bourassa, faced with their obvious bad faith, the FLQ has thus decided to move to action.

Pierre Laporte, Minister of Unemployment and Assimilation was executed at 6:18 tonight by the Dieppe cell (Royal 22nd). You will find his body in the trunk of the green Chevrolet (9J2420) at the end of St. Hubert.

We will win,
FLQ

P.S.: The exploiters of the Québec people take notice.

With this announcement the people of Québec learned that the *Front de Libération du Québec* had moved from its years of bombings and political manifestos into the realm of political murder. This document leading to the grisly dénouement of the October crisis contains the essential elements of French Canadian reality as seen by most radical *québécois:* the themes of the vendu, or the "sell-out," and, implicitly, of the "roi-nègre," the "nigger king," which the English have always sought and found to aid them in their goal of efficient exploitation of Québec's people. From the reference to Québec's Premier Robert Bourassa as a "valet" of the Federal Government, through reference to the assassinated Minister of Manpower and Immigration as the "Minister of Unemployment and Assimilation," to the reference to the group performing the "execution" as the "Dieppe cell" (Royal 22^{iem}) evoking memories of French Canadian losses in the disastrous raid upon that French coastal city in the summer of 1942, and the theme of Anglo-American imperialism and crushing exploitation of Québec's common man made possible by collaborators within his midst, the broad outlines of radical and, even, liberal Québec thought are drawn, drawn on a message indicating where the logic of their alienation has led.

For most Americans and some Canadians the kidnappings of October of 1970 were as incomprehensible as the exploding mailboxes in Westmount during the preceding decade. What had happened to the Québec of the travel posters, to the society walled within itself into a curious amalgam of the twentieth and seventeenth centuries, to the people in the process of assimilation to the English continent of North America? Had this people suddenly decided to reverse its death-train rushing toward the melting-pot and form a state of its own?

While Americans may have been puzzled to discover the crisis of a nation, heretofore considered serene, in its evening news and covering its magazines, few Canadians were. Understanding or not, almost every Canadian knew that something was happening in Québec, that it certainly was a province "pas comme les autres," although the familiar English Canadian cry "What does Quebec want?" indicated that few knew exactly what Québec really sought. Complicating things still further, different *québécois* wanted different things.

Suddenly all Canadian eyes are upon Québec and it is *the English Canadians* this time who speak most pleadingly of bilingualism and *bonne entente*. Why? The answer is disarmingly simple: French Quebekers are in the midst of a revitalization movement in which they have decided to take their collective destiny into their own hands, to assume full control of a society which is already de facto separate from the rest of the continent. The only real question is how best to do it: within Canada or within a separate French nation?

The Québec of the 1970's is a society alive with a sense of self, a society reveling in a first taste of freedom and unwilling to turn back to the days which English Canadians may now remember as the "good old days" but which many, many *québécois* now can only see as days of suffocation. The significance even of the word *québécois* reveals this new level of conscience: no longer do many French Quebekers refer to themselves as "Canadiens français" but as *"québécois,"* as citizens of what is to English Canada a "province" but to them is an "état." It is no accident that today's provincial assembly is called "l'Assemblée nationale," or that one hears the word "nation" roll easily from the lips of its citizens in designating Québec.

Québec today is a society divided more than ever before into its "two solitudes," English and French, but its French are no longer resigned to inferior status. This is not to say that every *québécois* is a revolutionary separatist, far, far from it, or that every *québécois* is a separatist, far from it, but only now that these options, and especially the latter one, are no longer so deviant as they once were. When a book such as Léandre Bergeron's *petit manuel d'histoire du Québec,* a revolutionary separatist interpretation of the history of the province, heads the best-seller list for the better part of a year, it is time to realize that the unthinkable is no longer so. Even today's reasonable man thinks long and hard of separation. When men of the stature of René Lévesque and Marcel Rioux declare themselves separatists it is a warning to those who think of men seeking Canada's dismemberment as occupants of a "lunatic fringe" that those days are gone. As Rioux (1971), who is perhaps Québec's leading sociologist, offered in the foreword to his recent book, *La Question du Québec:*

> Being a sociologist by profession I have examined some aspects of Québec culture and society. One will find in certain pages the perspective of a sociologist. In others, one will find that of a *Québécois* who has opted for the independence of his country.
>
> No one can remain in his ivory tower when questions which are a matter of life or death to his country are concerned. There comes a time when one must take a public stand. This little book gives me a chance to do so. (1971: 7-8).[1]

Québecois[2] today account for approximately 82 percent of the population of the province and for two-thirds of Montréal, the world's second largest French-speaking city. Numerically, Québec is their province. Financially, however, it is controlled by English-speaking interests. In fact, the earnings of French Canadians, *in their own province of Québec,* rank twelfth of the province's fourteen ethnic groups. Those male wage earners, engaged in non-agricultural occupations, of British, Scandinavian, Dutch, Jewish, even Ukrainian ancestry, all earn greater incomes than do the French. Only the Italians and American Indians earn less than the descendants of the original European settlers of "la belle province."

In 1968, a new political party, the *Parti Québécois,* led by René Lévesque, was founded in Québec with the sovereignty of the province "at the same time its end and means" (Lévesque, 1970:9). Proposing an independent Québec within a Canadian common market if possible, or, if necessary, an independent Québec free of all ties with English Canada, the *Parti Québécois* entered the April, 1970, provincial elections with three other major parties after less than two years of existence and gained 23.1 percent of all votes cast and nearly 30 percent of those cast by *québécois*. In 1973, in its second electoral outing, the *Parti Québécois* won 30 percent of the total Québec vote to become the official opposition party. Encouraged by the number of *québécois* willing to confide their future in a party scarcely established, the *Parti Québécois* has concentrated on preparing for future elections, claiming as a reasonable goal the gaining of enough seats to form a government by the end of the decade.

In 1972, the Montreal unit of *La Société Saint-Jean-Baptiste*—the national society of French Canada—announced a drive for 200,000 signatures on a petition demanding recognition of French as the *sole* official language of the province and the elimination of parents' rights to educate their children in the language of their choice under Lionel Groulx's call "Notre état français, nous l'aurons!" ("We will have our French state!") (Le Devoir 25 mars 1972:3). Only a decade ago, its leaders in Québec began preparations—later aborted—to "celebrate" the 200th anniversary of the English victory on the Plains of Abraham under the theme: "Two centuries of progressive cooperation." On July 31, 1974, the nationalists finally had their way and French became the official language of Québec.

While the youth of the United States rebelled against the sterile patriotism of a generation which led them to Vietnam, the youth of Québec were if anything more patriotic, more loyal to their province than were their parents! Patriotism has even come to rival love as the major theme of its poets, authors and artists.

Suddenly, all Québec seems peopled by those who no longer recognize Canada as their homeland. Each new day seems to bring more men, more books, more newspaper articles in this tradition. Even its Premiers now feel free, or perhaps impelled, to invoke the spectre of separation in making demands upon the Federal Government. Perhaps it is only a passing fad, perhaps once English Canada has been fully awakened *québécois* will gain enough within Canada that they hesitate to leave. Perhaps, again, it is a matter which will not stop short of fruition. Perhaps one day soon English Canadians and Americans will awake to discover an independent French state in North America.

What has happened—is happening—in Québec? It is a long and at times complex tale and, as always, it is best to begin at the beginning. . . .

LA NOUVELLE FRANCE: THE SETTLEMENT AND DEVELOPMENT OF QUEBEC AS A FRENCH COLONY

2

The Discovery and Settlement of New France

"Je me souviens," "I remember," the motto of Québec, strikes deep to the orientation of a people much of whose identity has always been in the past. Its sight evokes a long tale of settlement and French Empire, followed by English conquest and the litany of struggle which followed. Most of all, however, "Je me souviens" reminds each French Canadian that he is a testimony to the survival of generations of French, Catholic forebears in a hostile, English continent.

To the citizens of Québec the past is always anchored in what Wade (1968:1) has called the "golden age of French Canada": the discovery and settlement of *La Nouvelle France* from Cartier's first explorations in 1535 until its loss to Britain in the Treaty of Paris in 1763. Although Jacques Cartier was preceded by Cabot, who in 1497 explored Labrador, Newfoundland and Cape Breton establishing an English claim to North America, his explorations of the St. Lawrence, the "great highway of continental penetration on which the life of Nouvelle-France was to be concentrated" (Frégault and Trudel, 1963:13), placed him in the forefront of the French explorers. Despite Cartier's explorations, which began in 1535, the French made no serious effort to establish a colony until the beginning of the seventeenth century when an abortive attempt was made to establish a settlement in Acadia. European struggle dominated the thoughts of French Kings and a general feeling prevailed—a feeling later exemplified by Voltaire's reference to Canada as "quelques arpents de neige"[1] —that the rewards of North America were slim compared to those to be gained in Europe.

The French government, partly through lethargy and partly through the populace's general lack of interest failed to undertake a rapid development of Canada. What colonial adventures were attempted were small and minimally financed and, at that, by private sources interested solely in the region's potential natural resources. The major reason for French interest in America—missionizing the Indians—offered to generations of French Canadians by the authors of the province's history texts[2] would seem to account for this were it not for the fact that others have reported less altruistic concerns as being predominant. Marc Lescarbot, a French lawyer who accompanied De Monts on his expedition to Acadia complained in his *Histoire de la Nouvelle-France,* published in 1612, that settlement of the colony was being delayed by pecuniary concerns:

> The usual questions asked us are: "Are there treasures, are there gold and silver mines?" while no one asks: "Are the people there disposed to hear the Christian doctrine?" As for mines there really are some but they must be worked with industry, labor and patience. (quoted in Frégault et Trudel, 1963, vol. 1:17).

While Lescarbot was exhorting his countrymen to make some sacrifices for their riches, a small colony at Québec, founded in 1608, was beginning to ply the fur trade under Samuel de Champlain. From the beginning, Champlain was forced to ally himself with various Indian groups, chiefly Algonquin and Huron, against the Iroquois to gain fur contacts. Although the French managed to defeat the Iroquois initially, the involvement of the young colony in this internecine warfare subjected it to the horrors of war-by-massacre and served to drain it of its limited resources.

Until 1627, the colony continued to be the preserve of men

whose objective was fortune through the monopoly of the fur trade.[3] In that year, the French Cardinal Richelieu formed an association known as the "Cent Associés" to develop a strong, Catholic colony.[4] In exchange for perpetual monopoly of the fur trade and control of all other commerce except fishing, the group was to transport two to three hundred men of all trades to the colony in 1628 and to augment the number each year such that by 1643 the colony would have a population of at least four thousand. In addition, the "Cent Associés" bound themselves to provide for the colonists' needs for their first three years as well as to either grant them cleared land and seed for planting or otherwise assure their employment (Frégault et Trudel, 1963, vol.1: 22-23).

The "Cent Associés," despite Richelieu's efforts, met early failure. Their first attempt at settlement, in 1628, failed when war broke out between France and England as Charles I came to the aid of French Protestants. An English fleet commanded by a Franco-Scottish Huguenot entered the St. Lawrence and placed Québec under siege. While Champlain was successfully resisting, the initial flotilla of the "Cent Associés" with its cargo of colonists arrived and, after capture, turned back toward France. The following summer the English ships again returned to Québec and, on July 20, 1629, entered the city as conquerors (Salone, n.d.: 34).

Immediately upon capture of Québec the conquerors set about removing representatives of the French Crown and Champlain, himself, was sent to England. Upon his arrival there, however, he received the welcome news that a treaty of peace had been signed nearly three months prior to the capture of Québec and that it would be returned to France.[5]

Upon their formation the "Cent Associés" had levied an assessment of three thousand livres against each of its members for support of the colony after which expense the colony was to be a self-supporting, revenue-producing operation. This sum, which would have amounted to no more than three hundred thousand livres even if all assessments were paid, stands paltry beside the estimated five hundred thousand livres (twenty thousand pounds sterling) spent by the founders of Massachusetts to transport only a thousand colonists to the American colony at approximately the same time (49).

Perhaps the company might have been more fortunate had not Richelieu insisted upon an immediate beginning of settlement in the midst of war with England. The capture of the seven ships of Claude de Roguemont with their two hundred colonists cost the company 164,720 livres. The following year the company devoted 130,976 livres to armaments of the colony, which was also lost when the English captured Québec. As only 30,000 livres remained in the treasury in 1631 the company as a whole ceased its efforts, leaving only a few of its members and greatly reduced resources to carry on (51).

As a result of its early crippling, the company was forced to turn its settlement responsibilities over to individuals to seek colonists at their own expense in return for the granting of fiefs. Perhaps the most successful illustration of this means of settlement was to be seen in the example of Robert Gifford, a physician who had spent some time in Canada before being captured by the English. Upon his return to France he sought a *seigneurie* from the "Cent Associés" and was granted a league of land along the St. Lawrence near Québec extending a league and a half into the interior in exchange for a payment of one ounce of gold upon each change of *seigneur* and the equivalent of his income for one year after giving in fief or rent all or a part of his lands (55).

After receiving his concession, Gifford, now the *Seigneur de Beauport,* sought his colonists in his native Mortagne by advertising large grants of land for those willing to work them. On June 4, 1634, Gifford embarked for Québec with some thirty or forty colonists, including wives and children. During the next several years, others, not all of whom were needed on his seigneury, responded to his offer so that eventually Gifford seems to have been personally responsible for the settlement of fully fifty families in New France. Following the concessions of Beauport and Beaupré, an equally successful *seigneurie* located to the west of Beauport, the company of the Hundred Associates, hoping to be able to meet the terms of their agreement with Richelieu in this manner, granted another score of feudal concessions. By 1660, however, only twelve hundred immigrants had arrived since the original founding of Québec in 1608. Since the "Cent Associés" had obligated themselves to provide four thousand colonists during the fifteen-year period from 1628 to 1643 alone, control of the colony was removed from their hands by Louis XIV in 1663.[6]

Administration of the Colony

Under Louis XIV's reign France displayed a renewal of interest in America. After removal of the colony from the "Cent Associés," he established, in May, 1663, the *Compagnie des Indies Occidentales* to which he granted sovereignty to all French possessions in the New World. For the colonists who had gained a great deal of independence—one might even say a limited democracy—under the lax administration of the Hundred Associates, the assumption of royal rule meant a loss of liberties which had heretofore been greater than those of the mother-country and may have seemed despotic (Groulx, 1960:78-79). In fact, Eccles (1968:26) has pointed out, Louis XIV's concept of royal absolutism was at the time a very progressive one. In effect, it meant that the individual's primary allegiance was to the society as a whole, an allegiance later expressed in such royal instructions to the colony's chief administrator as "the rich must nourish the poor" and in his instructions given to Champigny in 1686:

> His Majesty wishes him to know that his entire conduct must lead to two principal ends; one to ensure that the French inhabitants established in that country enjoy complete tranquility among themselves, and are maintained in the just possession of all that belongs to them, and the other to conserve the said inhabitants and to increase their numbers by all means possible.

> His majesty wishes him to visit once a year all of the inhabitants between the Gulf and Island of Montreal to inform himself of all that goes on, pay heed to all the inhabitants' complaints and their needs, and attend to them as much as he possibly can, and so arrange it that they live together in peace, that they aid each other in their necessities and that they be not diverted from their work. (Eccles, 1968:14).

The administration of the colony was redesigned in the mold of a French province, with tripartite rule vested in a governor, intendant, and a Superior Council composed of the intendant and governor, the bishop, the attorney-general, a secretary and twelve other members holding royal appointments. Until 1726, the colony was governed primarily by the governor and intendant through a Superior Council which combined legislative, executive, and judicial functions. After that date, the Council receded in importance and effective rule was exercised through the offices of the intendant and governor.

New France was ideally to be governed by two heads: the governor and the intendant, or provincial administrator. Apparently the King's minister, Colbert, assumed that the relations between the two officials would follow the course of France in which the governors generally abandoned their powers to the intendant. What he had apparently not foreseen, however, was that, since the tendency for abdication of the governor's effective rule was largely the result of the vacation of their province by provincial governors to assume roles as courtiers in Versailles, the governor was in a very real sense trapped in New France with no place to which to withdraw. Not surprisingly, the overlapping powers of the two parts represented continual sources of friction throughout the colony's history.

Colbert's selection of intendant in the appointment of Jean Talon, further aggravated conflict between intendant and governor, as Talon, having the confidence of Colbert and not being inclined to accept a secondary role, felt free to extend the general mandate of the intendant beyond its traditional vague powers of general administration, control of commerce and the police, and impinge deeply upon those held by the governor and *counseil souverain* (Salone, n.d.:151-152; Groulx, 1950:81-82). Further adding to the executive division of the colony was the arrival in 1659 of Bishop François de Laval-Montmorency, an ultramontane who felt no need for the Church's removal from secular concerns. Indeed, Laval's influence was to become so great, causing the removal of three intendants including Jean Talon himself, that it is questionable whether effective secular control was not largely abandoned to the image of theocracy so deeply held by the Jesuits. Certainly the Church early gained control of the moral life of the colony as described by Baron de Lahontan:[7]

> Here we cannot enjoy ourselves, either at play or in visiting the ladies, but 'tis presently carried to the Curate's ears, who takes public notice of it in the Pulpit. His zeal goes so far, as even to name the Persons; and since he refuses the Sacrament of the Holy Supper to Ladies of Quality, upon the most slender Pretences, you may easily guess at the other steps of his Indiscretion. You cannot imagine to what a pitch these Ecclesiastical Lords have screw'd their Authority: They excommunicate all the Masks, and wherever they spy 'em, they run after 'em to uncover their Faces, and abuse 'em in a reproachful manner: In fine, they have a more watchful eye over the Conduct of the Girls and married Women, than their Fathers and Husbands have. They cry out against those that do not receive the Sacrament once a Month; and at *Easter* they oblige all sorts of Persons to give in Bills to their Confessors. They prohibit and burn all the books that treat of any other Subject but Devotion. When I think of this Tyranny, I cannot but be inrag'd at the impertinent Zeal of the Curate of this City. This inhumane Fellow came one day to my Lodging, and finding the Romance of the Adventures of *Petronius* upon my Table, he fell upon it with an unimaginable fury, and tore out almost all the Leaves. This book I valued more than my Life, because 'twas not castrated (i.e., it was unexpurgated); and indeed I was so provok'd when I saw it all in wrack, that if my Landlord had not held me, I had gone immediately to that turbulent Pastor's House, and would have pluck'd out the Hairs of his Beard with as little mercy as he did the Leaves of my Book. These animals cannot content themselves with the Studying of Mens Actions, but they must likewise dive into their Thoughts. By this Sketch, Sir, you may judge what a pleasant Life we lead here. (Thwaites 1905, Vol. 1:89-90).

The decision to assume royal control over the colony was apparently prompted by the realization that the French colony could not long survive any serious attempt on the part of the English to take possession of it in its current state. If a French territory was to be maintained in North America then substantial colonization would have to be undertaken. For the first time emphasis shifted from immediate commercial venture toward maximum population growth through immigration and indigenous fertility. Soldiers garrisoned in the province were encouraged to remain, marry, and take up farming. Louis XIV ordered a fine levied against all fathers who had not married their sons by the age of twenty and their daughters by the age of sixteen. If after reaching these ages the children were not married it was the father's duty to regularly present arguments as to why they were not to the council. To provide further inducement royal grants were given to those males who married early, and pensions were provided to those with large families. Whether result of such official sanction or no, the phenomenal growth rate characteristic of French Canada manifested itself early in Talon's report that the country "is full of native-born Frenchmen; the women are pregnant almost every year" (quoted in Salone, n.d.:170).

After the King assumed more direct responsibility for the colony French Canada blossomed into what was virtually a seventeenth-century welfare state, where the welfare and propagation of the colonists was of paramount concern. When the new colonists arrived to take their place among the other farmers and tradesmen of Québec they were fully cared for for a period of at least a year and often longer at the expense of the Crown. If, for example, once a man had begun the task of clearing the land and beginning cultivation he found himself unskilled in the task of farming he had recourse to instruction from aged farmers who were established in the outskirts of Québec to give aid to novices. Royal grants were also available to "persons of quality," to encourage them to settle and aid in the development of New France and, as additional inducement to those of wealth and influence to concern themselves with New France, Louis XIV began to distribute royal titles to those who distinguished themselves in this regard (173-178).

Ironically, one of the problems that had to be overcome in providing for the new settlers was the very basic one of where they should live. Under the old Hundred Associates a number of grants had been assigned to absentee landlords and much of the most fertile land along the St. Laurent remained uncleared and unavailable for settlement.

In order to provide suitable land for the new colonists it was obviously necessary to regain the property in the hands of these absentee landlords. By a decree issued in the *Conseil d'Etat,* March 21, 1663, the inhabitants of Québec were given six months to clear their concessions after which the land not under or not yet ready for cultivation was to revert to the crown. Unfortunately, the order was written in such a manner as to deprive many hard-working colonists of their land, as the decree did not take cognizance of the problems of settling in a new country where the task of clearing the land, difficult in itself, was interrupted all too frequently by Indian wars and by the myriad of other tasks incumbent upon the new colonists. As a result, the decree was ignored through legal manipulation (Salone, n.d.:180-181). Talon, sensing the importance of hastening the development of the country, was able to obtain a new royal order which clarified the situation and was to have resulted in the seizure of approximately half the land granted during the previous decade and its redistribution to those persons who were willing and able to clear and utilize it. Although some redistribution took place, primarily in the form of attenuation of the size of various holdings, Talon's departure prevented the kind of major revamping Louis XIV apparently had in mind (181-183).

In 1674, the *Compagnie des Indies Occidentales* reached the end of its resources and Louis XIV assumed full control of the colony. Engaged as he was, however, in the War of the Spanish Succession, he was unable to continue the vigorous support of the colony only so recently instituted, and the population fell back once again to augmentation of its members primarily by birth.

The Social Order of New France

Throughout the French Regime the society of New France was divided along lines of social status and degree of allegiance to France. The numerical importance of representatives of the Crown —the arrival of one military contingent of one thousand men, in 1665, itself, represented a one-third increase in the total population—all of whose officials were ranked in relation to one another, and the fact that the entire male population was formed into militia companies[8] resulted in a somewhat formal hierarchical

arrangement of the colony's male population. Concern with hierarchical ranking, apparently not limited to the upper segments of
the society, was of overwhelming importance to most of its
citizens:

> In all ranks of society there was a keen desire for status, for
> a title of office of some sort, from a seat on the Sovereign
> Council to the post of town crier. Many of the posts carried no
> salary, or a very low one, but it made no matter. If anyone
> was presumptuous enough to protest his inadequate salary or
> perquisites, he was informed he could resign. There were
> always others eager for the appointment. A keen awareness of
> the subtle distinctions in status was heightened as the number
> of posts and gradations in rank increased over the years. This
> was manifested continually by everyone, from the governor-
> general to rural church wardens. The governor-general quar-
> relled with the senior military officers over the type of salute
> he was to receive on tours of inspection; the intendant pleaded
> to be allowed to walk beside rather than behind the governor
> in processions; the governor of Montreal quarrelled bitterly
> with the bishop over the relative positions of their *prie dieus* in
> the parish church; the seigneurs disputed the right of captains
> of militia to occupy a certain pew; and the church wardens
> bickered continually over their exact place in religious cere-
> monies. Such things may seem ridiculous today but to the
> people of that age they were more important than money.
> (Eccles, 1968:25-26).

The importance of one's social status so greatly outweighed
pecuniary considerations for much of the population that individuals struggled to gain seigneuries, frequently not bothering
to collect the *cens et rentes* from those on their lands, even though
the responsibilities of a seigneur were such that most "had a hard
times making ends meet" (22) and certainly few, if any, seigneurs
could afford the luxury of not personally occupying themselves
with framing. The Colony, which had a greater number of nobles
in the mid-eighteenth century than all other French colonies
combined, also attracted a great number of individuals who,
apparently feeling secure from detection in their distance from the
mother-country, merely assumed titles and claimed their privileges. In 1684, a royal edict levying a fine upon any Canadian who
falsely claimed noble status was issued, but enforcement was

squelched by the intendant Champigny, who indicated "that there were many such in the colony, but in time of war he thought it unwise to initiate an enquiry lest it cool their ardour for military campaigns" (23).

A significant segment of the society, initially quite important if not dominant in its hierarchical structure, was composed of clerics and missionaries in various Catholic orders. Probably those Frenchmen most eager to come to Québec were members of religious orders imbued with the missionizing spirit of the Catholic counter reformation. By 1615, Recollets missionaries were beginning missionization of Indian groups along the St. Lawrence and by 1621 they had already completed a mission on the banks of the Charles River when they were joined by a group of Jesuits newly arrived from France. Not surprisingly, the major problem faced by the priests in their evangelical activities arose from opposition of the trading companies, who feared deep Indian involvement with the priests and even possible transmission of its pastoral doctrine (Reid, 1945:33-35). More significant for the Church's position within the society of New France, however, was the direction of the missionizing zeal of those who had crossed the ocean for Catholicism. During the early period, this zeal gave the colony a support which the Crown and trading companies could not, and it soon expanded into a virtual theocracy. As Wade has remarked:

> The Jesuits sought to establish in Canada the closed theocracy which they later achieved in Paraguay. . . . The fact that the superior of the mission was responsible only to the general of the order in Rome set the ecclesiastical life of New France in an ultramontane pattern which differentiated it sharply from the mother country with its gallic-minded clergy dependent upon the monarchy. (1968:15).

Indeed, so powerful had the Church become by the time of Louis XIV's assumption of royal control in 1663 that he included a reestablishment of civil authority as a matter of priority in Jean Talon's commission:

> It is absolutely necessary . . . to keep a proper balance between temporal authority, which resides in the person of the King and those who represent him, and spiritual authority, which

resides in the person of the Bishop and Jesuits, in a manner,
however, in which the latter's power is inferior to the former's.
(Voisine, 1971:15).

In time, with firm Crown support, French officials were able to
reestablish Gallic control over the Church and even expel clerics
whose presence was resented by the secular authorities. By the
time of the conquest, clerical power, strong as it was, primarily
derived from the strong religious devotion of most of the colonists.

The Rang Pattern of Rural Settlement

At the base of the colony's life lay its artisans, *coureurs de bois,*
and, especially, the mass of its *habitants,* the farmers who were to
become the backbone of the colony. Initially, the former groups
were of most importance as the colony's economy was firmly
tied to the fur trade. In time, however, with Louis XIV's decision
to begin settlement in earnest, the *habitant* became the basic
instrument of French claim to the land of New France and it was
he who, with his clergy, was to remain as a testimony to French
designs long after the Conquest.

Most important to the lives of the *habitants* and to the later
structure of French Canadian society was the development of the
rang system of settlement to meet the exigencies of the new
environment. The seigneurs, upon receiving their grants of land,
had to make them attractive for settlement, and in so doing had to
meet two principal needs: convenient transportation in a region
forested and without roads had to be provided, and settlement
had to proceed in such a fashion that individual families were
minimally exposed to the dangers which isolation would mean in
terms of Indian raids. The only ready solution to the problem of
transportation was to provide each *habitant* with ready access to
a river, while the exigencies of defense, and of companionship,
required some minimal clustering of farmhouses. The solution was
the development of the long, narrow farm lots peculiar to French
Canada arranged in a fashion known as the *rang.* In the beginning
of settlement each colonist was provided a lot with approximately
two hundred to two hundred fifty meters river frontage which
extended inland for an indeterminate distance. Houses were built

near the river centered in the narrow lots in such a fashion that the St. Lawrence came to assume the look of a "village street" on which Parkman later noted, "One could have seen nearly every house in Canada, by paddling a canoe up the St. Lawrence and the Richelieu" (quoted in Falardeau, n.d.:20). This solution was so logical in terms of the exigencies of the environment that when, in 1663, Louis XIV began his attempts to prevent the inhabitants from building their houses on their own land and to settle them in villages to be modeled upon the French wheel pattern, the *habitants* merely ignored these Royal edicts.

With the natural growth of the population the river frontage of the colony was soon exhausted such that by the late 1600's it was virtually impossible to find any available river frontage in New France. Soon second, and later additional, *rangs* were formed. The new *rangs* were laid out in essentially the same fashion as before, with the exception that their presence dictated a limitation of the length of the farm lots in previous *rangs* (of about one mile, yielding a length–width ratio of approximately 10:1, which became standard) and development of roads connecting fellow members of the same *rang*. At first, second *rangs* were formed in what was known as the *rang simple* pattern in which a single row of houses was arranged along a road and each settler found himself faced with woodland on the terminus of a lot of a member of the preceding *rang*. Soon, to alleviate isolation and to make road maintenance a simpler matter, *rangs doubles* were developed in which homes faced homes on opposite sides of the road. Thus, the "neighbourhood became more dense and the settlement began to take on the characteristics of an elongated village (*stassendorf*)" (Deffontaines, 1953:10).

The *rang* pattern of settlement brought with it numerous social ramifications. First, as primary interaction tended to be with those with whom one had ready access and, in the case of later *rangs,* with whom one shared responsibilities for maintaining the roads free of snow and in good condition, networks of social relations also tended to extend in an elongated fashion following the *rang.*[9] This sense of solidarity among neighbors, arising from the protection from Indians and solace from loneliness provided by one's neighbors during the long winters, resulted in close-knit neighbor ties best exemplified by the institution of *premier voisin,* or first neighbor, which:

> To the *habitant* . . . comes even before a relative; he is invited to all family gatherings, is consulted about important decisions, and helps out in all large projects. When a pig is slaughtered, he is given a piece, and when the bread is taken from the oven, a loaf is always sent over; if, on the other hand, some need arises, it is to the *premier voisin* that one has recourse. (12).

The *rang* also was not without its disadvantages. On the one hand it rendered much of farmwork quite difficult as, since properties extended in such an oblong fashion, much time and effort was wasted in transportation to and from the more distant portions of the lots. Furthermore, the narrow length of the lots made fencing a necessity if confusion on matters of property were to be avoided, and as a result much wood and labor were wasted in enclosing lots.[10]

Other important side effects of *rang* organization were the social equality it promoted among *habitants* and its discouragement of city development. *Rang* organization promoted social equality by providing an amazing degree of uniformity in extent of land holdings, and as a result of this uniformity no significant hierarchy among *habitants* ever evolved nor did any of the large estates so frequently established in newly settled regions develop. The adoption of *rang* settlement also served to retard development of villages of substantial size. For much of Québec's history, villages tended to consist solely of a Church, whose spire dominated the horizon, and the homes and businesses of a few tradesmen and of the older citizens of the area who, having passed on their farms to their children, retired to the small villages and Church-centered life (15-16).

While the *habitants* continued to reproduce and settle the virgin territory of the province, they did so under great hardship and without significant support from France. Despite the fact that the mother-country had twice the population of its chief colonial rival in the New World, England, its continual involvement in European wars and never-sufficiently-awakened interest led it— save for administrators and meager troop deployments—to abandon the colony. So meager was the amount of immigration provided by the home country that it is estimated that in the entire history of the colony immigration accounted for less than ten thousand colonists. Virtually all of the colony's growth which amounted to an increase from two hundred fifty inhabitants in 1635 to sixty-five thousand in 1763—insufficient as it was in the end to stave off English domination—came from natural reproduction (Henripin, 1954:13). That population was of paramount importance can be seen by the fact that even under conditions of internecine warfare with the English and their Iroquois allies—conditions which required the maximum possible mobilization of the population—the year 1714 saw only 4,484 men between the ages of fourteen and sixty and 628 soldiers and naval troops which could be mustered against English colonies already able to call upon upwards of 60,000 men (6). Little wonder that under the pincer land and sea tactics favored by the English (who approached Québec by land up the Hudson River Valley and through the Richelieu and by sea across the Atlantic and up the St. Lawrence), the colony eventually fell.

MAINTAINING A FRENCH IDENTITY IN THE BRITISH EMPIRE: COPING WITH FOREIGN DOMINATION

3

Aftermath of the Conquest

After a century of struggle with English colonists and the British nation a frightened Canadian people found itself finally prostrated before their armies. Remembering the sad lot of the deported Acadians and the militant protestantism of New England, the newly vanquished feared the worst. Surely the British would move quickly to attack their language, customs and, especially, their religion.

Surprisingly, the Conqueror showed himself immediately concerned with their welfare. Brigadier General James Murray, who became the military governor of Québec after Wolfe's victory on the plains of Abraham, responded with concern to the "miserable situation" of the Canadians after the Conquest:

> . . . to describe it is really beyond my powers and to think of it is shocking to Humanity. It has afforded the King's British Subjects an opportunity of exerting that Benevolence and charity inseparable form the Sentiments which the freedom of our laws of Church and state must ever inspire. The merchants and officers have made a collection of five hundred pounds Halifax currency and the Soldiers insist on giving one day's

provision in a month for the support of the indigent, without these aids many must have perished and still I fear (in spite of all we can do) a famine unless a supply of corn is sent from Montreal or the British Provinces. (Wade, 1968:48).

After a struggle which "had been long and without mercy . . . [in which] the official propaganda never ceased repeating to them that the English Conqueror would show no compassion" (Brunet, 1953:507), the colonists suddenly found themselves faced with benevolent rule. Soldiers paid for their purchases in cash, all possible care was taken to assure adequate market provision and an end to speculation of necessary goods, freedom of religion was recognized and British officers were told to indicate respect for Catholic religious processions. On the whole, rights of Canadians were so scrupulously attended to that an Englishman, sued by a colonist in a Québec court, found himself ordered to have the charge translated into English and to reply to it in French, as "such was the language of the country" (Wade, 1968:51). Such concern, motivated largely as it may have been by a desire to gain the colonists' loyalty, was more than they had received during most of the preceding French regime and certainly more than that exhibited during the latter years, when the name of the Intendant Bigot became synonymous with venality and subjugation of Canadians to French officials.

Certainly, however, the Conquest was not without immediate repercussions harmful to the colonists. Indeed, captured by people of different laws, religion and language—not to say temperament— a transition wholly favorable to the colonists would have indicated a benevolence rarely if ever seen in a victor. Yet, even the most fateful immediate result of the Conquest—the loss of the Colony's administrative and economic elite—cannot be wholly blamed upon the English.

A good portion of the loss of New France's bourgeoisie came in the direct wake of the Conquest as perhaps one thousand to twelve hundred of the colony's inhabitants chose to return to France rather than submit to British rule. Among those leaving the colony were the bulk of its administrators as well as much of its cultural and business elite. This exodus has assumed something of a mythic quality in French Canadian history: in desperate times the bourgeoisie deserted the poor *habitants* of North America, leaving them in the care of their only real allies, the clergy. Frances-Xavier Garneau mourned that: "The merchants, the lawyers, the old administrators, indeed most of the distinguished citizens who were still in the country left for France" (quoted in Brunet, 1958:56), while Michel Bibaud concluded that the loss of these individuals

> was all the more regrettable because of the fact that it took place in the highest class, the only at the time, with few exceptions, where there were to be found developed talents and educated men. The change was for the worse and in the arts and sciences it was long felt in the country. (56).

While there can be no doubt but that the colony did suffer some loss of its bourgeoisie as a result of emigration it seems evident today that the boats back to France may have been invested with more importance and talent than they in fact carried. It appears that the myth of total emigration of the colony's directing class served as a convenient excuse to explain the colony's easy capitulation and long period of stagnation. As Baby has noted in his study of the "Exodus,"

> 130 seigneurs, 100 gentlemen and bourgeois, 125 notable merchants, 25 legal authorities and lawyers (of whom several had belonged to the Superior Council), 25 to 30 doctors and surgeons, and nearly as many notaries

chose to remain in Québec (quoted in Wade, 1968:50). Indeed, it is apparent that most of the emigration was composed of French soldiers and administrators supplemented with perhaps no more than a hundred of the colony's leading *noblesse* who chose to return to France upon losing their roles in the fur trade and the military (50).

The loss of most of the colony's middle class should not be viewed as the result of massive emigration, but rather as a slow draining which resulted from a series of shocks. The first, and perhaps most profound, setback suffered by the business elite was the refusal of France to provide payment on approximately 41 million livres of paper currency held by the citizens of New France at the time of the Conquest (48). Economic ruin was everywhere and inventories stood drained without capital to re-plenish them. Adding to this ruin was the fact that large orders of many Canadian merchants remained stored in warehouses in France, unable to be delivered in French ships. As these inventories (most representing a year's order) were all that remained between many businessmen and total ruin, desperate efforts were made to gain their transportation to the colony. Several of the merchants journeyed to France and then to Britain only to meet British refusal to permit French ships to carry the merchandise and claims of the impossibility of sparing British ships for the task.[1] As the products were destined to the market of a colonial society, efforts to recoup losses by selling them on the French market produced little, and much was left to deteriorate in ware-houses. One of the merchants, Louis Perrault, desperate to avoid loss of his entire order, sailed to London where his offer to pay all tariffs on the merchandise was rejected, whereupon, he loaded it upon a ship and departed for Louisiana (Brunet, 1958:63-65).

Faced with the impossibility of continuing to transact business with the mother country, those French Canadian businessmen still able to continue sought contacts in Britain. Under the guidance of former French business associates, the merchants were directed to various British commerical outlets, many of which were owned by Frenchmen who had settled in England. Unfor-tunately for the future of an indigenous bourgeoisie, however, most of those contacts willing to deal on some level of credit with their new Canadian associates were of very little importance and as readily subject to bankruptcy as were their Canadian corres-pondents. The remaining French Canadian merchants:

> were only small businessmen with many irons in the fire but
> without relatives of importance and credit and of no influence
> in their own country. Moreover, their London contacts were
> not themselves among the most important in the city. These
> modest businessmen—those of London and those of the
> colony—were not of sufficient size to rival their English
> competitors. (68)

In contrast to the miserable state of the indigenous bourgeoisie, the newly arrived British merchants flourished and, not limiting themselves to the fur trade, invaded all business domains. Adding to the ease of the British commercial takeover of the colony was the fact that the burden of economic suffering was not distributed evenly over each social class and, thus, a wedge was driven between classes. Also in contrast to the lot of the middle classes was that of the farmer, which was brighter than ever in the years after the conquest. In 1773, demand for wheat forced the British Parliament to reduce tariffs on its import and its price quickly doubled on the Canadian market. This new-found prosperity served to provide additional evidence to the population that they had come under the domination of a people with good "business sense." The prosperity and relative freedom brought by the British were such that, as Mgr. Briand reported,

> Everything appears very peaceful to me here [Montréal] and I don't remember to have heard, since my departure from Québec, a single word of complaint against the government. The people and everyone in general appear to me to be as happy as if they had never known another. (78)

With the acceptance by the *habitants* of the new ruler and the fall of the middle classes, only two significant social groups remained which might have posed a threat to British government: the *seigneurs* and the clergy. Neither did, and each became a mainstay of foreign rule. As Rioux (1971:48) has noted in providing the answer to his question "The businessmen eliminated, what happened to the nobility?":

> The greatest cordiality soon reigned between seigneurs and English officers and the numerous marriages that the officers contracted in the colony testify to the intimacy of their relations . . . the wife of the chaplain of the Québec garrison remarked that French Canadian women demonstrated an "extreme penchant for English officers."

Finding themselves reduced in status in the eyes of their compatriots as a result of the French defeat and unfavorable comparison between past and present government, the *seigneurs* appear to have become collaborators with the largely military administrative bureaucracy of the post-conquest period. Its loss of prestige with the *habitants* eventually was translated to a loss in British eyes as well, however, as the *seigneurs* showed themselves unable to rally substantial numbers of colonists to repel the American invasion of the colony during the Revolutionary War.

More and more the British and the clergy turned toward each other for mutual protection: the clergy to safeguard the religion against the dangers of discriminatory laws likely to be promulgated if their support should appear lukewarm, and to protect itself against the new wave of republicanism beginning to manifest itself in America and France; the colony's administrators to gain the support of the one most reliable source of control over the province's *habitants*. The entrance into force of the Quebec Act in 1775 gave Catholics free exercise of their religion, "which was no longer to be an obstacle to preferment to any office or position, since a new form of oath was provided which did not offend Catholic principles" (Wade, 1968:64). Even the right to collect tithes was guaranteed in the Act, which also, in effect, granted French colonists virtual equality with the province's English inhabitants.

In general, with the exception of some support—and this largely centered in Montréal—for the American colonists during their revolution, most *habitants* appeared to be satisfied with their new nationality in the years immediately following the Conquest. Haldimand, the governor of Trois-Riviéres, wrote of the colonists' adaptation to the new political climate: "I am persuaded that they would be in despair were they to see a French fleet and troops arrive in this country in any number whatsoever; they begin to taste too well the sweets of liberty to be the dupes of the French" (quoted in Wade, 1968:76). Concern with learning the language of the new Empire was such that Mgr. Hubert, Bishop of Québec, announced the establishment of a free English parochial school in 1792, an adventure which sorely taxed the Bishop's resources but which was deemed necessary to prevent French children from frequenting Protestant schools. The complaint of the day among those attempting to learn English was that there were not enough English in the colony to make ready practice available! Brunet argues that it was this absence of English, at a time when assimilation might well have been favorably received, rather than any attempt to maintain a separate identity, which prevented assimilation. "There was not," he says,

> a total assimilation because there was not an assimilating core.
> Some Canadian families, with the means to do so, sent their
> sons to study in England or the United States. Charles-Michel
> de Salaberry used the English language to correspond with his
> father. (1958:109)

The British had gained a conquest of fantasy proportion: the
colonists and their priests expressed acceptance and often enthusi-
asm over the policies of their new rulers while the bourgeoisie
crumbled almost spontaneously without strenuous effort on the
part of their English competitors or the need for the promulgation
of punitive restrictions against them. As Brunet has concluded:

> For the Canadians of 1760, the Conquest led to a simple
> change in the succession to the throne. Louis XV had aban-
> doned the colony. The old king was dead. The new subjects
> of His British Majesty showed themselves ready to shout:
> "Long live King George." (1953:516)

Revival of Nationalist Sentiment

This easy acceptance of British dominance was not to last long.
During the American Revolution, fears that Québec might be lost
to colonists fighting as allies of France ran high among British
residents. These fears were especially strong among United Empire
Loyalists who fled to Canada in the years immediately following
the Revolutionary War and were further exacerbated by the outbreak of Revolution in France, and the subsequent Reign of
Terror. To the new immigrants especially, the French presence
came to represent all they had fled from in fear, and more:
"papism." "They were," Wade says,

> badly scared men, who had lived through one revolution in
> America and dreaded another in Canada as the old eighteenth-
> century order crumbled. Their nervousness led them to con-
> fuse a growing French-Canadian nationalism and North Ameri-
> can republicanism with a loyalty to France which had died
> with the Terror. (1968:93).

Their presence, coupled as it was with the realization that Britain
was engaged in a struggle for survival against republican France,
injected "an ethnic tension hitherto unknown in Canada . . . which
left its mark on the French-Canadian mind" (93).

Ethnic tensions became evident almost from the beginning of the entrance into force of the new constitution on December 28, 1791. Immediately, the French found themselves slighted in the new Assembly as, although only some ten thousand of the province's population of one hundred fifty-six thousand were English, sixteen of the fifty-six elected delegates were English-speaking. Ethnicity immediately became an issue as the choice of Speaker of the Assembly was taken into consideration. Jean-Antoine Panet was nominated by the French members, while William Grant, James McGill and Jacob Jordan were the candidates of the English. The nomination of Panet, the eventual winner, who operated with only a limited command of the English language, created an immediate stir. As one of the few French delegates who opposed him, Pierre-Louis Panet (a cousin) declared:

> There is an absolute necessity for Canadians to adopt the English language in time as it is the only means to dissipate the hostility and suspicion that the diversity of language will always maintain between two peoples united by circumstances and forced to live together. But while awaiting this happy revolution, I believe that decency demands that the orator whom we choose be able to express himself in the English language when he addresses the representative of our sovereign. (Chapais 1921, Vol. II:52) [2]

The wedge between French and English was driven further by the French Republicans' use of Vermont as a base for attempts to rally the colonists against their new masters. Rumors of a French fleet bound for Canada once again circulated through the province and civil disorders were widespread during the mid-1790's. Fears of massive Canadian support for a return to French rule, however, failed to materialize as the clergy stood firm against the religious changes wrought by Republican France. The bonds, Bishop Hubert wrote in a circular letter to his clergy,

> which attached them to France had been entirely broken, and that all the loyalty and obedience which they formerly owed to the King of France, they now owed to His Britannic Majesty . . . [and, furthermore, it was their duty] to drive the French from this Province. (Wade 1968:99)

Repugnance for the French Revolution had its effect as the assembly offered in 1799 to provide twenty thousand pounds to aid England in its war against France and, shortly thereafter, numerous French Canadians added their names to the patriotic fund designated to provide support for British arms.

The English-speaking business and appointed administrative elite of the colony, however, had not forgotten its minority fear and embarked on a course designed to minimize French influence and, hopefully, lead to assimilation. The French elected officials of the Assembly found themselves faced at every turn by the "chateau clique"—a group of British administrators and *seigneurs* who carefully dispensed favors and lucrative public offices to their members—in efforts to exercise the democratic rule guaranteed them.

The appearance of the journal *Le Canadien* added a strong voice to the growing feeling that the colonial administrative structure of the colony had gained an unjust power which it exercised to promote English interests. It reported instances of abuse of executive power and massive land speculation in which members of the chateau clique were engaged, chief among which was the granting of two million acres of land to English speculators in the wooded region between the St. Lawrence Valley and Vermont later to be known as the "Eastern Townships." The effects of laying out land along township rather than *rang* lines and advertising for settlers in American newspapers were the influx of English speakers and the long delay of natural French expansion into the area. At this time, many of the elected French officials began to fear that the goal of the British was "to drown the *Canadiens* while respecting all the while for form the liberal constitution which they claimed to have given to the *Canadiens*" (Bergeron, 1970: 77).

The 1807 elections produced several members of what had become the French party who, due to their modest financial situation, were unable to attend the sessions of the legislature. In order to remedy this a bill was introduced providing subvention funds for those whose presence required extended travel, a measure which was combatted by Judge DeBonne, leader of the *"chouayens,"* or *"vendus"* ("sell-outs") who had allied them-

selves with the English elite. In response to his opposition the
Assembly passed a bill excluding judges from sitting in the
Assembly. The bill was promptly rejected by the Legislative
Council. The *Parti Canadien,* or popular party, won a majority
in the Assembly in the elections of 1808 and 1810, but in both
cases, the fight over the seating of judges caused Governor Craig
to dissolve Parliament.

Several days after the dissolution of the session of 1810, Craig
seized the press of *Le Canadien* and imprisoned its printer. Troops
were marshalled in the streets of the city to assure order and three
of the paper's founders were jailed without trial. Frustrated with
his inability to control the elected Assembly of Lower Canada,
Craig wrote London complaining of the fact that the "Avocats
and Notaries" who predominated in the Assembly were attempting to cast off British rule—an endeavor in which he felt that they
had succeeded in gaining the alliance of the great mass of the
population. The members of the Assembly, he reported,

> consist mostly of a set of unprincipled Avocats, and Notaries,
> totally uninformed as to the Principles of the British Constitu-
> tion or parliamentary proceedings, which they profess to take
> for their Model, with no property of any sort, having every-
> thing to gain, and nothing to lose by any change they can
> bring about. . . . That these people have gradually advanced in
> audacity, in proportion as they have considered the power of
> France as more firmly established by the Successes of Bona-
> parte in Europe is obvious to every one, and that they are
> using every endeavor to pave the way for a change of Do-
> minion, and a Return under that Government, is the general
> opinion of all ranks with whom it is possible to converse on
> the Subject; Even the very few of the better sort of Canadians
> themselves who have sufficient information to be aware of the
> misery that would ensue on such an event. . . . Unfortunately,
> the great Mass of the people are completely infected, they
> look forward to the event, they whisper it among themselves,
> and I am assured that they even have a song among them,
> which points out Napoleon as the person who is to expel the
> English. . . . It seems to be a favourite object with them to
> be considered as [a] separate Nation; *La Nation Canadienne*
> is their constant expression, and with regard to their having
> been hitherto quiet & faithful subjects, it need only be
> observed that no opportunity has presented them an encour-

agement to shew themselves otherwise. (Kennedy 1930: 228-230)

Once again, however, the threat of war with the United States forced the British to conciliate its French colonists, and Craig's proposals to govern without an elected parliament were dismissed.

On the eve of the War of 1812, Craig was replaced by a new governor of Swiss-Huguenot extraction, Sir George Prevost. Prevost gained the all-important support of the clergy by formally recognizing the Catholic Bishop of Québec and granting him an annual salary of one thousand pounds. Thus, upon the outbreak of war in 1812, the Assembly voted financial support and Canadians rallied to resist the several feeble attempts made by the Americans to invade the province.

Despite support of the war, the Assembly showed itself disposed to inquire into abuses of the Legislative Council during Craig's "Reign of Terror" and in no mood to cease pressing its demand for control over the administration of the colony. Unfortunately, for the stability of the government, Prevost was recalled in 1815 to answer charges, largely promulgated by the chateau clique, that he had taken an unnecessarily cautious military stance during the war in limiting his efforts to the defense of the province.

Prevost was succeeeed by Sir Gordon Drummond, a man more in the mold of Craig. After Drummond's dissolution of the 1816 Assembly, Sir John Sherbrooke arrived in the colony to replace him and, hopefully, reestablish a stable government. Although his efforts to gain moderation were partially successful, the natural division of the colony between French colonists allied with a few English republican supporters—the leader of the popular party was, for a time, English—and the English merchant and administrative establishment continued to press toward violent confrontation.

That the good will of the colonists might easily have been won if the rights which their numbers granted them under British law had been respected may be seen in the eulogy pronounced upon the death of George III in 1820 by Louis—Joseph Papineau, the speaker of the Assembly and later the major figure in the 1837-38 Rebellion:

George III, a sovereign respected for his moral qualities and his
attention to his responsibilities, succeeded Louis XV, a prince
justly despised for his debaucheries and his lack of attention
to his people's needs, for his senseless prodigality for his
favorites and mistresses. Since that epoch the reign of law has
replaced that of violence, and the treasure, the navy, and the
army of Great Britain have been employed to provide us with
effective protection against external danger; since that day its
best laws have become ours, while our religion, our property,
and the laws by which they were governed have been pre-
served; soon after the privileges of its free constitution were
accorded to us, infallible guarantees of our domestic prosperity, if it is observed. Now religious tolerance, trial by jury,
the wisest guarantee which has ever been established for the
protection of innocence, protection against arbitrary imprisonment, thanks to the privilege of the *habeas corpus*, equal
protection guaranteed by law to the person, honor, and goods
of citizens, the right to only obey laws made by us and
adopted by our representatives, all these advantages have
become our birthright, and will be, I hope, the lasting heritage
of our posterity. To conserve them, let us act like English
subjects and free men. (Chapais, 1921 Vol. III:92-93)

Instead, however, of suggesting moderation, the control of the
Assembly by French interests only pressed the chateau clique to
seek support from London to negate it. The year 1820 was
marked by the arrival of the Governor Dalhousie, a man later to
be regarded simply as a tyrant by French Canadians, and a firm
determination of the Assembly to assume complete financial
control of the colony, borne of the discovery that the accounts of
the Receiver-General were ninety-seven thousand pounds short,
apparently as a result of land speculation. Fearing loss of the
power of the purse, the English administrators decided the time
had come to complete the project of union between Upper and
Lower Canada[3] to gain English control. When news of the introduction of the bill in Parliament reached Québec in the fall of
1822, a petition opposing it was signed by over sixty thousand
individuals, mostly with their marks, and delivered to London by
Louis-Joseph Papineau and John Neilson, a Scottish ally of
Papineau in his struggle for representative government. Faced with
the obvious opposition of the colonists to the project of unifica-
tion, it was defeated. Several years of tranquility followed, aided

by Dalhousie's temporary replacement as governor by Sir Francis Burton. Upon his return, Dalhousie again clashed with the Assembly on the matter of fiscal control and again prorogued the Assembly. Papineau promptly censured Dalhousie's address of dissolution and heated elections followed. Upon the elections, with their now familiar result, and the reelection of Papineau as speaker—a choice which Dalhousie refused to accept—the new Assembly was dissolved after a session of only two days. Again thousands of signatures were gathered against the Administration and presented to Parliament. In the midst of general turmoil and the beginning of political trials, Dalhousie was replaced by Sir James Kempt, who followed a policy of conciliation during his brief tenure, only to be replaced in the fall of 1830 by Lord Aylmer.

Aylmer attempted to calm the situation by offering Papineau and Neilson positions in the executive council, which they declined, and by including eight French Canadians among his first eleven nominees to the Legislative Council. On the crucial matter of revenue control he agreed to yield to Assembly priority on condition that a permanent civil list be accepted. The Assembly refused, contending that the spirit of an earlier report of the British House of Commons granted them full fiscal control. In the midst of this struggle three French Canadians were shot by troops in Montréal election riots, and indictments against the officers for the action were dismissed by a grand jury, to Aylmer's expressed delight. In a furor, the Assembly recessed without approving a budget which would permit the government to continue.

Further adding to the crisis was the realization by French Canadians that their province was becoming a dumping ground for immigrants fleeing poverty in the British Isles. Placed in timber ships as ballast for the return trip to Canada, most arrived in a state of such poor health that they were forced to become public charges. "The real crisis of the immigration situation," Wade reports,

> came in 1832 with an outbreak of Asiatic cholera brought by
> the newcomers which spread like wildfire along the St.
> Lawrence and decimated both immigrants and natives. Immi-

gration became, to certain wild French-Canadian eyes, an English conspiracy to wipe them off the face of the earth. (141)

The Assembly had had enough and arose in near rebellion. The 1834 session saw the introduction of the "ninety-two resolutions" designed to provide it with all the power of the British House of Commons. Upon the passage of the resolutions—two of which called for his impeachment—Aylmer dissolved the Assembly. The resulting elections brought the full head of radicalism as Papineau and his followers swept to victory and even such a formerly respected leader as Neilson was cast aside as being too moderate. In the face of certain conflict, a new governor, Lord Gosford, was appointed and dispatched to Canada as the head of a commission of inquiry. Gosford's conspicuous moderation, evidenced in such actions as his disbanding of the British Rifle Corps, a group of English Canadian irregulars dedicated to maintaining a British Union, succeeded to the degree that at one point Papineau found his majority reduced to a single vote. The ever-volatile situation soon changed, however, with the premature disclosure by the governor of Upper Canada of Gosford's policy of moderation and appeasement and the fact that he had no intention of recommending real reform. When Papineau received report of Gosford's intentions from the leader of the English reformists in Upper Canada he immediately transmitted it to the Assembly and once more confidence in the government waned.

Gosford's Commission presented its report to Parliament in early March, 1836, with recommendations that the principal demands of the Assembly—that the Legislative Council be elected and fiscal control be wholly vested in the Assembly—be rejected on the grounds that they would open the floodgates to further reform and possibly dissolution of the imperial tie. Rather than create substantive changes, however, the Commission suggested that the ends of order might be achieved by appointment, and subsequent co-option, of French leaders. Four days after the tabling of the Royal Commission report, Lord Russell presented ten resolutions based on the report which clearly rejected the ninety-two resolutions of 1834 and, in effect, rejected all efforts directed toward democratization of the Legislative Council and Assembly control of the province's revenues.

News of the acceptance of the resolutions by Parliament reached a Canada in the midst of depression and a people heavily sensitized to political issues. Province-wide assemblies were held to decide upon a response. The first of the assemblies, held in Saint-Ours on May 7, 1837, produced a decision to boycott goods imported from England and thus deprive the government of taxa⁻ tion revenues. Purchase of contraband imported from the United States was openly encouraged, the French Canadian deputies themselves taking the lead by dressing in clothes of obvious American origin. In addition, the Assembly accepted a series of resolutions prepared by the *Comité de control permanent des Patriotes de Montréal* labelling the British government as

> an "oppresive power, a government of force" which violates with impunity the constitution of the country . . . since the Russell Resolutions, [the *Patriotes*] no longer considered themselves bound to the English government except by force. (Bilodeau, *et al.*, 1971:340).

During the months of May and June, similar Assemblies sprouted throughout the province. Finally, in an attempt at reconciliation, Gosford called an Assembly only to find summoned before him men dressed "d'étoffe du pays" and in items of American contra- band, intransigent on all positions. A moderate resolution, agree- ing to provide funds for the continuation of the government on the condition of reforms, failed, while a resolution cosponsored by Papineau, informing London that if it carried out the Russell resolutions the Assembly would consider its loyalties to the Crown severed, passed. The Assembly of Lower Canada was then sus- pended for the last time.

The Rebellion of 1837-38

In response, several young *Patriotes,* André Ouimet, Amédée Papineau (son of Louis-Joseph), and Thomas Brown, born in New Brunswick and raised in the United States, organized a paramili- tary group, the *Fils de la Liberté.* Also at this time the *Patriotes* began to form parallel institutions. At Deux-Montagnes, a dozen miles to the northwest of Montréal, the population elected its own justices of the peace. War seemed imminent. On October twenty-third, five thousand persons assembled at Saint-Charles only to hear Papineau, all-too-aware of the imminence of hostilities, caution against legal efforts to gain control of the province. Events, however, had passed even Papineau by, and the day was carried by the suggestion of an English physician allied with the *Patriotes,* Wolfred Nelson, "that the time has come to melt our pewter plates and spoons to make balls from them" (Bergeron, 1970:92). The Assembly recessed with the recommendation that citizens of the Richelieu elect their own judges and that a constitutional convention be held to draft a new constitution for Québec.

Once again the Church leaders rallied to the side of the government. Mgr. Lortigue published a letter distributed throughout the province forbidding Catholics from complicity with the "rebels." In response, twelve hundred *Patriotes* marched before Montréal's Saint-Jacques Cathedral while Mgr. Bourget was booed on the Church steps in Chambly and *curés* elsewhere met with groups shouting the Marseillaise. On November 6, members of the English Doric club attacked a group of *Fils de la Liberté* as they were leaving a meeting and, gaining the battle, proceeded to sack the office of the Vindicator, a pro-patriot English-language newspaper. Gosford sent troops into the streets to prevent the attack from escalating into general battle and sought reinforcements from the Maritimes and from Upper Canada, which was experiencing similar troubles as its Assembly rebelled against the tight rule of the group known as the "Family Compact."

On November twelfth, public assembly was prohibited. Several days later arrest warrants were issued against twenty-six *Patriotes.* Papineau, O'Callaghan, Desrivières, Brown, and Perreault, among others, fled toward the Richelieu, while André Ouimet, president of the *Fils de la Liberté*, was arrested and thrown into prison. When the Montréal Volunteer Cavalry attempted to arrest several *Patriotes* at Saint-Jean they found themselves ambushed and fled.

The colonists began to form militias to overthrow the government. A planned attempt by the English to take Saint-Denis by surprise during the night of November twenty-second was turned to failure as the troops found themselves bogged down on a muddy side road and forced to attack during the day. Alerted, waiting *Patriotes* turned back the weary army. At Saint-Charles, two hundred *Patriotes* under the command of T. S. Brown fortified themselves in a manor, only to be decimated by British soldiers equipped with cannons. This battle crushed the resistance in the Richelieu as its survivors fled toward the United States to join Papineau and O'Callaghan, who had earlier fled to avoid capture. At this time, the only remaining *Patriote* group of any size gathered in the church at Saint-Eustache, near Deux-Montagnes, to await British attack. On December thirteenth, Colborne, with an army of two thousand regulars and volunteers, attacked the church, setting fire to the rectory and rear of the church and firing at the *Patriotes* as they attempted to escape. Chénier, the leader of the group, and seventy others were killed in this fashion, while many others perished in the fire. After the battle the church was desecrated, the town looted and burned, and the rebellion terminated for the remainder of the winter.

Despite the clergy's pleas for calm and the mid-winter arrival of troops from the Maritimes, hostilities broke out early the following year with an abortive invasion led by Nelson. Aroused by the events of the previous year into a political frenzy, *habitants* both within Canada and among those who had fled to the United States formed themselves into associations known as *Fréres Chasseurs,* whose intent was to lead insurrections throughout Upper and Lower Canada. After several minor battles which took place during the short post-harvest period, before the rigors of the Canadian winter fully set in, the *Patriotes* were totally defeated and the houses of known patriots in the region immediately south of Montréal placed in flames.[4]

Lord Durham's Report
In the midst of the Rebellion, on February 10, 1838, the British Parliament suspended the constitution of Lower Canada and named Lord Durham (John George Lambton) governor-general of Upper and Lower Canada and high commissioner to investigate the rebellion. Durham immediately faced the crucial problem of the fate of the imprisoned *Patriotes.* To submit them to trial by jury would have meant either certain conviction by a British

jury or certain acquittal by a French one. Choosing to avoid the problems due process would entail, he pardoned most of the prisoners and banished the major leaders still remaining in Canada. Opposition to this policy arose ostensibly on the basis of the lack of due process—although almost certainly anger over his lenience was the major factor responsible for it—and his ruling was reversed by London. Feeling that he had been subjected to a vote of no confidence, Durham resigned his commission and returned to Britain to write his report before passing even his first winter in the colony (Craig, 1963:iii–vi).

Despite his short tenure, Durham's grasp of the realities of Canada was amazingly perceptive, and his report, together with its recommendations for the union of the two Canadas, the final establishment of fully responsible government, and the eventual assimilation of the French, stands as a milestone in Canadian history. In his report, completed in January of 1839, Durham stated that he had expected to find in Lower Canada that:

> the original and constant source of the evil was to be found in the effects of the political institutions of the Provinces; that a reform of the constitution, or perhaps merely the introduction of a sounder practice into the administration of the government, would remove all causes of contest and complaint. (Craig, 1963:21)

Instead, to his chagrin, he found that a contest raged "between a government and a people":

> I found two nations warring in the bosom of a single state: I found a struggle, not of principles, but of races; and I perceived that it would be idle to attempt any amelioration of laws or institutions until we could first succeed in terminating the deadly animostiy that now separates the inhabitants of Lower Canada into the hostile divisions of French and English. (23)

"We are ready," said Durham,

> to believe that the real motive of the quarrel is something else and that the difference of race has slightly and occasionally contributed aggravated dissensions. . . . [But] the national feud forces itself on the very senses, irresistibly and palpably, as the origin or the essence of every dispute which divides the

community; we discover that dissensions, which appear to have another origin, are but forms of this constant and all-pervading quarrel; and that *every contest is one of French and English in the outset or becomes so ere it has run its course* [emphasis mine]. (23)[5]

After the attempted revolution, Durham found, not surprisingly, that virtually no moderate faction remained and that English who had previously been liberals had for the most part allied themselves with other English-speakers who were determined never again to permit themselves to fall under the hands of a French majority in the Assembly. On the French side only a few, chief among whom were the clergy, condemned the actions of their countrymen.

Faced with this irreconcilable dilemma and with the ever-present possibility of the outbreak of further disorders, Durham offered his solution: Lower Canada must be made English. Rather than attempting to appease the French Canadians by permitting them retention of their language, law, and religious institutions, he argued, pressure to assimilate must be brought to bear immediately. For Durham, it was either a question of yielding the province to the French or drowning them in an English world. "The error," he continued, "to which the present contest must be attributed, is the vain endeavor to preserve a French Canadian nationality in the midst of Anglo-American colonies and states" (50).

> A plan by which it is proposed to ensure the tranquil government of Lower Canada, must include in itself the means of putting an end to the agitation of national disputes in the legislature, by settling, once and for ever, the national character of the province. I entertain no doubts as to the national character which must be given to Lower Canada; it must be that of the British Empire; that of the majority of the population of British America; that of the great race which must, in the lapse of no long period of time, be predominant over the whole North American Continent. Without effecting the change so rapidly or so roughly as to shock the feelings and trample on the welfare of the existing generation, it must henceforth be the first and steady purpose of the British government to establish an English population, with English laws and language, in this Province, and to trust its govern-

ment to none but a decidedly English legislature. (Craig, 1963:146).

Elaboration of a Rural Ethos

To many French Canadians the handwriting was finally clearly exposed for all to see: the goal of the English in Lower Canada was nothing less than the extinction of the French "race" in America. The wide dissemination of Durham's report in Lower Canada, soon to become only a part of a union of Upper and Lower Canada and, in 1867, of the Canadian confederation, served the notice which aroused the intellectual and, especially the clerical elite of the province to turn inward more than ever before, to lean heavily upon the myth of a rural, French Catholic *destiny* in North America—a destiny which demanded above all else *la survivance*.

In a sense, with the exception perhaps of the heated two decades of involvement immediately preceding the rebellion, the vast majority of the population had always subscribed to an ideal of survival coming naturally to a people isolated in rural *rangs* from the disturbing forces of ethnic conflict. Their "survival" consisted of the natural replication of the language, religion and customs of one generation by the next. The rural withdrawal which provided the mechanism for survival and came to represent the idealized pattern of French Canadian life, however, was not always dominant. During the era of New France fully one quarter, and a dominant quarter at that, was urban. Only with the conquest and the collapse of the opportunity structure of urban life did the rural life so pervade the society that it became synonymous even with the life of the elite. In response to the conquest, French Canadian society, whose population was 83 percent rural by 1825,

> far from continuing to develop as other western societies of the period in industrializing, urbanizing and secularizing themselves organized itself to the contrary upon its popular and rural elements so that in lieu of turning in the direction of urbanization *elle se folklorise davantage*. (Rioux, 1971:49)

Thus, while the need to gain a livelihood oriented the population to the agricultural life with its inherent isolation and favoring of the legendary levels of fecundity which guaranteed ethnic survival, this rural withdrawal was glorified by the province's elite as if it were a conscious act on the part of the population to preserve the language and faith from English, Protestant contamination. "Agriculturalism," Brunet argued in his favorite posture of demythologizer of French Canadian life, "only became the national credo after the first half of the nineteenth century" (1958: 124).

> Because they could not direct themselves towards other domains of economic activity, the Canadians nourished an exaggerated love of agriculture. They wished to maintain, no matter what the cost, the old rural and village social order that had provided them refuge after the Conquest. They had acquired a limited conception of economic life. Incapable of continuing the commercial and industrial tradition of the founders of the French Empire in America, they convinced themselves that the cultivation of the earth would furnish them the economic basis of a prosperous society, *obliged to make colonists and peasants of themselves they concluded—or rather their leaders concluded for them—that they had an agricultural vocation* [emphasis mine]. (124)

With the arrival of masses of English colonists in the other regions destined to become Canada and the loss of control of the economic life of their towns, the French of Canada turned inward toward what Brunet has called, "les trois dominantes de la pensée": the language, agriculturalism, and the Faith. The periodic events of national importance penetrating the barrier, such as the formation of the Confederation with attendant increase in English dominance of the economic and political life, the execution of Riel, indicating that Québec was to become a French reservation in North America,[6] and the continual failure to gain sufficient recognition of French rights outside Québec to avoid assimilation of those established elsewhere in Canada, reinforced the belief that rural withdrawal was the only viable defense against assimilation.

URBANIZATION AND INDUSTRIALIZATION: THE END TO RURAL WITHDRAWAL AS A VIABLE RESPONSE

4

Maria Chapdelaine, torn between two men of Québec, began to falter. One had left for the "states" and had the riches of a factory-worker to offer; the other was her quiet, pious *premier voisin,* who could only promise a continuance of the hard, short life in the winters of Québec that she had always known. Perhaps the "states," with its paved streets, social life, and even its alien people was the answer. Perhaps life and the world were passing by the people of Québec trapped in their cycle of planting, harvesting, and freezing for generations. ". . . c'est un pays dur, icitte. Pourquoi rester?"[1] Maria thought as she yielded to the call of an easier life.

> Alors une . . . voix plus grande que les autres s'éleva dans le silence: la voix du pays de Québec, qui était à moitié un chant de femme et à moitié un sermon de prêtre . . .
>
> Elle disait: "Nous sommes venus il y a trois cents ans, et nous sommes restés. . . . Ceux qui nous ont menés ici pourraient revenir parmi nous sans amertume et sans chagrin, car s'il est vrai que nous n'ayons guère appris, assurément nous n'avons rien oublié.

Nous avions apporté d'outre-mer nos prières et nos chansons: elles sont toujours les mêmes. Nous avions apporté dans nos poitrines le coeur des hommes de notre pays, vaillant et vif, aussi prompt à la pitié qu'au rire, le coeur le plus humain de tous les coeurs humains: il n'a pas changé . . .

Autour de nous des étrangers sont venus, qu'il nous plaît d'appeler les barbares; ils ont pris presque tout le pouvoir; ils ont acquis presque tout l'argent; mais au pays de Québec rien n'a changé. Rien ne changera, parce que nous sommes un témoignage. De nous-mêmes et de nos destinées, nous n'avons compris clairement que ce devoir-là: persister . . . nous mantenir. . . . Et nous nous sommes maintenus, peut-être afin que dans plusieurs siècles encore le monde se tourne ver nous et dise: Ces gens sont d'une race qui ne sait pas mourir. . . . Nous sommes un témoignage.

C'est pourquoi il faut rester dans la province où nos pères sont restés, et vivre comme ils ont vécu, pour obéir au commandement inexprimé qui s'est formé dans leurs coeurs, qui a passé dans les notres et que nous devrons transmettre à notre tour à de nombreux enfants: Au pays de Québec rien ne doit mourir et rien ne doit changer. . . ." (Hémon, 1924:212-13)

Then a . . . voice more profound than the rest arose in the silence: the voice of the land of Québec, which was at the same time half the song of a woman and half the sermon of a priest. . . .

It said: "We came here three hundred years ago and we have remained here. . . . Those who led us here would be able to return among us without sorrow or bitterness, because *if it is true that we have scarcely learned anything it is also true that we have forgotten nothing.*

We brought our prayers and our songs from overseas: and they are still just as we brought them. We carried in our breasts the heart of the men of our country, brave and passionate, as quick to pity as to laugh, the heart the most human of all human hearts: this, too, has not changed. . . .

Around us strangers have come, whom it pleases us to call barbarians: they have taken almost all the power; they have accumulated almost all the money; but in Québec nothing has changed. Nothing will change, because we are a testimony.

> For ourselves and our children, we have only understood clearly but one duty: persist . . . maintain. . . . *And we have maintained ourselves, perhaps so that after several more centuries the world will turn to us and say: These people are a race that doesn't know how to die. . . . We are a testimony.*
>
> That's why we must stay in the province where our fathers stayed, and live like they lived, to obey the unexpressed commandment which was formed in their hearts, which has passed into ours and which we will transmit in our turn to our many children: "In the land of Québec nothing must die and nothing must change [emphasis mine] . . . ." (Hémon, 1924: 212-213)

Caught by the call of Québec Maria yielded to duty and returned her mind and body to the land.

Even at the time Louis Hémon wrote what must surely be considered the classic novel of Québec, the world which he recorded was in fast decline. The world he described of the pious Maria living and working with her father, mother and brothers in newly cleared land far from the overcrowded *rangs* of the St. Lawrence, struggling just to survive, dreaming of the long sled ride to the rural church for mass and talk on the church steps, had already lost its crucial battle to the factories of New England and the cities of Québec itself. The call of the Church for the taking of the land ("Emparons-nous le sol!") and the drowning of the English through a *ravanche des berceaux* ("revenge of the cradles") had only hastened the process of absorption into the industrial economy by creating a surplus of population too great for the agricultural society to maintain. Even colonization—represented by the efforts of Maria's father to gain a foothold in the northern country of Lac Saint-Jean—scarcely provided any relief. The ethos of withdrawal had not taken cognizance of its ecological ramifications.

In a sense, the dilemma of Maria Chapdelaine: to remain with the land—which with all its hardships still provided a secure setting in the kinship, friendship and religious network that was rural French Canadian culture—or leave it under the pressure of a population growth which was steadily forcing the exploitation of more and more marginal land and the reliance upon non-farming winter activities (principally logging) to supplement a meager farm income, was the dilemma of all *québécois* during the latter half of the nineteenth century and the beginning of the twentieth. Although Maria elected to remain with the land and the past, the push from the lack of rural opportunity and—probably to a much lesser degree than was true of most of North America—the draw of the cities forced most of her peers to seek an urban life.

French Canadian Fertility

In the initial days of New France population grew slowly as a result of very limited settlement and the fact that, because of disease and wars, births did not exceed deaths until 1638. By 1666, the population had reached a total of 3,215 (Keyfitz, 1960: 129). The 1698 census indicated a population of 14,000, while only thirty-eight years later, in 1736, the population totaled 40,000.[2] The striking factor is not the trebling of the population in less than forty years but the fact that virtually all of this population growth was the result of natural increase rather than immigration. It has been estimated that *total* net immigration from France to New France during the entire period of the colony did not exceed 10,000 individuals and was perhaps as low as 4,000 (Henripin, 1957:206; Keyfitz, 1960:130).

By 1763, the population had grown to 70,000. This, coupled with our knowledge of the extremely low level of immigration (accounting for *at most* only 66 colonists a year during the entire French period), leads Keyfitz to the conclusion that the rapid growth

> implies fairly settled conditions and a rate of fertility among the highest ever reached, even among small populations occupying practically limitless areas. That the 70,000 of 1763 could be the recognized ancestors of over 4-½ million Canadians and perhaps 1-½ million Americans implies a continued high fertility, as well as a degree of cultural continuity in the face of majority pressures of many kinds that has few parallels in world history. (130-131)

As noted above, after the conquest, Québec, unlike other western areas which were just beginning the process of industrialization, urbanization, and secularization, fell back on its rural strengths. Again, in Rioux's words, rather than continuing in the urban direction, the entire society "se folklorise davantage" (1969:49). Coupled with this rural withdrawal was a baby boom of epic proportions—a boom so great that it came to be known as "une revanche des berceaux," a revenge of the cradles.

The fertility level of French Canadians has always been markedly high. During the French regime Henripin has estimated that the average married woman bore more than one child every two years, so that during the entire child-bearing span a woman married at the age of fifteen had, on the average, thirteen children. As noted by Henripin, "This figure, at the mortality rates of that time, represents a doubling of the population every twenty-two years; at the rate of mortality now prevailing, a doubling every nine or ten years" (1957:208).

Of course, most French Canadian women at the time did *not* marry at age fifteen. It appears that a more reasonable estimate of population growth may be based on an estimate that the average mother who survived until the age of fifty had 8.5 to 9 children. At the mortality rates of the day it is apparent that the birth rate yielded a population doubling every thirty years (208).[3]

In comparison with recent studies of the fecundity of rural Iran, where knowledge and practice of contraception was as lacking as in seventeenth-century New France, the fertility rates of the latter still stand as being remarkably high (209). Why?

Aside from the fact that high fertility had the specific sanction and encouragement of the government, it was

> also a socially prevalent and a generally and individually internalized value [and] "it was still the time when children were economic assets; in New France, they were also potential defenders against the Indians and the English colonists who were growing in strength and threatened to absorb New France." (209)

After the English conquest, when the French colonists might have been expected to respond to the presence of foreign domination with a diminution in the rate of fertility, the rate of population growth actually increased and from 1760 to 1850 doubled

every twenty-five years, producing a population growth of Mal-
thusian proportions (209). While it is tempting to subscribe to the
Church-inspired theory of *revanche des berceaux* and conjure
images of French Canadians actively waging war against the
English Canadian invaders in their bedrooms, it is most likely that
the increase in population growth was the result of the process
of ruralization itself. Given the differences in fertility found by
Henripin in urban and rural populations in general and in French
Canada (1960:168), and the importance of children in performing farm labor, it is much more likely that individual decisions to
marry and produce large numbers of children were the result of
the exigencies of rural life rather than any effort to survive as a
group.

In itself, this astonishing level of population growth seemed to
present no threat to the integrity of French Canadian society. On
the contrary, a population growth of this size might well have
tipped the population balance forever in the French favor, as the
clerical elite—and through them, the populace—hoped. However,
the English, while unable to match the birth rate of French
Canadians,[4] had the trump of immigration to provide them with
their own *revanche*. Thus, while the French population continued
to grow geometrically, immigration from the British Isles and
massive emigration of French Canadians to the United States
beginning in the middle of the nineteenth century resulted in a
steady decrease in the proportionate importance of the French
population.

While the rapid birth rate failed to meet the hopes of those who
wished to drown the English in a tide of births, it was not without
significant and unexpected effects. Although the population
explosion arose from the ethos of the French Canadian rural life,
the excess population it produced returned at first to haunt and
later to destroy it.

To understand the devastating cultural effect produced by this
rapid population growth, it is first necessary to understand what
the growth meant in human terms. What did these people do?
How were they provided for?

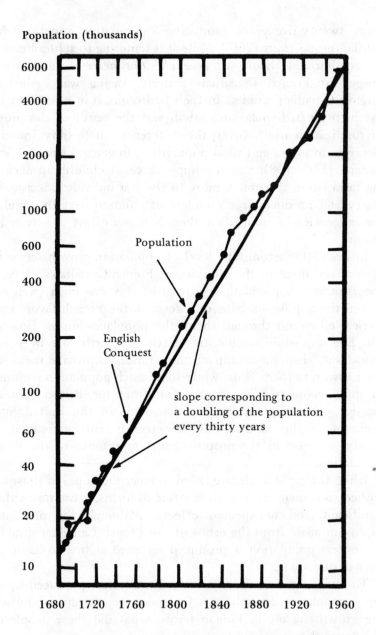

The Growth of French Canada's Population
Henripin 1957: 14

Persons of French Origin and Total Population

Year	Total Population (000's)	Immigration during Preceding Decade	Emigration during Preceding Decade	French Population	French Percentage of Total
1851[a]	1,842	——	——	696	37.8
1861[a]	2,508	209	86	881	35.1
1871[b]	3,486	187	377	1,083	31.1
1881	4,325	353	439	1,299	30.0
1891	4,833	903	1,110	1,405	29.1
1901	5,371	326	505	1,649	30.7
1911	7,207	1,782	1,067	2,062	28.6
1921	8,788	1,592	1,330	2,453	27.9
1931	10,377	1,195	967	2,928	28.2
1941	11,507	150	241	3,483	30.3
1951	13,648	548	380	4,319	30.8
1961	18,238	1,543	463	5,540	30.4
1971	21,568	1,429	707	6,180	28.7

[a]Upper and Lower Canada only.
[b]Nova Scotia, New Brunswick, Quebec and Ontario only.
(Keyfitz, 1960:135; Canada Yearbook 1974:160, 167)

Ecological Ramifications of French Canadian Fertility

Horace Miner (1939), in his monograph of a rural French Canadian parish on the lower St. Lawrence, *St. Denis: A French-
Canadian Parish,* describes a typical rural family cycle characteristic of Québec in the 1930's. Except for the later date of marriage
and the lower infant mortality rate, it seems unlikely that there
is any significant difference to be found between his description
drawn from the early twentieth century and the rural lifestyle of
Québec's past.

> A young man of twenty-six marries a girl of twenty-five, and
> in the marriage contract he receives the title to the paternal
> land. His father is sixty years old now and, as he is not able
> to do the work as he used to, has been planning for several
> years to turn over the farm to his son . . .

> By the time the young people have been married eight years,
> they have had five children, one of whom has died. The eldest
> child is seven years old, the youngest a babe in arms. The
> family cycle is so regular that native expression gives voice to
> such a remark as "He is just a young man. He has only four
> or five children." At this point the man still has the vigor of
> his thirty-four years to carry him over the hardest period of
> the cycle . . .

In eight more years the father is forty-two and the couple has had ten children, three of whom have died. The eldest sons are helping in the field, and there is no labor problem. By this time the father has begun to think seriously of plans for the future of his children . . .

In selecting which son will remain at home, it must be remembered that the choice of one of the eldest boys would be unwise, as his own children would soon overcrowd the house when he is married [and] a son near the middle of the sequence of children is chosen to inherit the farm . . .

There remain five children unestablished, two boys and three girls; one of the latter will normally marry a local farmer. The girls, as far as is financially possible, are sent to near-by convents for two or even three years to secure their *diplômes* after they complete the local schools. There is occasional opportunity for girls with such education to get teaching positions in local schools. . . . A girl may go on and become a nun if she so desires. If the family has sufficient money, one or more of the boys will be given some schooling beyond the local schools . . .

Thus far, the ten children have the following outlook: four die before reaching twenty-five years; one inherits the paternal land; one marries a farmer; and one (if a boy) enters priesthood, or profession, or (if a girl) enters convent, becomes a schoolteacher, or marries a professional man. There are still three children unaccounted for. The father, during his management of the farm, although passing on the responsibility to his successor in the latter's first years, tries to buy another farm or save the money for a son to get a farm somewhere. A local informant estimated that one-quarter of the farmers establish two sons on lands. This failing, the father gives the boy some technical training or sends him to cities or industrial centers where he can get work. (Miner, 1939:80-84)

As can readily be seen from Miner's description of the problems of placement of children, the high fertility rate was a mixed blessing. The labor gains achieved through having a number of offspring to perform chores were offset by the need and the difficulty of providing them adequate life-placements of their own. If we accept Miner's analysis as being generally accurate for the past as well as for St.-Denis of the 1930's—and, except for the more recent emphasis upon the possibility of providing technical training for the male offspring, I see no reason not to—then it is obvious that with each farm producing one successor, and a spouse for an unrelated successor, four of the six living children are left unaccounted for. At the very most, only one child will be absorbed by the church or in a professional occupation. If the remaining three choose to remain on the land, as they did until the nineteenth century, when industrial occupations first became a reality, then 1½ farms must be found to house them. Where could these farms be found?

Owing to the geographical structure of Québec, only a small portion of the province is truly suitable for agriculture. By far the most arable land was to be found in the wide, flat valley of the St. Lawrence. As previously noted, the first settlers arranged themselves in the *rang* pattern, which gave the St. Lawrence the look of a village street which it still retains today. Even with the narrow river frontage (three or four *arpents,* or about six hundred to eight hundred yards) occupied by each settler, by the time of the British conquest the rapid population growth had already taken its toll, and virtually all the waterfront along the St. Lawrence and its major tributaries had been occupied (Deffontaines, 1964:7).

Already as early as 1668, all of the river holdings had been exhausted at Sillery, Cap Rouge and St. Augustin in the lower St. Lawrence, and by 1681 almost the entire coastline at Lauzon (near Québec city) had been settled (8). In 1722, at St.-André-de-Tilly, the second *rang* was begun. By the period of the conquest, the area of Trois Rivières already had begun a third *rang* (8).

With the rapid spread of settlement, by 1820, all of the old seigneuries had been occupied. The only available land remaining upon which new farms might be established to absorb the non-inheriting children of each generation was in the virgin areas, such as Lac St.-Jean on the Saguenay, which meant a very harsh and marginal existence, or land removed from the possibility of settlement and held by speculators who denied others access. Most of the latter land had been gained by British investors with governmental connections and was held *en friche* (uncultivated) with the intention of retaining it for future capital gains.[6]

Denied a source of land upon which to continue to live their traditional life, the non-inheriting children were forced to leave Québec, at first for the farms and later for the factories of New England. As Rameau (1859) indicated, masses of non-inheriting children remained in their parishes making do as best they could as laborers, a "situation bien précaire dans un pays où le manque de capitaux et la rigueur de l'hiver rendent le travail salarié rare et peu fructueux" (169).

Initially, most of those who left for the "States" left only for a season—to harvest crops in Vermont—but with employment possibilities relatively plentiful, what began as a temporary emigration became a permanent resettlement. A number of emigrants with ready cash even left Québec to purchase farms in Vermont and New Hampshire. Of those who journeyed to the states with the intention of earning enough capital to return and purchase a farm, few returned with the savings to do so. Despite the large wages reputed to be offered in the United States

> the more extravagant spending habits existing in the south had often absorbed all or part of their wages, and few among them drew a real profit from their journey to purchase and clear *une terre* on their return.[7] (169)

Many of those who migrated to other parts of Canada with the desire to maintain their rural French orientation were in time as lost to the French cause in the New World as those who were swallowed in the melting pot "en bas."[8] Few of the descendants of the tens of thousands of Québec farmers and trappers who migrated to Ontario, Manitoba, and the Western provinces have been able to resist the dominant English population of the continent. In 1961, 49.9 percent of those of French Canadian origin in Alberta claimed English as their maternal language, compared with 43.1 percent in Saskatchewan, 37.7 percent in Ontario, and 30.3 percent in Manitoba. Clearly, the exodus from Québec has made it very difficult for those who were part of this exodus to resist the temptation to give up their "mission" and assimilate to the majority.

In retrospect, it seems clear that the pattern of ruralization and expansion could not long continue in a region with such limited arable land. If the goal of Québec's intellectual elite was to assure the survival of the *canadien* culture and language, then once the barrier of the *limiting factor*[9] of land had been breached and large numbers of individuals had had to leave the system in order to survive, some effort should have been made to provide a modified or alternate system by encouraging industrial development. In fact, however, any shift from the quasi-sacred agricultural life was fervently rejected.

Even at the beginning of the twentieth century, when hundreds of thousands had already fled Québec, the French Canadian economist, Edouard Montpetit, whom Michel Brunet described as "l'un des plus brillants élèves du collège de Montréal" (1958:132), was encouraged by his advisor to take up the agricultural vocation: "Mon cher Edouard, vous ne ferez rien de bon à moins du devenir agriculteur, de vous installer sur une terre" (132). Far from being exceptional advice, this was the logical extension of an educational system whose lectures, readings, arithmetic, and memorized passages made constant reference to the farm. As the Jesuit Alexandre Dugré warned: "We must cut lumber or die, sow or lie fallow . . . our race will be agricultural or it will no longer grow, it will disappear" (Trudeau, 1956:28).

The Failure of the Indigenous Bourgeoisie
to Direct Québec's Industrialization

French Canadian society, even in the nineteenth century, consisted of numerous small villages and several cities of moderate size. Obviously, the commerical populations of Trois-Rivières, Québec, and Montréal, not to mention the villages of the province, were not all English. Not all of the petty bourgeoisie of New France was forced to "return" to the land. Not all of those who left the land left to assume the life of the wage earner. French Canada has always valued the life of the small merchant as a lesser alternative to careers as notaries, doctors, and priests. In the past, and certainly today, it can be said that Québec is a province of the small enterprise, whether it be an *épicerie,* a *pharmacie,* a *quin-caillerie,* or even a small *casse-crôute* specializing in *chiens chauds* and *patates frites.* These men, as much as the farmers, have been the backbone of Québec and as such have enjoyed clerical favor.

Everett Hughes noted this clerical sanctioning of the small businessman in his recording of part of a St. Jean-Baptiste day sermon given by the *curé* of Ste. Anne:

> The patriotic way for the true French Canadian to live is to save and become a small proprietor. English methods are not ours. The French became great by small savings and small business. Don't borrow the commerical ways of others. The prosperity of this community lies with us, not with the industries of England and the United States, but in the number of small proprietors. (1943:151)

Much of Québec's economic isolation during the nineteenth century was the result of the shift of the basic material of transportation from wood to iron. As this shift was made, Québec, lacking coal and known iron reserves, lost its only important industry, shipbuilding, and ceded its place behind the Canadian tariff wall to Ontario. Only with the depletion of pulpwood, copper, and iron, the demand for aluminum for airplanes, and development of hydro-electric power as an inexpensive substitute for coal, was the possibility for the location of major industry in Québec reopened (Faucher and Lamontagne, 1953:23-27).

When industrialization came, it came under an English tongue and continued in that tongue. Why? Why was Québec's potential urban population permitted to leave the province *en masse* until the *English* decided to enter and make use of the labor and resources of the province?

Obviously, the fact that there were no existing French Canadian industrial combines able to provide the capital needed to develop the resources of the province and that the heavily rural society—which was in many ways economically comparable to the southern United States—hardly had the resources to finance its own development, limited the possibilities for indigenous development. In seeking to explain the failure of French Canadians to develop Québec, however, it is important to look toward the social structure of the society itself. Granted, in the beginning industrialization by French Canadians may have been difficult, yet why do the industries of Québec still remain so firmly in Anglo-American hands?[10]

The blame for the continued, if not the initial, failure of the *québécois* to take hold of their industry lies primarily in the failure of the French Canadian elite to grant managerial, engineering and other industrial occupations the social sanction needed to make them attractive vocations. While Québec was yielding its economic base to foreign control, its most skilled minds were turning, as always, to the liberal professions. With the limited portion of the population who attended the *collèges* and universities—only 33 percent of those in the second grade in 1952 were to be found in the eleventh nine years later—there was no "backup" population to fill the business occupations, and they passed without challenge, from president to foreman, to the English.

As for those individuals who did occupy positions in the business milieu, their outlook was little suited for the major tasks of organization and capital expenditure which industrialization required. As Nöel Vallerand has noted, these men suffered from the fact that they:

> [were] used to the more or less serious requirements of the small and medium-sized enterprise, to a slow rhythm of industrialization, too few and always having too little capital at their disposal, surrounded by economic structures in which they were the valets not the masters, and finally, prisoners of a philosophy of action dominated by the idea of "fair-play," individualism and laissez-faire, the French Canadian plutocrats were totally unable to respond to the challenge of the century. (*La Souveraineté et l'économie*, 1970:56)

In addition to the low prestige value placed upon business vocations in French Canadian society, the failure of French Canadians to play a proportionate role in the economy of Québec can be attributed to a family-oriented, conservative approach to business, stressing the kind of primary relationships characteristic of pre-industrial economic organization. A French Canadian business, whether it be a (potentially great) brewery or meat-processing house, is likely to be limited by a non-expansionist outlook. Norman Taylor, in his study of French Canadians as industrial entrepreneurs, provides numerous excerpts from interviews with businessmen exemplifying this orientation:

> I don't want to get too big. I'm happy so long as I get a comfortable living for myself and my family. This business has done well—better than I expected—and if I were rich, I would

have more work and worry. It's no use being a millionaire in the cemetery. [Shoe manufacturer, forty-seven years old, 160 employees.] (1964:275)

The attitude of these French Canadian businessmen, who saw expansion as something to be very wary of and, in most cases, to be avoided, contrasts markedly with English Canadian entrepreneurial attitudes as sampled by Taylor:

If I thought there was no intention to expand, I wouldn't be staying here. You have to expand or decline, you just can't stand still. [Junior member of a family business, manufacturing shoes, twenty-seven, 320 employees.] (1964:277-78)

French Canadian businessmen, rather than viewing profits as something which should be "plowed back" into the business on the theory that "you have to have money to make money," often choose to invest their profits—the means of potential growth—in real estate, blue-chip securities, or a summer home for the family (Taylor, 1964:278; Melançon, 1956:503-22).

Monetary risks, however, are by no means the determining factor in deciding whether or not to go ahead with expansion. A major consideration is likely to be whether or not there are qualified family members who can be placed in positions of responsibility to manage the new posts created by expansion:

Some years ago we did start another plant, but the family wasn't organized for it; I mean to say that *we had no one available in the family to look after it, so we closed it down.* [Furniture manufacturer, fifty-six, 390 employees.] (1964: 279; emphasis Taylor's)

Another factor noted by Taylor limiting French Canadian business expansion is an individualism ironically—in the larger context of Québec—motivated by fear of yielding control to outsiders:

... there was this fellow in Montreal. He wanted to let me have lots of money, as much as I wanted. But he wanted to have a controlling interest. I said no. I can get plenty of money any day, but it means taking a partner. I don't want that. You get the ideas and do the work and he shares the profit. [Manufacturer of baseball bats, tool handles, etc., forty-three, 9 employees.] (282)[11]

This preoccupation with individual control of the business is often represented by company directors who stymie growth through their reluctance to delegate authority even within the family. Taylor records the case of an insurance company operating throughout French Canada in which the president constantly entered the offices of high-ranking company officials to give advice or to remove correspondence from their desks to personally draft replies. Excerpts from his interviews dramatically demonstrate the concern of his sample of French Canadian business leaders with personal control of even trifling matters:

> I'm supposed to be managing director, but in effect I'm assistant manager, since my father, who is president and general manager, makes absolutely all the decisions. We have a company secretary, a production superintendent, and a superintendent of lumbering operations. They can't take any decisions on their own. That's crazy, eh? But it's a fact. (1964:286)

on the emphasis on personnel policies which stress non-business aspects of employees' lives, such as their kinship network:

> Sometimes you won't fire a worker because he might be related to someone in the plant you like very much and you don't want to hurt the relative's feelings. [Hockey-stick manufacturer, thirty-six, 55 employees.] (289),

On workers' private lives:

> In hiring a worker we make sure there is stability in his family; that is, no family problems. For instance, does he live with his wife or not? We take good care of morality. It's more important than skill on the job. [Woodenware manufacturer, fifty-five, 150 employees.] (289),

On seniority:

> My manager is inept, but he has been with us a long time; he was hired by my father. So what can I do? [Description withheld.] (289),

also have had major ramifications limiting the efficacy of French Canadian industry.

The failure of French enterprises to appreciate English business methods has stymied Pan-Canadian commercial relationships.

French Canadians differ from English Canadians in seeing inter-personal relationships as necessary corollaries to business relation-ships. Thus, they are uncertain of the motives of other ethnic groups:

> Of course, we are never sure when we get an order whether it's because we know the man well or because he thinks our shoes are better or a better price. My feeling is that in Toronto it's simply a question of business. In B.C., however, they will consider you as a person. [Shoe manufacturer.] (290)

Another, perhaps central, problem affecting the relatively low degree of French Canadian business success relative to that of the English is a sense of "business inferiority" found among the French. It is not at all uncommon for French Canadians to openly remark that they don't have an aptitude for business. In commer-cial relationships with English Canadians, the French often seem to be on the defensive, behaving as if they are certain that the English have some special knack or special way of thinking con-ferred by the English language which gives them an edge in com-mercial affairs.

This sense of "business inferiority" often results in behavior, of small French businessmen at least, in which the French entre-preneur behaves in a tentative fashion, indicatiing that he expects to lose ground in the transaction. French businessmen, perhaps uncertain of their ability to "make a sell," usually present them-selves in such a manner that it is clear that there is a great deal of price flexibility in situations in which an English businessman would set a price and mean it. One often has the sense that the businessman is reluctant to say "no" for fear of losing the sale, however close his profit margin might become.[12]

A final handicapping problem in the approach of French Canadian entrepreneurs to the business of business is the ten-dency toward product conservatism indicative of a lack of market orientation:

> (a) firm continued to make cast-iron wood stoves and ranges despite the well-known long-run decline in demand. The sons of the three or four older directors pleaded, "If we are going to make stoves, then let's make gas or electric stoves," but were able to achieve this only when the retirement or death of their fathers left them free to do so. (293)

Thus, a variety of economic and cultural factors prevented French Canadian businessmen from developing the industrial potential of Québec and providing with this industrial base a source of employment for those leaving the land. Ironically, at a time when Québec's progeny were leaving in massive waves of emigration and eventually becoming part of the English sea, it was English capital that lessened the flow and gave the province a chance to keep its own offspring.

The English-Directed Industrialization and Urbanization of Québec

With the shift of the base of industry from wood to coal and iron in the mid-eighteenth century, Québec's entry into the industrial age was delayed until the beginning of the twentieth. During this period what industry the province had—agriculture accounted for 65 percent of the total product, forestry products 25 percent, fishing and mining about 2 percent, and industry only 4 percent (Bilodeau, *et al.,* 1971:455)—was localized in such labor-intensive industries as shoe and textile manufacturing, lumber milling, and the loading and unloading of the cargo ships and trains.[13]

With the beginning of Québec's limited industrialization in the 1860's, the province also tasted its first union struggles. As early as 1867, "les Chevaliers de Saint-Crispin," an American-organized labor union, attempted to unite the workers of Québec, only to collide with the Church in its first strike. A strike which was organized in the shoe industry produced a rapid affirmation that "the solution to the problems of the workers is based on Christianity, which establishes the obligation of sacrifice and the law of renunciation" (Bilodeau, *et al.,* 1971:461). In 1884, the Church, under Mgr. Taschereau, obtained a papal condemnation of the "Chevaliers du Travail" which, while later revoked under the pressure of the American church and the English press of Québec, left no doubt as to the Church's stance toward unions (463).

The American economic invasion of Québec and of Canada as a whole came during World War I as Britain was forced to divest itself of many of its large Canadian holdings. The invasion continued until in 1934, when 394 American businesses were in operation in Québec, representing fully one third of the industrial capital of the province (Wade, 1968:864).[14] In Québec, its development included numerous major enterprises, chief among which was the Canadian International Paper Company, a subsidiary of International Paper and Power of Boston. The control this single corporation wielded over the paper and pulp industry was such that the governments of Québec and Ontario were forced to set up a cartel of fourteen competing companies, many of which were on the verge of bankruptcy, to restore a semblance of competition.

Other areas of Québec industry tell the same tale. The Aluminum Company of America (Alcoa), which bought its Shipshaw site in 1925 and developed it during the second World War, owned 80 percent of its Canadian subsidiary. E. I. duPont de Nemours and Imperial Chemical each held 40 percent of CIL. The asbestos mines of Québec, which produce 43 percent of the world's and 85 percent of Canada's production of asbestos, are controlled for the most part by Johns-Manville. The newsprint, paper, and pulp industries of Québec are virtually all owned by English Canadian and American firms. Canadair, which has recently received major subventions from the Québec government in an effort to reduce *mise en pieds* ("layoffs") and subsequent unemployment, has been owned by General Dynamics since the end of World War II. The textile industry, too, is American and English Canadian, as is the sugar refining industry. The list is endless, comprising everything from the major department stores (Eaton's, Simpsons, and recently, Miracle Mart) and supermarkets (Dominion, Steinberg's) of the province to its public utilities.[15] It is obvious to the eye of every *québécois,* even in an era when public relations calls for advertising in his own language, that his economy rests in the hands of others: the English Canadians and the Americans (Chapin, 1955:44–52; Bilodeau, *et al.,* 1971:603).

Although this list is most frequently used to condemn the Anglo-American "exploitation" of Québec, the fact that Québec would not have been industrialized without this foreign investment is rarely emphasized. An issue of the separatist weekly *Point de Mire* (4 décembre 1971) detailed American and English Canadian ownership of Québec corporations in one article, traced the

A perspective on American investment at the time of American withdrawal from Vietnam: Assistant to Québec's Premier Bourassa: "These gentlemen have been sent by Mr. Nixon . . . They are ready to invest." (Jean-Pierre Girerd; *La Presse*, 30 mars 1971:A2)

relationships between the largest French-language daily in the Western Hemisphere, *La Presse*, its holding company "Power Corporation," and various other firms in the province in another, and in a third referred to Québec as "La poule aux oeufs d'or des colonisateurs" ("The colonizer's chicken with the golden eggs"),[16] illustrated this tendency to neglect the fact that foreign (non-French Canadian) investment was sought by Québec leaders in lieu of what would have been a preferable indigenous development.

A few voices were raised against English development of the resources of the province such as that of Errol Bouchette, who, in his 1901 text *Emparons-nous de l'industrie* ("Let's take control of our industries"), was among the first to recognize that the future lay in the industrial sphere. On the whole, these warnings fell on the deaf ears of a people little attuned to economic realities. Concerted opposition to the policy of the Taschereau government (1920-1935), for example, which was the first provincial government to actively encourage foreign investment, was more the result of a lingering fear of industrialization *per se* than of resource alienation or foreign exploitation (Wade, 1968:863).

Viewed from the vantage point of today, in which it is clear that the industrialization of Québec was essentially Anglo-American, it is easy to conjure an unholy cabal of English industrialists and unscrupulous Québec politicians:

> Le gouvernement du Québec aurait pu exploiter les ressources du Québec au profit du peuple canayen. Il aurait pu emprunter du capital pour lancer notre économie. Mais il ne pouvait pas le faire, parce qu'il était dominé, à travers le clergé et les petits politiciens canayens comme Sir Lomer Gouin, par la bourgeoisie anglo-saxonne. Le gouvernement provincial était au service du capital anglo-saxon. (Bergeron, 1970:185).

On the whole, however, despite certain instances of corruption, it is probable that the close industrial-provincial relationships which have existed during the past half-century were followed by provincial governments desirous of aiding the French Canadian people. As Brunet (1954: 115) has noted, one could hardly expect men with no economic training whatsoever to develop elaborate plans to both industrialize and retain control of the province. Wasn't it enough that the tide of emigration to the States had been largely halted and turned toward the cities of Québec? Weren't people getting jobs, *and in Québec?*

The government was not alone among the major institutions of Québec in smoothing the path of the English-speaking industrialists. With American industry faced with socialist-dominated unions and bloody strikes in the states it must have been reassuring to discover that in Québec the most powerful of all social institutions, the Catholic Church, was just as wary of unions. In 1921, the *Conféderation des travailleurs catholiques du Canada* was organized under a plan to develop Catholic unions throughout Canada (Bilodeau, *et al.,* 1971:535-36). These "syndicats de boutique" were organized largely by Jesuits as the Catholic response to the "communist" inspired foreign unions under constitutions which called for cooperation between labor and management. From Chapin's description, in terms which are not exaggerated, we can appreciate the fear which their presence might have inspired in the minds of potential investors habituated to American unions:

> In their early years their leaders were picked for them, and their chaplins had a veto power in their executives.
>
> For a long time they were little better than glorified company unions. The boss would give the local organizer a donation for the annual picnic and he would sign on the dotted line.[18] (1955:54)

French Canadians were a docile lot, ready to work and grateful for the chance to work at home. That they offered the qualities investors sought is readily seen in the following prospectus issued by a large power company:

> Ste. Mathilde is mainly an industrial centre of quite recent growth. Ample power, contented and industrious labour combined with good transportation facilities and the generosity of the city authorities in easing the burden of new industries are rapidly building this city into an important industrial centre.
>
> Ste. Mathilde is also well known as a point to which pilgrims converge every year. . . . to venerate the shrine of Ste. Mathilde.
>
> Total population: 10,000 (approx.)
>
> Total number employed: 600 (approx.)
>
> Number to be drawn from the surrounding territory: male, 750; female, 250
>
> Race: French-Canadian (95 per cent)
>
> Degree of unionism: No unions
>
> Annual labour turnover: Practically nil
>
> Strikes or shut outs in last few years: None in ten years
>
> Usual hours of work: male, 60 hours; female, 55 hours
>
> (from Hughes, 1943:26)

And investors came. From 1901 to 1931 the urban population

Comparative Increase in the Rural and Urban Population of Québec, 1871-1931

	1871	1881	1891	1901	1911	1921	1931
Rural and Village	921,946	1,006,678	1,023,422	1,046,654	1,100,602	1,158,728	1,190,855
% increase		9.2	1.7	2.3	5.2	5.3	2.8
Urban Montréal and Jesus Islands	132,477	180,684	264,566	348,211	545,115	719,315	993,477
% increase		36.4	46.4	31.6	56.5	31.9	38.1
Other Urban	137,093	171,665	200,547	254,033	360,059	482,622	689,923
% increase		25.2	16.8	26.7	41.7	34.0	42.9

	1941	1951	1961	1971	
Rural and Village	1,222,198	1,326,883	1,352,807	1,166,520	Rural= unincorporated places
% increase	2.7	8.5	1.9	−13.8	Villages=unincorporated places with less than 1,000 population
Urban Montréal and Jesus Islands	1,145,282	1,395,400	2,215,627	2,743,208	Urban=incorporated places with more than 1,000 persons
% increase	3.8	21.9	51.2	34.0	
Other Urban	964,402	1,333,398	1,796,895	2,118,032	
% increase	39.8	30.8	34.8	17.8	

(After Hughes 1943:27; Canada Year Books)

of Québec soared while the rural areas barely maintained their own. The industrialization and urbanization of the population of Québec, long hidden by the exodus of urban migrants to the States, at last brought the industrial revolution home. During the first decade of the twentieth century alone the population of Montréal increased from 348,211 to 545,115 (an increase of 56.5 percent) while the other urban centers of Québec, in increasing from 254,033 to 360,059 (a 4.17 percent increase), were not far off pace.

Number Employed in Agriculture per 1,000 Occupied Persons in Québec, 1871–1931

1871 . . . 470.8	1901 . . . 382.6	1931 . . . 224.8	1961 . . . 107.4
1881 . . . 466.1	1911 . . . 313.2	1941 . . . 251.8	1971 . . . 56.2
1891 . . . 455.1	1921 . . . 281.4	1951 . . . 189.1	

(After Hughes, 1943:22; Canada Year Books. Figures from 1941–1971 represent the proportion of individuals living on farms to that of the population as a whole.)

The decline in agricultural employment in Québec, which is recorded in only miniscule drops until the last decade of the nineteenth century, suddenly began to show the rapid increase of non-farm opportunities in the province. Thus during the decade 1871–1881, a decrease of less than 1 percent in the number of males gainfully employed in agriculture in the province is shown. The next decade gives indication of only slightly increased non-agricultural opportunities in the province, with a decrease in agricultural employment of 2.4 percent. The decade 1891–1901, however, yielded a decline of 15.9 percent, indicating a drop of almost one-sixth of the percentage of males gainfully employed in agriculture over the previous census. The next decades saw continued decreases of major proportions: a decline of 18.2 percent from 1901–1911, of 10.2 percent from 1911–1921 during the war years, and of 20.1 percent during the decade of 1921–1931. During the great depression, the proportion of the population actually engaged in agricultural activity may have increased slightly. During the thirty year period from 1941 to 1971, however, there has been an astounding decline in the proportion of Québec's population living on farms: from 25.2 percent in 1941 to only 5.6% in 1971. While Québec's rural regime continues to survive in the hearts of many urbanites, in reality it is over. Today, Québec is an urban society.

The Place of Québécois in the New Industrial Hierarchy

Where was this recently urbanized population arranged in the structure of Québec's new corporations? Most of the corporations of the province were those specific to the natural resources of the area or were labor-intensive industries (especially textile and shoe manufacturing) which, because of higher labor costs elsewhere, localized in Québec to find new life. Thus, the mass of these newly urbanized workers entered the realm of the semi- and unskilled.

Everett C. Hughes (1943), in his classic study of the effects of Anglo-American industrialization upon a French Canadian town (Drummondville, or "Cantonville," as Hughes chooses to refer to it to preserve its anonymity), traced the relative positions of the town's English and French population in the industrial hierarchy. The town was originally settled after the War of 1812 by British soldiers in an area which was to become known as the "Eastern Townships," in which the English were guaranteed representation in the provincial assembly in excess of what their numbers would warrant.[19] These English reserves did not last long, however, and soon the agricultural expansion of *québécois* deluged the area's English. By the 1850s the French enjoyed a clear majority of the township's council positions and in the 1871 census represented three quarters of the population. In 1911 the population was more than 90 percent French, and by the time of Hughes's study in the 1930s it was approximately 95 percent French (31).

The replacement of English settlers by French, a phenomenon which has repeated itself everywhere in the Eastern Townships, in Drummondville as elsewhere, proceeded from the bottom of the social scale through the influx of French wage-earners, then of French shopkeepers who gained the patronage of their fellows eventually forcing most of the English competitors out of business, and finally to the professional level as English lawyers, notaries, and doctors found themselves in a losing competition with their French counterparts for clients. In Drummondville the process of succession was effectively completed in 1900, when there were no longer any English professional men remaining in the community. In the next year, a meeting of the town's business and professional men for the purpose of the formation of a Chamber of Commerce only produced two English among the thirty-two founders and the organization was naturally titled a *chambre de commerce*, with the minutes being recorded only in French (30–31).[20]

Thus the community whose social structure Hughes was to investigate was for all practical purposes an indigenous French-Canadian community.

Hughes found 4,118 (64.5 percent) of the gainfully employed French population of Drummondville employed in industry while 2,270 (35.5 percent) were employed in non-industrial occupations. Of the town's 345 employed English, fully 306 (88.7 percent) had industrial employment, while only 39 (11.3 percent) were employed in non-industrial occupations (47).

In an extensive analysis of the major industry of the town, a mill producing artificial silk goods, Hughes found an organizational structure clearly dominated by English-speaking individuals:[21]

Employees of Drummondville's Major Silk Mill by Nationality, 1937

Rank	English and Other	French	Total
1) Staff, above foreman	24 (96%)	1 (4%)	25
2) Foremen	57 (69.5%)	25 (30.5%)	82
3) All others:	308 (11.8%)	2,311 (88.2%)	
a) main office	65 (40.1%)	97 (59.9%)	162
b) engineering and chemical	92 (30.9%)	206 (69.1%)	298
c) personnel, final examination, programming and shipping	28 (18.2%)	126 (81.8%)	154
d) textile production	123 (6.1%)	1,882 (93.9%)	2,005
Total	389	2,337	2,726

(Hughes, 1943:55)

All of the English-speaking executive and staff personnel were foreign to the region, having relocated in Drummondville for the purpose of the establishment and administration of the mill.[22] The heart of the operation consisted of a nucleus of approximately seventy employees of the home plant in Great Britain, which included in its number about fifty individuals who headed the various manufacturing and finishing departments.

While the management of the company was wholly English, the supervisory personnel, or foremen, contained a liberal sprinkling of French personnel within their ranks—of the plant's eighty-two foremen, twenty-five were French. When the relative importance of the positions occupied by French and English foremen was placed under closer scrutiny, however, it became obvious that these figures indicated a greater importance of the French at the supervisory level than they possessed in actuality, as most were minor, or assistant, foremen. The major function of the French foremen in this plant was to render literal the function of foremen as translators of the wishes of their superiors. The reason for hiring English foremen and French assistants is often put as follows:

> We tried to have French foremen, but it has not worked out. They pay too much attention to family and friends; the British foreman does his job, is friendly with no one, and is just. He doesn't speak French, and that is probably a good thing, too. As it is, he has to work through a French assistant foreman. The foreman might go directly to a man and say: "The next time you do so and so, you will be kicked to hell out of here." As it is, he says to the French assistant foreman: "Tell so and so if he does that again I will kick him to hell out." The assistant goes to the man, and says: "Look here, the boss is pretty sore. You better watch your step." The French assistant foreman acts as a cushion.[23] (55)

Another genuine concern of the employers was with the fact that French Canadians in supervisory positions would be under heavy pressure to recruit relatives and bestow favors which would impair production. The promotion of an English employee to foreman, on the other hand, carried with it no such fears unless he had married into a French family.

The "rank and file" of the mill, while French in the great majority, contained a considerable number of English. Interestingly, here, too, there was a ranking in favor of the English as their relative frequency increased from line production through the more socially prestigious personnel, engineering, chemical, and main office positions. French employees not employed "on the line" were usually clerical workers. In the main office, for example, a number of the daughters of Drummondville's French elite—who could not work in the factory under any conditions, even for wages which averaged twice as much as their clerical earnings—had found employment as secretaries and clerks (59). The genuine rank and file, providing the cheap and reliable labor which encouraged the mill's location in Drummondville in the first place, was 94 percent French.

While the English were the Captains and Sergeants of industry, the non-industrial sphere of Drummondville, which provides goods and services to its people, belonged to the French:

Distribution of French and Non-French in Non-industrial Occupations in Drummondville, 1938

Occupation	French	Percent	Non-French	Percent
1) Professional and quasi-professional	101	4.4	9	21.4
2) Proprietors and managers of business concerns	238	10.5	13	31.0
3) Agents and clerks	463	20.4	10	23.8
4) Proprietors and persons engaged in service shops and trades	445	19.6	7	16.7
5) Servants	295	13.0	1	2.4
6) *Rentiers* and public functionaries	111	4.9	2	4.8
7) Laborers	617	27.2	0	0.0

Nationality of Owner or Manager of Business and Service Units in Drummondville, 1938

	French	English	Jewish and Other
1) Utilities and Banks	8	3	0
2) Businesses:			
a) Wholesalers and distributors	47	2	1
b) Retail	142	2	14
c) Hotels and recreation	37	1	2
Total Businesses	226	5	17
3) Services:			
a) Professional	33	1	0
b) Quasi-professional	33	0	2
c) Service shops	116	1	1
d) Trades	29	0	0
e) Agents	12	0	0
Total Services	223	2	3
Grand Total	457	10*	20

(After Hughes, 1943:68)

*one-half of these men are hired managers, while only about 5 percent of the French total are in this category.

In the entire non-industrial occupational sphere of Drummond-ville, Hughes found that

> no English person conducts an enterprise or offers a service in this community without either some special advantage with the English population or some support from an outside appointing agency, or both. (71-72)

Of the 345 employed English in Drummondville only 2 were under French authority.[24] Clearly the role of the English in Drummondville was the direction and management of the city's industry while the non-industrial sphere of goods and services was primarily French.

While French representation in the higher industrial ranks has increased somewhat since Hughes' study the situation is still not a bright one for French Canadians. Today, in the rest of Canada outside Québec, French Canadians comprise 10 percent of the work force but control only 5 percent of the administrative posts. Within Québec, excluding Montréal, only 7 percent of the total labor force is English while 30 percent of all administrative and 80 percent of the highest administrative positions are occupied by this group. In Montréal, French Canadians form 60 percent of the employed manpower but occupy only 17 percent of the high administrative posts. Eighty percent of all administrators earning more than ten thousand dollars are English, and of this group only one in five serve in positions which require them to be bilingual. The French who have gained administrative rank are overwhelmingly employed in English-owned or controlled corporations and are required, or course, to be bilingual (Rioux, 1969: 124-125). No wonder Rioux argues that despite superficial changes French Canadians are still "scieurs de bois et de porteurs d'eau" in an industrial hierarchy in which French are victims twice over. "One knows," he says,

> that Canada is dominated economically by the United States; Québec is not only dominated by the United States but by English Canada, itself. Thus if Canadian corporations live off the crumbs of American industry, the French enterprises of Québec live off the crumbs of the crumbs.[25] (123-124)

A number of recent studies have only confirmed the persistence—albeit slightly ameliorated—of the situation Hughes drew in microcosm for Drummondville for Québec and Canada as a whole.[26] D. L. C. Rennie, in an unpublished master's thesis, has extended the tale of French underrepresentation to Montréal, noting that, in a city in which French Canadians are clearly in a majority, the directorships of the city's major corporations are overwhelmingly held by English-speaking individuals.[27]

The most thorough analysis of relative French-English occupational status, however, has come from the Royal Commission on Bilingualism and Biculturalism formed to analyze and report upon the current state of the major ethnic groups of Canada. Volume Three of the *Report of the Royal Commission on Bilingualism and Biculturalism* concerns itself with "The Work World" and finds that French Canadians continue to rank well below English Canadians in occupational status, as the following tables indicate:

Occupation and Ethnic Origin—Canada, 1961 (Percentages)

	British	French	Italian	Ukrainian	Jewish
Professional and technical	9.3	5.9	2.8	5.8	13.7
Managerial	12.1	7.6	6.6	7.1	39.4
Craftsmen and Production Workers	25.5	31.4	43.7	29.6	15.6
Laborers	4.6	7.5	19.2	6.9	1.1
Others	48.5	47.6	27.7	50.6	30.2

(After Figure 1, RRCBB, vol. 111:39)

Occupation and Ethnic Origin—Québec, 1961 (Percentages)

	British	French	Italian	Jewish
Professional and technical	15.0	6.3	3.5	11.7
Managerial	15.4	7.9	6.1	37.7
Craftsmen and Production Workers	23.1	32.0	44.7	16.8
Laborers	3.0	7.2	17.4	0.9
Others	43.5	46.6	28.3	32.9
Number	151,852	999,798	34,211	21,998

(After RRCBB, vol. 111:43)

Occupation and Ethnic Origin
Montréal Metropolitan Census Area, 1961 (Percentages)

	British (all)	British non-Roman Catholic	British Roman Catholic	French	Italian	Jewish
Professional and Technical	16.9	19.3	11.4	7.6	3.2	11.6
Managerial	17.9	19.6	14.0	9.0	6.1	38.5
Craftsmen and Production Workers	23.1	21.9	25.9	36.4	44.9	16.7
Laborers	2.3	1.7	3.4	6.3	18.7	0.8
Others	39.8	37.5	45.3	40.7	27.1	32.4
Number	98,927	68,459	30,468	331,734	30,596	20,616

(After RRCBB, vol. 111:44)

Supplementing the fact that French Canadians are under-represented in the professional and managerial fields is the fact that those French in these occupational categories in most cases earn significantly less than their English counterparts. Thus, British engineers in Montréal had average incomes of $8,508 in 1961, while French engineers earned $7,919. Among architects the discrepancy was even more marked, with the British earning $12,339 and the French $8,500 per annum. The same trend was found among physicians and surgeons, with the British earning $15,206 and the French $12,770 annually (RRCBB, vol. III: 65-67).

While a number of factors such as relative levels of schooling, of unemployment, and age differentials join with that of occupation to explain much of the discrepancy in French and English income levels, a significant proportion of this still must be attributed to ethnicity. For Montréal, Raynauld, Marion and Béland, in their "La répartition des revenus" prepared for the Commission, concluded that ethnicity carried an important weight in the determination of income (see table).

Discrepancy between French and English in occupational level has by no means been limited to private industry. Even within the Federal Service, where numerous efforts have been made to make French Canadians really feel a part of the national government, there still remain significant discrepancies in employment and income between the two major groups.[28]

Of all the tabulations of the condition of the French Canadian

Net Contribution of Ethnic Origin—Metropolitan Montréal, 1961

	Deviation From Observed Average of $4,443	Net Contribution of Ethnic Origin
English-Scottish	+ $1,319	+ $606
Irish	+ 1,012	+ 468
French	− 330	− 267
Northern European	+ 1,201	+ 303
Italian	− 961	− 370
Jewish	+ 878	+ 9*
Eastern European	− 100	− 480
German	+ 387	+ 65*
Other	− 311	− 334

*=not statistically significant.

(Net contribution of ethnic origin refers to the increase or decrease in average wage and salary attributable to ethnic origin when all other factors are held constant.)

(After RRCBB, vol. 111:77)

within his own province, however, none have been as telling as the tabulation of income according to ethnic group revealed by the 1961 national census:

Ethnic Origin	Income	Index
1. British	$4,940	142.4
2. Scandinavian	4,939	142.4
3. Dutch	4,891	140.9
4. Jewish	4,851	139.8
5. Russian	4,828	139.1
6. German	4,254	122.6
7. Polish	3,984	114.8
8. Asiatic	3,734	107.6
9. Ukrainian	3,733	107.6
10. Other Europeans	3,547	102.4
11. Hungarians	3,537	101.9
12. French	3,185	91.8
13. Italian	2,938	84.6
14. Indian	2,112	60.8
Mean Income for Québec	3,469	100.0
French (80% of total population)	3,185	91.8
All other groups	4,605	133.2

(Comité de documentation du Parti Québécois, 1970:22-23)

Twelfth of fourteen. Only the newcomers, the Italians, and the only group preceding them, the Indians, fared worse than the French Canadians, *les québécois,* at home in *La Belle Province.*

CRISIS IN BLANC AND WHITE

5

J'imagine mal qu'on ne se rende pas compte que c'est notre langue française qui est à la source de tous nos problèmes politiques, économiques et sociaux. Je veux bien que la langue crée une mentalité nord-américaine. Ce bilinguisme que l'on veut imposer au pays (le Canada) est trop dispendieux.

Le cas est typique: pendant que nos politiciens se débattent pour protéger le français, les Américains se débattent pour nous déposséder. C'est sur ce plan que je ne puis pas voir comment des gens intelligent peuvent défendre une langue qui n'est plus à la mesure du progrès.

Comme c'est bizarre de constater n'est-ce pas que c'est celui qui parle français qui est le moins instruit, le plus pauvre, le plus dominé et qui chôme le plus... etc. Je suis persuadé que l'anglisation finale règlerait tous ces problèmes. Il n'y aurait plus de disputes aussi inutiles que coûteuses sur la question du français-langue-de-travail.

Il n'y aurait plus de querelles politiques Ottawa-Québec sur le biculturalisme. Les relations Québec–USA ne se feraient plus au niveau du gouvernement et des institutions mais au niveau de la masse et nous pourrions en tirer un immense profit.

Je disais que la langue par sa structure crée une mentalité. Vous voulez devenir un commerçant riche et puissant?

Anglicisez-vous. That's all! Abandonnez votre français de salon et de ruelle et dans 10 ans le Québec ne connaîtra plus de problèmes stupides comme le bill 63.

La solution est radicale, elle n'est peut-être pas la meilleure, mais elle est la seul d'après moi qui soit apte à revaloriser le Québec. Chacun doit prendre conscience de cette anglicisation qui doit se faire.

Vous riez des guerres de religions en Irlande [reference to a recent *La Presse* editorial ridiculing religious wars] et moi, je ris de vos guerres de langues. Toutes les guerres font des morts, et c'est la langue française qui crèvera la première et c'est tant mieux. Quand l'anglicisation sera complétée, vous aurez vraiment la certitude de participer à la vie économique, puisque vous aurez acquis une nouvelle mentalité.

Si nos ancêtres avaient compris la nécessité de l'anglicisation, vous ne seriez pas dans un tel pétrin aujord'hui. Vous voulez la prospérité pour vos descendants? Envoyez-les à l'école anglaise. S'ils ne parlent plus français ensuite, ils pourront toujours se vanter d'avoir du sang joual qui coule dans leurs veines.

Vous croyez peut-être que je suis un fanatique. Au contraire, je ne suis qu'un paisible étudiant qui va au CEGEP ou "trou commun pour les francophones québécois." J'attends tranquillement l'heure de la libération . . . linguistique. De toutes façons, que vous défendiez ou non la langue française, vous ne la parlerez plus dans 50 ans. Mais si ça vous enchante de jouer les dupes pendant les cinquante prochaines années, ce ne sera pas de ma faute et je m'en lave les mains. A vous de prendre une décision!

NON, les Anglais ne m'ont rien donné pour écrire cette lettre et je suis sûr qu'il y a d'autres francophones qui sont prêts à faire le grand saut; à ceux-ci je leur dis, faites faire part de vos idées dans ce journal afin que tout le monde puisse prendre conscience de la nécessité urgent d'implanter l'anglais langue-maternelle-et-langue-de-travail.

Yves Landry, Laval

(La Presse, 26 mars 1971:A4)

It's difficult to believe that we never take note of the fact that it is *our* French language which is at the root of all of our political, economic and social problems. I really wish that our language created a North American mentality. This bilingualism that everyone wants to impose on Canada is too costly.

It's typical: while our politicans debate among themselves as to how to protect the French language, the Americans are debating how best to dispossess us of what we have. How intelligent men can continue to defend a language which has been bypassed by progress under these conditions is beyond me. It's funny how it's always those who speak French who are the poorest, the least educated, the most exploited and the most unemployed, isn't it? I'm convinced that anglicization will solve all of these problems. There won't be any more disputes as useless as they are costly on the French-language-of-work issue. There will no longer be any Ottawa-Québec quarrels on biculturalism. Québec–USA relations would no longer be limited to the governmental and institutional levels but would extend to every Quebeker and, from this, we would all draw an immense profit.

I maintain that language, itself, by its structure creates a mentality. Do you want to become a rich and powerful merchant? Learn to speak English. "That's all!" Give up your French which you can only use at home and in the alleys anyway and in 10 years Québec will no longer be bothered by problems as stupid as Bill 63.[1]

The solution is perhaps radical and not the best, but it's the only one which I think is likely to revitalize Québec. Everyone should be aware of this anglicization which must take place.

You laugh at the Irish religious war [a reference to a recent La Presse editorial ridiculing religious wars] and I laugh at your wars of language. All wars cause casualties, and it's the French language which is going to die first and so much the better. When anglicization is finished, you will have the certainty of being able to participate in the economic life, since you will have acquired a new mentality.

If our ancestors had understood the necessity of anglicization you would not be in such a mess today. Do you want your descendants to be prosperous? Send them to an English school. If afterwards they can no longer speak French, they can always brag that they have joual blood flowing in their veins.

Perhaps you think I'm a fanatic. On the contrary, I'm only a peaceful student attending a CEGEP [Collége d'enseignement général et professionel, part of a newly established network of community colleges leading either to a terminal degree or to admission to further university study], or "common hole for

French Quebekers." I'm waiting patiently for the moment of liberation . . . linguistic, that is. In any case, whether you defend the French language or not, you won't be speaking it 50 years from now. But if you enjoy playing the role of fool for the next 50 years, it won't be my fault and I'm washing my hands of any responsibility. It's up to you to make your own decision!

NO, the English haven't paid me to write this letter, and I'm certain that there are other French-speakers who are ready to make the great leap; to them I can only say, let others know your feelings by writing this paper so that everybody will realize the urgent necessity of establishing English as the maternal language and language of work.

Yves Landry, Laval[2]

(*La Presse*, March 26, 1971:A4)

While there can be no doubt that this letter represents an unpopular, if not aberrant, opinion in Québec, it deserves lengthy quotation as it touches squarely upon the central issue, the central battleground, which separates French and English in Canada. The struggle is not, as Landry sees it quite clearly, one of two cultures struggling for hegemony, but of two languages spoken by peoples who have far more in common than the terms "French" and "English," conjuring images of two great cultures of Europe, would suggest. [3]

Without doubt there are cultural differences between English and French Canadians. It is a mistake, however, I think, to isolate and treat differences in religion, importance of kinship as a social base, and general group solidarity as indications of clear cultural differences. In so doing, one finds it quite easy to attribute the inferior French social position in Canada to these factors. Thus, we have the image of a French Canadian trapped in the oppressive environment of his religion and kin which prohibit him from exercising the selfishness of purpose central to vertical mobility in an industrial society. No one can doubt that there is truth in this description, just as there is in the old argument that French employees refuse to leave Québec to acquire the necessary managerial skills in all aspects of a corporate operation and therefore find themselves at a disadvantage vis-à-vis their English counterparts in matters of promotion. What these culturally based arguments neglect, however, is that none of them is responsible for the continuance of the inferior position of the French in Canada. This honor belongs to the French language. It is the language itself which is the criterion for ethnic classification in Canada, as the terms "French" and "English" clearly indicate. What is an urban, Protestant, French-speaking Canadian? A French Canadian. And the son of a Catholic, English-speaking farmer who has just arrived in Montréal from the Québec countryside? An English Canadian.

While it can be shown that English-speaking Protestants descended from the earliest English settlers of Montréal occupy more central positions than their more recently arrived Irish countrymen, it is as much a mistake to attribute this to Irish culture or Catholicism as it is to dwell upon cultural criteria other than language as determinants of relative French–English social position.

Perhaps the clearest example of the tendency to maximize cultural differentiation between Canada's two major ethnic groups can be seen in Phillipe Garigue's article "French–Canadian Kinship and Urban Life," which appeared in the *American Anthropologist* in 1956. In analyzing the extent of kinship knowledge of fifty-two individuals, mostly of middle income, residing in Montréal, he discovered that the mean number of relatives whose name and/or sex and kin relation were recalled was 215 and ranged from 75 to 484. In view of the fact that Codere has discovered recognition networks of between 30 and 33 kin in a survey of two hundred American university students aged between seventeen and twenty, Garigue noted that there appear to be marked cultural differences between the two groups. While college students, because of their age and consequent lack of descending generations and assumed emphasis on upward mobility and non-kin-based relationships, probably represent the extreme of minimal kinship recognition in America, the difference is still impressive. Considering that:

> One of the most widely accepted generalizations about kinship is the proposition that the greater the urbanization, the smaller the kinship range, and that this apparent result of city life is everywhere the same, (Garigue, 1956:371)

why hasn't the kinship basis of French Canadian society been radically altered by urbanization? Garigue feels that these differences

> are not due to more extensive rural survivals among the French
> Canadians, or to longer urban conditioning in the United
> States, but in each instance seem to be part of the established
> urban way of life, with its cultural values, (372)

and are due to the presence of

> a cultural complex which included the French language as
> spoken in Quebec, a specific system of education, membership
> in the Catholic Church, and various political theories about the
> status of French Canadians in Canada. (370)

"It seems," he says, *"that the crucial factors in diminishing kinship recognition are the cultural values of the society, not its degree of urbanization"* (372; emphasis mine). In other words, cultural factors, in Garigue's opinion, have prevented French Canadians from being subject to the common urban phenomenon of the reduction of the importance of kin in an urban individual's life.

Marcel Rioux, on the other hand, in an article speaking to the same issue, "Kinship Recognition and Urbanization in French Canada," which appeared in the National Museum of Canada's *Contributions to Anthropology* (1959), takes issue with Garigue on French Canadian cultural immunity to the effects of urbanization. Arguing that French Canada is less urbanized than the United States and that:

> Owing to the partial physical and cultural isolation of French
> Canada in the nineteenth century, urbanization processes have
> been at work over a shorter period than in the rest of North
> America; this society has only started since 1940 to become
> more individualistic and secularized, (379)

Rioux demonstrates that there exists a great deal of rural–urban variation within French Canada with respect to kinship recognition and that on this basis it is unwise to view French Canadian-American variation on this score exclusively in terms of cultural values.[4]

Rioux concludes:

> there are extensive spatio-temporal variations within French
> Canada on the question of kinship recognition and . . . these
> variations are due primarily to a difference in the degree of
> urbanization in the various segments of this socio-cultural
> whole; cultural values might be affected by the social trans-
> formations that urbanization brings about, but in the case of
> kinship recognition it seems that the urbanization factor is
> primordial. (385)

Is it not possible, however, that the reduced importance of
French Canadian kinship recognized by Rioux in the wake of
urbanization serves to mask an original cultural base? After all,
a recognition level of over two hundred in Montréal as compared
to just over thirty for American college students *does* represent
a major difference. Perhaps it would be best to seek an analogous
geographical region in the United States and investigate the
importance of kin-based interaction there. The author is, himself,
familiar with several small- and medium-sized towns in the southern part of the United States in which there is a *marked* tendency
to maintain regular kin interaction with relatives classed as second
cousins and even beyond. While the basis for this interaction could
be classified as "cultural," or "subcultural," the principal factor
accounting for its presence is the *lack of spatial and vertical
mobility* common to the region. People still tend to live and die
in the same place and status in which they were born. Regular
contact is thus maintained with large numbers of relatives, so that
one's second cousin's personality as well as his name and relationship can be easily brought to mind. Today, a change can clearly be
seen to be under way in the region as many individuals—while
reluctant to move to the North as it is often viewed as a cold,
ruthless environment where one's very linguistic capacity is likely
to be called into question[5]—have moved from the towns and
farms of the South to its major cities: Atlanta, Birmingham, and
New Orleans. Even in the cities, however, patterns of visiting and
maintenance of other kin contact appear with sufficient strength
to suggest that the recentness of urbanization is a major factor in
their maintenance.

The lack of spatial and vertical mobility which has typified
Southern life has also been clearly represented *in an intensified*

fashion in Québec. Whereas the Southern white fears ridicule or isolation because of his accent when he leaves his region, the *québécois* is forced to change his language in order to communicate at all. Consequently, the spatial mobility freely enjoyed by English-speaking North Americans who can feel themselves at home virtually anywhere north of the Rio Grande has never been possible—short of assimilation—for French Canadians. There are, to be certain, major French–English differences in the relative importance of kinship ties among the two groups, as Garigue has noted, but these differences are primarily the result of spatial isolation enforced by the barriers of language. To conceive of them in cultural terms is to miss the essential point.

This lack of essential cultural difference between French and English in North America has been repeatedly emphasized by French Canadians themselves. Indeed, it is the similarity and easy incorporation of things American that has most troubled French Canadian nationalists. Most obvious is a *rapprochement* of vocabulary due to the significant presence of English loan words, so that it is absolutely obligatory to utilize expressions like "je vais prendre un shower" rather than "je vais prendre une douche" if one wants to avoid a queer look, or to ask a service station to "mettez l'air dans les tires" rather than "gonflez les pneus" if one wants service, huge segments of the population seem to have virtually no ethnic screen which signals dissonance in the face of the "latest" thing from the States. Drive through any small or medium-sized Québec town and much of what you will see in terms of tastes in cars, which are invariably "jacked-up" and laden with decals, and in food—*chiens chauds, patates frites, hamburgers, poulet frit,* and Pizza—will immediately impress you as representing a unique variant upon the life style of a small Southern or Western town. When one considers the difficulty in extracting anything uniquely French, other than language, from the situation in which a *gars* (boy) takes his *char* (car) down to the *Baron de Boeuf* after school, it is easy to grasp the traditional complaint of those engaged in the revitalization of French language and culture in America that their efforts are being repeatedly undermined by the vogue for things American.

Adding to the problem is that, in spite of all efforts to establish relations with France, the French themselves have no more, and perhaps among most *québécois,* less, popularity than do English Canadians and Americans. The path backward is halted by ties long since severed in the wake of the Conquest and the French Revolution, and bridges being built today are weakened by the feeling that France is a nation of aloof "snobs."

Indications of this distance felt by *québécois* vis-à-vis the French are frequently encountered. I have, myself, had several extended conversations with Frenchmen, male and female, in the presence of *québécois* in which it was clear that the dynamics of the situation saw the French individual looking to me, as an American, as someone who could at least be passably viewed as a cultural equal while glaring condescendingly on his "pauvre cousin" who insisted on breaking all social proprieties and failed to understand that "On ne dit pas 'tu' à *tout* le monde." Invariably, the French individual expressed a sincere desire to leave Québec, and the obviously felt taint of association with this peculiar variety of Frenchman and live for a time in the United States. On the other hand, the relationship in which there was the most rapport for me, but also the most possibility for tension, was the one with the *québécois* who recognized the values of easy familiarity and humor with which I am most comfortable.

André Marrauld, in a letter published in the March 30, 1971 issue of *La Presse,* headlined "Problèmes d'adaptation de l'immigrant français," complained that not enough attention is paid to the plight of French immigrants in Québec. Upon arrival at Dorval International Airport, he says, the French immigrant encounters people who speak French, which assures him that he is in a French country. What he doesn't understand is that:

> The words are just the same but the mind is different. . . . Just as the Parisian, braggart and quarrelsome as he is, shocks a *québécois,* so does the habitual discretion of the latter in the street shock the Parisian. Just picture a Montréal taxi driver screaming "Ta guele, empereur!" ["Shut up, emperor!"] to a bus driver. . . .

> Bit by bit, the entire Canadian context reveals itself to him. The disappointments begin when he starts to look for work. He's rather proud of his French references and diplomas and

even of his driver's license. He immediately discovers that all these have no value in Canada. He has to begin again. . . .

It seems evident to me that there should be a counselor in the Canadian immigration bureaus in France to *mettre les Français en garde.* . . .

His patterns of thought and speech make him poorly understood; he has to learn to systematically keep quiet and listen. . . .

[Because of the false similarity of language] it takes him a while to see that a barrier, a wall, exists, and therefore he suffers, is impatient and frustrated all the more by it. Therefore, don't forget the French immigrant in your prayers! (Marrauld, *La Presse,* 30 Mars 1971:A4)

A common area of frustration arising from failure to recognize that Québec is not as closely connected to France as its language suggests arises in the "dubbing-in" of American films and the production of American plays in the French of Paris. In a recent review following the appearance of the play *Libres sont des papillons* ("Butterflies are free") in Montréal, Michel Beaulieu complained of the ineptitude represented by the production of an American play in Parisian French in Québec. In translating it into the language of the metropolis, Beaulieu felt that it had lost "even in its language all connection with us." "Is it necessary," he wondered, "to keep repeating that we are a part of American life and that our perspective would only be more open than that of our too celebrated 'cousins.' " The enjoyment of such a play is also impaired by the "constant impression that the comedians are having to force themselves to speak well ["Bien parler"]," that is, speak in Parisian French (Beaulieu, *Le Devoir,* 14 février 1972: 10).[6]

Even, or perhaps most of all, the segment of the population which is assumed to be most radical—the CEGEP and university students—is preoccupied with things English and, most particularly, American. The smell of hashish, the sound of American and British pop music, the dress and style of the "hip" generation have all been adopted by French Canadian youth, so much so that a visitor to a student coffee house or bar might never realize he was entirely surrounded by French-speaking individuals unless he turned his ears from the jukebox to his immediate surroundings. Here, too, the spread of "the drug culture" has taken its toll among confused parents, whose concern has resulted in the proliferation of texts on drugs which purport to explain "pourquoi votre enfant se drogue."

Even the left-wing separatist weekly *Point de Mire*,[7] which is primarily student-oriented, devotes the majority of its record and motion picture reviews to English products. It is not unusual to find a detailed article on English domination of some aspect of French Canadian life followed by a review of the Rolling Stones' or John Lennon's latest record. In twenty issues chosen at random from 1971, I found a total of fifteen record and nineteen motion picture reviews. Of the records reviewed, fully fourteen of the fifteen were of English or American groups, while only one was recorded by a French performer (Robert Charlebois, often deservedly described as "Québec's Bob Dylan"). In the category of motion picture reviews, French films fared better but were still in the minority, as ten of the nineteen films reviewed were English. A letter which appeared in the April 30, 1971 issue of the magazine indicates that the irony of this situation has not escaped notice:

> How can a magazine preaching the liberation of peoples from American imperialism, which works to support the real Québec theater, testimony of our daily life, in the same breath under the "Record" section speak to us about: Faces, with Rod Stewart and Ronnie Lane, You're Not Alone, To Be Continued (cf. April 2nd issue), not to mention previous reviews which follow the same lack of logic?
>
> Is Michèle Comtois unaware of all the ideology which permeates your journal or, worse yet, of the importance of music in a culture?
>
> Are you a part, Mademoiselle, of the international (!) youth movement for which all good music must carry the seal "made in USA"?
>
> Don't misunderstand me. I know that music doesn't know frontiers and I enjoy a good soul record now and then. But reserving your critical section exclusively for American or British records at the expense of Québec and French ones

says a lot about your degree of Americanization and has no
place in a magazine like yours.

Joe-Ann Ouellet, St-Amable

(*Point de Mire,* 30 Avril 1971:4).

Clearly, French Canadians are primarily French-speaking North
Americans. What separates French and English in North America
is not so much a difference of culture but of language. But when
one thinks what separation a language can bring. . . .

Bilingualism and Ethnic Identity

English, as the dominant language of North America and today's
universal language, has a certain appeal which would attract a
significant number of French Canadians toward its mastery in
any event. The pressures, however—and herein lies much of the
Canadian problem—have been far from limited to internal ones
directed toward self-betterment. French Canadians feel and *know*
that in order to advance within Canadian society, including French
Canadian society, a mastery of English is virtually indispensable.

Everywhere in Québec, except perhaps in such completely rural
areas as the lowest part of the St. Lawrence Valley, English exerts
a pressure far, far in excess of the numerical importance of the
English-speakers of the region. In Sherbrooke, a major industrial
town ninety miles to the east of Montréal, the Royal Commission
on Bilingualism and Biculturalism found that a constant complaint
of French Canadians was that: "You have to know English to earn
a living. . . . English is spoken so much around Sherbrooke, a
French Canadian has trouble getting ahead if he doesn't know
English" (1965:38). This in a city in which 88 percent of the
population is French. In Trois-Rivières, a city 95 percent French-
speaking, halfway between Québec and Montréal on the north
shore of the St. Lawrence, the Commission heard again and again
complaints that:

> English Canadians make no effort to learn French; some of
> them have lived in Three Rivers for fifty years and still don't
> know a word of French. They think themselves culturally
> superior; they own 75 percent of the local capital. The
> English-speaking bosses don't encourage French Canadians to

rise to managerial positions—not through ill-will mind you, but because *they forget the very existence of the French Canadians, in spite of their overwhelming numbers in the area.* (Preliminary Report of the RCBB, 1965:38; emphasis mine)

In general, and especially among French Canadian youth,[8] the Commission found a great deal of bitterness in Québec toward English Canadians who "feel no need to learn French" and are "camping here like some imperial army" (38).

Again and again, I was faced with the complaint by French Canadians that they were forced to learn English to find work. Indeed, as in many cases the work itself does not demand a command of English, the insistence on bilingual employees and the general preference shown bilinguals in matters of salary and promotion often seem to result from a "knee jerk" reaction demanding knowledge of English followed by even French employers. One computer operator in his mid-twenties summed up this feeling in a rather typical response:

> *Tabernac!* Why should I have to learn English and even speak better English than most English Canadians can just to get a good job in Québec? Even if all the directors are English there are still ten times as many of us as there are English. Why can't they learn French? I don't mind learning English but it's always "*must* be bilingual."

The roots of this bitterness lie in the English domination of the province. Whereas an English-speaking individual expects to be able to travel anywhere in North America in his own language, and is quick to comment that a French Canadian in Rivière-du-Loup "speaks English very poorly," the French Canadian knows his language will open few doors for him. He has learned to be defensive, even ashamed, of his inability to communicate in English, but without this knowledge his grasp on the choicest jobs and his ability to rise through the industrial and commercial ranks is marginal.[9]

I found this sense of personal linguistic inadequacy to be rather deeply ingrained among many French monolinguals. Even among radical nationalist youth there was a sense that one was not quite a complete individual unless he was bilingual. Thus, I found repeatedly that even individuals who consciously identified themselves as "québécois" rather than the less nationalistic "canadien-français" expressed to me a feeling that it was *they* who should be speaking English with me and not me speaking French with them. In the words of one monolingual *québécoise* of the Université de Montréal: "C'est moi qui devrais parler ta langue pas le contraire." In permitting me to speak French and not attempting to struggle along in English, a sense of guilt that one was letting the opportunity to practice pass was often evident. (See also the section on reciprocal exploitation below.)

Despite some indications (cf. footnote 9 above) which, I am rather certain, greatly exaggerate the level of bilingualism among English-speaking Montrealers,[10] virtually all French Canadians seem agreed that bilingualism is *à sens unique* ("one way"). Rioux notes that 96 percent of French-language administrators are required to be bilingual by their contracts while only half of Québec's English are required to know French and, in Montréal, 86 percent of English-speakers earning above five thousand dollars a year are unilingual (1969:126). In any event, it is well known that an English Canadian generally can easily find work in Montréal—a city two-thirds French—with little or no effort, while it is not quite so easy for a French Canadian to do the same. As one farmer struggling to survive on a small farm told me: "I can't go to Montréal to find work because I can't speak any English. You always have to speak English there."[11]

The parents of Québec, not surprisingly under these conditions, are unwilling to trust to the Provincial government's much vaunted efforts to make *le français-langue-de-travail* in the matter of their children's future. Many may have felt themselves hampered by an inadequate knowledge of English and are unwilling to see their children's future so stymied. Thus, a Gallup poll published in the September 7, 1965 issue of *La Presse* indicated the following results in response to the question:

> In your opinion, do you think that the teaching of English should or should not be obligatory in the same way as is Reading, Writing and Arithmetic, in the schools of French Canada?

	General Opinion	East	Québec	Ontario	West
Yes	84%	89%	92%	84%	76%
No	13	9	7	11	21
No response	3	2	1	5	3

It was Québec parents rather than their English Canadian neighbors who felt most strongly that English should be a mandatory subject in Québec's schools.

In conversations which I have had with French Canadian students it seems that it is often the student's mother who is the major familial force encouraging the learning of English. This impression is confirmed by Pierre Vallières in his *Nègres blancs d'Amerique: Autobiographie précoce d'un "terroriste" québécois.* While he was attending a *collège* studying classics, ostensibly for a religious vocation, his mother

> Absolutely insisting that [I] study English and math never ceased to hassle me—"Leave this day school! When you're finished studying then where are you going to work, especially if you don't speak English?" (Valliéres, 1968:175)

Not surprisingly, the encroachment of English upon the daily lives of French Canadians appears to have significantly heightened the *psychic intensity*[12] of French identity. While temporal evidence of this is difficult to obtain, there can be little disagreement that preoccupation with French identity, always present, appears to have increased significantly in the past fifty years. At the Conquest, after an initial period of uncertainty, French Canadians appeared to have been "fort tranquilles et paraissent attendre la décision de leur sort sans aucune inquiétude" (Haldimand quoted in Brunet, 1958:43). Indeed, if Burton's report is to be believed, and there appears to be no indication to the contrary, "the *habitants,* particularly the peasants, appear very happy to have changed masters" (43). The Rebellion of 1837–38, which produced the *patriotes* revered by today's separatists, was more a bourgeois than a true ethnic revolt, and its leadership was shared by English colonists. With the hanging of Riel and the increased subordination of Québec brought on by Confederation, however, the tide began to change and subsequent national crises evidenced more and more of an ethnic base. World Wars I and II brought draft riots and massive evasion of French Canadians from conscription, while their English counterparts volunteered in droves. Indeed, as François-Albert Angers has noted, the plebiscite held April 27, 1942 was "un vote de race" in which French Canadians refused to come to the aid of "Mother England."

Do you consent to free the government from all obligation resulting from previous commitments restricting the methods of mobilization of the military services?[13]

Percentage of the Population Voting "No" According to Province

Quebec	71.2[14]	Nova Scotia	21.3
Yukon	31.7	British Columbia	19.6
New Brunswick	29.1	Manitoba	19.5
Alberta	27.1	Prince Edward Island	16.6
Saskatchewan	26.6	Ontario	16.1

(After Laurendeau, 1962:119; Bergeron, 1970:198)

The relative psychic intensity of French identity in Québec also appears to vary significantly with the degree of urbanization. In criss-crossing the province of Québec I found that the level of antagonism toward English seems to be significantly less in rural areas. It was not unusual in my experience for French Canadian farmers and rural dwellers to receive me in a much warmer fashion than would their counterparts in the city. The fact that I was American and from the English world—to the degree that it was a factor at all—seemed to drop quickly from the consciousness of both parties in conversations which began with "tu" and some- times lasted for almost an hour in the periodic intensification and lapse of dialogue peculiar to the countryside and small towns. Indeed, at one point during the course of my research, a farmer of my acquaintance made quite obvious efforts to serve as a match- maker between me and a *québécoise* of whom he was very fond.[15]

Attempting to empirically substantiate a rural–urban increase in psychic intensity of French identity is by no means an easy matter. One criterion, however, whose investigation might be fruitful is that of adherence to separatist political beliefs. If the process of urbanization, which is assumed to be coupled with increased pressure to accommodate to the English world, results in an increased awareness of "Frenchness" and a bitterness toward the current Canadian entity which devalues that identity, then it should be assumed that a separatist political party will receive a higher percentage of votes in urban than rural areas.

The 1970 Québec provincial elections, in which the separatist

Parti Québécois was pitted against three union parties: the *Parti Libérale, Union Nationale* and the *Ralliement Créditiste,* offers us the opportunity to trace the relative support for this party on a rural–urban dimension. When a voting analysis is made among the French electorate it is evident that support for the P.Q. was strongest in urban and weakest in rural areas:

Total Québec Vote Among Francophones in April, 1970 Provincial Elections

	Number of Votes Cast	Percent of Total
Libéral	752,696	32.6
Parti Québécois	660,818	28.7
Union Nationale	558,227	24.2
R. C. (including others)	332,007	14.5
Total	2,303,748	

(After Smith, 1970:103)

Vote According to Québec's Major Regions[16]

	P. Q.	Libéral	U. N.	Others
Island of Montréal[17]				
East	48.5%	30.3%	17.0%	4.3%
West	41.8	38.5	14.3	5.3
Rive Nord de Montréal	35.0	37.3	22.8	4.9
Rive Sud de Montréal	33.4	36.8	23.7	6.0
Region de l'Estrie (incl. Most of Eastern Townships)	19.4	20.3	30.8	29.5
Western Québec	13.8	45.7	25.0	15.6
Côte Nord	50.8	25.2	19.8	4.1
Regions de l'Abitibi, Mauricie, Gaspé, Québec, etc. (58 counties)	227,031	367,749	324,004	239,794

(After Smith, 1970:100–103)

If it is possible, as I think it is, to make a general equation between votes cast for the *Parti Québécois* and degree of French identity, then it is clear from the results of the 1970 election that there is an increase in French identity associated with urbanization. Not surprisingly, the French working-class ridings of East Montréal provided the *Parti Québécois* with six of its seven seats—

the only victory outside of Montréal for the P.Q. coming from the largely rural Saguenay riding on the lower north shore of the St. Lawrence.[18]

Undoubtedly, a major factor increasing the intensity of recognition of French identity in Montréal is the awareness of a major status differential between French and English Montrealers. While not all English Canadians live in the luxurious mansions of Westmount or the only slightly more humble homes of the Town of Mount-Royal, it is they and not their poor cousins of Point St. Charles who represent the English presence to Montréal's French population. La Ville d'Outremont, as a point of French aspirations, pales before these English quarters; yet, even here, few of the city's French Canadian families are likely to enter as residents. For the most part, they are likely to pass their lives and rear their children in the drab tenements and *taudis* (slums) which sprawl across the entire eastern sector of the city.

Adding to this sense of inferiority is the fact that most obvious loci of economic power in the city are English: Steinberg's and Dominion grocery stores, with their city-wide branches; Eaton's, Simpson's and Morgan's (Hudson's Bay Company) department stores; the Bank of Nova Scotia, the Bank of Montreal and the Royal Bank of Canada, which, even with their careful efforts to translate their titles into French, remain symbols of the English presence. Despite the fact that the English number only one fifth of the population, they clearly exert a very forceful influence upon the life of Montréal. Of the city's four television stations, two serve the more than two thirds of the population which is French while the remaining two *presumably* serve only that fifth of the population that is English. As Maheu, summarizing the opinion of *le Père* Bernard Mailhot, has expressed it:

> The French Canadians sense that they live in a city which doesn't belong to them, which doesn't resemble them; this feeling is so real that it often happens that they address one another in English without noticing it. . . . The English community is conscious of being a privileged minority, it sees its existence questioned and threatened by the discontented mass which surrounds it and whose anger can break out at any time. . . . Montreal always appears to be *la ville des autres*.

> The two communities who live there have a defense psy-
> chology *vis-à-vis* each other, Père Mailhot continues, no one is
> at home there. (Maheu, 1964:17)

Exemplifying this sense of alienation experienced by *québécois*
in Montréal is an experience which one of my *québécoise* informants had as a young girl in Eaton's, a major department store
located in the central shopping district. When she approached a
saleslady to negotiate a purchase she was told haughtily: "I don't
speak French." Switching to English she fared no better and was
told that she wasn't understood. She held back her tears and anger
until she reached home, when she broke down sobbing to her
mother, "Mother, I am never going to be able to speak English."
Her relation of the story, fifteen years laters, showed that its
impact, coupled presumably with later real or imagined insults,
still roused a strong well of bitterness.

Yet Montréal is not an English city. Quite to the contrary, the
French outnumber the English in a ratio of five to two, and the
apparatus of city government is wholly in French hands. Most
English feel ill at ease in Montréal; it is certainly not their city.
Paradoxically, many French, in spite of their numerical superiority, feel the same way. As one French Canadian farmer told
me: "On n'a pas besoin de parler français à Montréal. On y parle
anglais." Whatever the objective reality, the journey from the
small towns and farms of the province to Montréal is too often
seen as a journey to an English bastion—technically French, "mais
une ville anglaise quand-même."

A further phenomenon accenting the differences separating
French and English in the city is the tendency for each group to
go its way ignoring the presence of the other. As one well-to-do
Jewish notary who has been a lifelong resident of Montréal
lamented: "There is a whole world that will never be open to us
here."[19] The city, being as it is largely based on secondary contacts, only exaggerates the natural tendency for those of different
languages to isolate themselves. Establishing a close, continuing
relationship with someone from the other language group requires
an effort and an uncomfortable foreknowledge that the difference more often than not foredooms the relationship—eventually
it will become easier to fall back on one's ethnic fellows, where
there are no indelible criteria upon which to fix one's paranoia.

As Maheu has also noted: "Montrealers seem centered upon the ethnic problem and the closing off of each group from the other seems almost total" (1964:17).

Montréal thus serves as a point of contact between two peoples. The French Canadian who enters it faces, in all probability, a greater sense of linguistic dissonance—a greater devaluation of his native language—than he has ever known in his search for a livelihood there. Coupled with this linguistic dissonance is the fact that the learning of English does not permit him genuine access to the expressive sphere of this world but only to its instrumental region—in learning English he does not really gain the possibility of making English friends but, rather, gains the right to serve them. Under this situation of linguistic dissonance and interethnic isolation it appears that the sense of "Frenchness," of the psychic intensity of French identity, has been heightened so that it is possible to speak of an increase in ethnic identity associated with urbanization in Québec.

Caste Aspects of French-English Relations

> To be a "nigger," is not to be a man in America but to be someone's slave. For the rich white man of Yankee America the "nigger" is subhuman. Even the poor whites think of the "nigger" as their inferior. They say: "to work as hard as a nigger," "to smell as bad as a nigger," "to be dangerous like a nigger," "to be as stupid as a nigger". . .

> In Québec, French Canadians don't know this irrational racism which has caused so much harm to the white and black workers of the United States. No credit is due them for this, however, as there is no "Black problem" in Québec. The liberation struggle undertaken by American blacks is, however, of growing interest to the French Canadian people because the workers of Québec are aware of their condition as niggers, as exploited, second-class citizens. Haven't they been since the founding of New France the "white niggers of America"? Weren't they, like all American Blacks, imported to serve as cheap labor in the New World? Only color and continent of origin distinguishes one from the other. (Vallieres, 1968: 25-26)[20]

> Québécois are beginning to realize that they are the niggers around here. (conversation with a French Canadian radical)

Is the assertion that *québécois* and French Canadians in general are the "white niggers of America" merely radical rhetoric of the all-too-familiar "student as nigger" or "woman as nigger" genre, or is this comparison valid? To what extent, if at all, does the analogy between American blacks and French Canadians hold true?

The notion of a French "race" in North America is by no means a recent one. Again and again throughout French Canadian history it has made its appearance. French history texts have traditionally carried titles like *La race française en Amérique* (Desrosiers et Fournet, 1911), and Lionel Groulx chose as a title for his major novel *L'appel de la race*. The term "race," however, is employed with the full breadth of its meaning as a "people" or "nation" rather than in the more restricted sense its use immediately evokes in the United States today.[21]

When Vallières refers to French Canadians as "white niggers," the analogy he is making, while limited to an extension of the Marxist concept of "class consciousness" to "race consciousness," is not strictly one of race at all but rather one of *caste*.[22] In speaking of "white niggers," he describes a group of people isolated from the remainder of North American society according to the criterion of ethnicity which channels and maintains them in the most dismal and unrewarding positions which the society has to offer. Following this argument, caste can be seen to be defined in the United States primarily by race or color and in Canada primarily by language.

In seeking to establish the limits, or indeed even the legitimacy, of the assertion that French Canadians represent a caste or even a quasi-caste in North America, it is useful to investigate the Canadian situation in the light of several of the major criteria whose presence can be used to define caste systems cross-culturally: "occupational prescription," concepts of "caste purity," and "caste endogamy."

For the criteria of occupational prescription, as well as those of caste purity and endogamy, the traditional caste system of India can be seen as the limiting case. Caste, as ideally practiced in India, *determined* occupation, degree of ritual purity, and the range of acceptable marriage partners. In the United States, as in India, birth-ascribed "casting" no longer operates with legal sanction, and blacks find themselves facing few legal boundaries. Occupational discrimination has been prohibited by law, concepts of purity are no longer permitted to determine public commensality or toilet use, and anti-miscegenation statutes have all but been eliminated by the Federal court system. Yet, of course, caste remains with us. There remain distinct taboos against black-white intermarriage, there continues to exist among both blacks and whites a deep sense that blackness is equivalent to filth and lack of order—an association rooted deep in the American psyche and only gradually, if at all, in the process of change—and there continues to exist an occupational channeling—one cannot any longer say prescription, as it is in this sphere that some change has been effected.

From our previous discussion it is evident that the occupational channeling of American blacks has its analogue in Canada among French Canadians. While a French Canadian youth can, through talent and sustained effort, make his way out of the occupational ranks most of his fellows occupy, as can any similarly talented American black, the effort required is clearly much greater than that which would be exacted from his English counterpart.

While there are breaches of the racial barriers in the United States in brief sexual encounters, marriage between blacks and whites is quite rare.[23] There can be no question but that cultural prescriptions against French–English intermarriage do not approach the intensity of those directed against black-white marriages. Yet, proscriptions clearly exist. As Colette Carisse, in an article "Orientations culturelles dans les marriages entre Canadiens français et Canadiens anglais" appearing in *Sociologie et Société,* has remarked:

> The cultural resistances to such unions are so strong that when they don't succeed in preventing the union, they make certain that the road of those who dare to violate these barriers will be a series of disappointments and misfortunes.

> In *les Anciens Canadiens* [1890, Philippe Aubert de Gaspé], Blanche d'Haberville refuses, immediately after the Conquest, to marry her childhood friend, an "anglais" who wished to become "canadien." "There is between us now an abyss which

I will never cross." Her friend of yesterday has become the conqueror and she refuses to "light the torch of marriage on the smoking ashes of [her] poor country."[24]

Several years later, once the embers cooled, however, her brother married an English woman. (Carisse, 1969: 39-40)[25]

And French-English marriages are relatively rare. Ross has noted that: "One of the remarkable features about the French and English in the Province of Quebec is that intermarriage between the two groups has not developed to any great extent" (1941:67). Henripin, Charbonneau and Mertens, in their analysis of the 1961 national census, have found that, for Canada as a whole, 86.7 percent of French Canadians marry within their own group while 81.4 percent of "British" Canadians do the same.[26] Among French Canadians 9.1 percent take "British" spouses and 5.4 percent of the "British" marry French partners.

In Québec, where French ethnicity receives its maximum expression and environmental support, the level of French endogamy is fully 95.6 percent while "British" endogamy is only 74.9 percent. Eighteen and seven-tenths percent of all "British" marriages contracted in the province are with French Canadians while marriages with "British" spouses account for only a miniscule 2.9 percent of all Québec French marriages (RRCBB, vol. IV:281, 285).

A most interesting, and telling, feature of French-English marriages when they do occur, however, is the fact that, contrary to the image projected in novels and movies produced by French Canadian males, the preferred marriage seems to be that between an English male and a French female. Thus, one finds that for all of Canada, 5.8 percent of "British" males take French spouses while only 4.9 percent of the females choose their husbands from among the ranks of French Canadians. Among French Canadians 9.7 percent of marriages entered into by French females are with "British" males while 8.5 percent of those undertaken by French males are with "British" females. In Québec, 20.7 percent of "British" males married French females while 16.7 percent of "British" females were married to French spouses. Among the French population of the province, the rate of "British"-directed exogamy was 3.3 percent for the females and 2.6 percent for the males.

Perhaps most interesting of all is that among the twelve major ethnic groups of Canada all save three are characterized by greater rates of female than male endogamy—the females of nine of the twelve groups are more inclined to marry within the group and evidence a greater anchoring to their ethnic origins. The three groups which demonstrate a reversal of this tendency are the Ukrainians, Germans, and French. The sexual endogamy differential for Ukrainians is 1.2 percent in favor of a tendency for females to marry out with greater frequency than males, while for Germans it is 1.0 percent. Curiously enough, however, the French, the ethnic group with the longest period of settlement among the twelve considered in the census endogamy tables, show a male-female endogamy differential of 3.2 percent, *with the males tending to marry within the group with greater frequency* (RRCBB, vol. IV:293).[27]

While it is difficult to be certain of the reasons which underlie the observed tendency of French-English intermarriages to be English male-French female and for endogamy to be greater among French males than among French females, various possible explanations suggest themselves: (1) English females may reject marriage with French males as beneath them, perhaps thinking of their children's future; (2) French males, because of the traditional focus upon male offspring, especially in matters of inheritance, may have a greater interest in preservation of their ethnicity through their progeny than do French females; (3) English males may find French females desirable sexual partners who, in choosing an English spouse, have anticipated rearing their children in English; (4) French Canadian women, seeing a dim future for their children, decide to "sell out" or, perhaps better put, "bail out."[28]

The final criterion of caste to be considered here—that of pollution—yields the most tenuous ground of all upon which to base a theory of the "nègres blancs d'Amérique." This is not to say that concepts of French as polluting are not present. On the contrary, they are very much in evidence. Indications of French "pollution," however, are most generally seen in a class perspective. The fact of the French-English economic differential itself means that French Canadians are more likely to have attributes associated with poverty ascribed to them. Thus, French Canadians are less well educated and have acquired, partially as a result of this, a stereotypic conception in English thought best summed up in the expression "stupid frog." The currency of this stereotype is such that I found even well-educated French to be sensitive on this score. One conversation with a French professional was interrupted by an English individual of similar status who made a joking comment about the "stupid French." After responding with appropriate good humor, the French woman turned to me and asked in French: "there's a grain of truth to what he said in his mind, isn't there!?"

Dental standards, partially as a result of poverty and partially the result of a rural tradition, are extremely low. It is rare indeed to see a French Canadian who does not have obviously caried or false teeth. Until recently, poverty and a desire to enhance personal beauty induced some French Canadian girls to have their teeth extracted and replaced with straight, white, cavity-free false teeth.[29] Poor dental care, possibly as a result of the symbolic element it represents, produced perhaps the closest to a disgust, and thus a "pollution," response which I was able to record:

> French girls may be sexy but they always have bad teeth. I remember going out with a really tough girl a couple of years ago, frenching her, and *Jesus*, her teeth came out. I almost threw up. (English male, 25)

> One of the reasons I go here (Le chat noir) is that you can see if a girl has her real teeth [due to the identifying effect of the ultraviolet light which differentiates false from real teeth]. J's girl is beautiful but look at her teeth [indicating a girl seated at the table with several false incisors]. (Yugoslav male, 23)

The dating of a French male by an English female often appears to evoke sentiments of disgust among the girl's parents even when they are Catholic, and is the Canadian equivalent, diminished in affect to be certain, of a white female dating a black male in the United States. That the motive is oftentimes a desire to evoke parental anger, or a sentiment of any kind, can be seen from the statement of a twenty-year-old English Catholic girl who told me that she and her parents (especially her father, whom she saw as very aloof) rarely interacted except in heated argument over her French boyfriend. The girl, whose closest friend was a black female who always dated whites and according to her own testimony couldn't "stand to have a black man touch me," had had unfortunate experiences in her selections of boyfriends for years: they always seemed to be either French or Jewish.

While aspects of the three caste criteria discussed are represented in French–English relations in Canada, conception of the situation in caste terms alone does violence to the reality at hand. French Canadians are not, after all, really "white niggers." To conceive of them as such may capture some of their experience on this English-speaking continent but it does great injustice to the much deeper psychic trauma of the American black. It also fails to take account of the fact that even with French–English cultural similarities these differences are greater than those found between so-called "black culture" and American culture in general. Most important of all, the French have their language to retreat to as a clear symbol of group identity and a screen against outsiders.[30] As George DeVos has remarked:

> A caste can't escape psychologically because it has no separate culture to harbor to—but an ethnic group can mobilize itself both psychologically and politically in terms of its separateness—rather than fighting lower status with the system. (personal communication)

French Canadians, unlike blacks, may choose to retain the quasi-caste identification which is coupled with their ethnicity or cast it off and assimilate. While the first generation French Canadian in the process of assimilation is very unlikely to completely shake the telltale accent and the capacity to speak French which will identify him, his children, even with a French Canadian surname, can be accepted as English. This fact alone makes it quite obvious that French–English relations must be viewed on an ethnic, class, or, at most, quasi-caste rather than on a true caste or racial level.

While the discussion of caste or racial aspects of French–English relations might well be left at this point, it is worthwhile to note two related phenomena: (1) the universal use of "tu" in Québec; and (2) André Laurendeau's theory of "le roi-nègre" which is embraced by French Canadian separatists.

Perhaps the first thing which strikes the French-speaking individual upon arriving in Québec is the almost universal use of "tu," of the familiar form of address, among *québécois,* in general, and especially among those in the lower classes of Québec society. It is the rule, rather than the exception, for a stranger to address another stranger with the familiar form and, even among strangers, age and status differences are likely to be ignored. Thus I found myself, much to my pleasant surprise, "tu'ed" by service station attendants and professionals alike—although the latter tended to show more restraint, and several minutes of conversation or a second meeting in informal surroundings were usually required to switch to the familiar form. Needless to say, in places frequented by students "vous" was only heard when conversation required the plural form, and negotiating a path through a crowded bar or coffee house was accomplished with "excuse."

One becomes so habituated to the use of "tu" in Québec, especially among age mates, that the presence of an individual from the one group which absolutely refuses to accept or use it— the "real" French—is somewhat jolting. Use of "tu" with these individuals seems to wreak havoc with their autonomic nervous systems. The French appear to have as hard a time, perhaps even a much harder one, "tuing" casual acquaintances as a white American would in adopting the "brother" and "sister" forms of the black ghetto. One French woman of my acquaintance suffered under this annoyance for years until a policeman in the process of ticketing her car referred to her as "toi."[31] That was too much. She took his badge number, wrote the police department (where it presumably received a hearty laugh) and *Le Devoir,* where it was probably received with a sad shrug of resignation.

Maurice Duplessis, the long-time ruler of Québec, in exercising his customary concern for democratic institutions, spawned the theory of "le roi-nègre," which has since been extended to interpret all of French Canadian history. Duplessis, in 1958, the year before his death, tiring of the presence of the *Le Devoir* reporter Guy Lamarche at his press conferences, told him to leave. When

Lamarche refused to budge he had him ejected by the police. *Le Devoir* was joined in its strenuous objection to this incident by the other major French papers of the province, while the English press let the matter pass seemingly without concern. Responding to what he felt was a typical indifference of English Canadians toward the rights of their French fellow citizens, André Lauredeau, then editor of *Le Devoir,* editorialized:

> Usually the English are more sensitive than we are to assaults of all forms of liberty. This is why Mr. Duplessis has a bad press outside of Québec. . . . This is often caused by the old prejudices of "race" and language but we would be wrong to explain everything on the grounds of ethnic prejudice. The English conquered their political liberties little by little; they know better their price; they are usually more sensitive to threats against them.

> *Usually,* we emphasize. Because in Québec this tradition seems singularly anemic. At least if we can judge by the English newspapers when they assess Québec events.

> If Ottawa tried to muzzle speech by majority vote then all the journals would chorus their protests . . .

> In Québec's legislative assembly such incidents are the daily fare, yet our English language newspapers let them pass with almost no protest. Why?

> Québec's English newspapers act like the British in the heart of one of their African colonies.

> The British have a strong sense of politics; they rarely destroy the political institutions of a conquered country. They surround the Negro king, but they leave him some illusion of control. They permit him on occasion to cut off heads if such is the custom. One thing would never occur to them: to demand of a Negro king that he conform to the high moral and political standards of the British.

> It is important to find a Negro king who will collaborate and protect British interests. Once this collaboration is assured, the rest is unimportant. Does the little king violate the rules of democracy? One would know not to expect anything more from a primitive . . .

> I do not attribute these sentiments to the English minority of Québec. But things happen as if their leaders subscribe to the

> theory and practice of the Negro king. They pardon in Mr. Duplessis, chief of the natives of the country of Québec, what they would not tolerate in one of their own . . .

> The result is the regression of democracy and parliamentarianism, an arbitrary and no longer contested reign, and a constant collusion between Anglo-Québec finance and the most rotten aspects of this province's politics. (*Le Devoir*, 4 juillet 1958:4)

The idea that the English had been ruling Québec for two centuries through "Negro kings" quickly caught on. "So that is what the problem has been! That is what has held us back!" many seem to have thought-wished. The thesis of "le roi-nègre," however, had to wait until 1970 to receive the ultimate and logical extension given it by Léandre Bergeron in his *Petit manuel d'histoire du Québec*. This paperbound book of 249 pages, sold at a maximum price of one dollar per copy, received a truly phenomenal acceptance and led the Québec best-seller list for nine months. Bergeron saw the grand scope of Québec history as being shaped largely by English efforts to simultaneously exploit the "cheap labor" of the *québécois* and to maintain him in continued subservience. In order to accomplish these goals, at each moment in history the British had to search within Québec society for those elements most sympathetic to their interests, support them and give them free rein within the province. While at various times they leaned toward politicians, as Duplessis, their chief ally through the post-Conquest period, Bergeron maintains, was the one which could always be counted upon to deliver the tranquil, reactionary province they sought: the Catholic church, described by Bergeron as "le parfait roi-nègre."

Today, not surprisingly, Québec's Premier Bourassa is the focus of theorizing concerning his role as "roi-nègre," something which his own frequently publicized meetings with American businessmen to attract capital has not diminished. "Bourassa is here," one of my informants insisted, "because the English like him. As long as he does what they want he can stay."

"Reciprocal Exploitation" [32]

> How come you shut me out as if I wasn't there?
> What's this new bitterness you've found?

However wronged you were, however strong it hurt;
It wasn't me that held you down. . . .

Why can't you understand I'm glad you're standing proud?
I know you made it on your own,
But in this pride you've earned,
I thought you might have learned,
that you don't have to stand alone.
("Song for Canada," Gzowski and Tyson, ASCAP,
Copyright Warner Brothers Music, 1965)

"Song for Canada," as the liner notes on the Ian and Sylvia album *In the Early Morning Rain,* in which it appears state, is "for the French listeners. . . . It is a genuine effort to bridge the widening gap between two peoples but . . . the French Canadians do not hear it—they have their own singers." The gulf, not to say abyss, separating French and English in Canada is such that the two peoples are often said to be living in "two solitudes." Chauveau has perhaps best captured the sense of physical proximity yet great psychic distance reminiscent of a Rousseauvian painting:

> English and French, we climb by a double flight of stairs toward the destinies reserved for us on this continent, without knowing each other, without meeting each other, and without even seeing each other, except on the landing of politics. In social and literary terms, we are far more foreign to each other than the English and French of Europe. (Chauveau in Wade, 1964:2)

While French and English worlds remain largely closed one to the other, French and English outside of Québec and in Montréal must interact constantly. Here there is too much proximity, too much economic interdependence to permit a complete turning inward. The necessity of this interaction, however, does not mean that it is entered into without reserve. Indeed, in most daily French-English encounters—those fleeting contacts with sales personnel, supermarket checkers, postal clerks—a kind of holding back as part of an ethnic barrier can readily be observed.

The essence of reciprocal exploitation of members of one group by another requires that there be some binding element resented by members of one of the groups, yet, for all practical purposes, unbreakable. In Québec, that element is primarily French economic dependence upon the English and secondarily the fact that the French, themselves, occupy only a small section of an English continent. At present the bond seems secure and the economic tie seems as invulnerable to rupture as is the geographic one.

Under a situation of economic dependence upon another group, symbolized in Québec by the need to know English, a preservation of an adquate self-image stipulates that some method of back-pedaling, of resisting necessity, be found. Thus, while the French are clearly subjected to instrumental exploitation they see themselves as dominant, within Québec, in the expressive arena. Ground lost by the French in the arena of self-image through inferior economic power is made up in the realm of *esoteric* and *exoteric*[33] stereotypes and, if possible, in individual encounters with members of the English group.

On the esoteric level, the French see themselves as *gens sympathiques,* as warm, pleasant people more concerned with the enjoyment of life than with the accumulation of material possessions. Their exoteric image of English Canadians portrays their compatriots as calculating and aloof people given over to the world of the mind and failing that of the body.[34] Clear superiority to the English is recognized in the expressive spheres of life, while reality, an unpleasant intrusion into stereotypes concerning oneself, intervenes in the instrumental sphere and grants the English superior business ability best summarized in the word "clever." As Aellen discovered in her analysis of questionnaires administered to schoolchildren: "French Canadians see themselves as more interesting, brave, dependable and happy, but less smart or successful" (1967:95).

Aellen has also found that English Canadian school children felt that French Canadians were "less friendly, pleasant, stable, popular and ambitious, but . . . more honest than English Canadians" (95). With maturation, this cluster, while retaining its essential integrity, is subsumed to the perception that English Canadians, perhaps more than any other, carry of French Canadians: that of a childlike, vaguely infantile group of people.[35] From this exoteric stereotype arises the preferred fashion of interaction with French: bemused toleration of their tendency to be carried away with every novel idea or persuasive argument.

It is this belief, in fact, which removes some of the edge from the vitriolic separatist attacks, as it sees them as arising more from the character of French Canadian personality than from real grievances.

Stereotypes of French Canadians as being swept away with their own rhetoric, which can be seen in such phrases as "The frogs love to talk," are by no means limited to English Canadians. French Canadians themselves frequently make comments which indicate that there is some internalization of a similar stereotype on an esoteric level, as did one middle-aged informant, originally from a largely French village in Ontario, who complained to me that:

> We French have mouths like this [indicating with a gesture of his hands a mouth several feet across] and arms this long [touching his right arm above his elbow with an open left fist.] We're always talking about what we're going to do but we can't do anything.

Not surprisingly, most efforts of French Canadians to even the score take place on the linguistic level. English Canadians, as a rule, make little effort to conceal their belief that English is a superior language well adapted to the scientific world of the twentieth century. Their disparaging attitudes toward French may be as subtle as a refusal to learn it, even though they may come from a line which has lived in Québec for generations, or on rare occasions as blatant as a reference to French Canadians as people who don't "speak white." Even the most charitable English, who grant the French language *as it is spoken in France* a place along-side English in a ranking of the world's languages, make explicit reference to Québec French as a dialect or a patois and offer as their major argument for refusing to learn French that, even if they did learn "real French," no one in Québec would understand them anyway.

There is no need for *québécois* to be alerted to the attitude the English harbor toward their language—they know it all too well and subscribe to much of it themselves. One of the major efforts of Québec's various French revitalization movements has always been directed toward convincing the people of French Canada that their language is as good, better in fact, than English and that it is in fact *the* language of culture.

One of these revitalizationists, Professor Raymond Barbeau, quoting Phillipe Garigue to the effect that:

> The usage of French as a criterion of identity today exceeds the importance given to religion, territorial residence, family name or even place of birth. The notion of the French Canadian nation is itself connected to the concept of the priority of the French language as a sign of national identity, (Barbeau, 1965:12)

argues that the major problem of the French Canadian people is their belief that their language is inferior. "The weakness of our language," he says, "touches our most intimate being: as a people we have not yet learned to speak, we are a people who stammer, curse and talk jargon." (10) While the language spoken by many *québécois* may be inferior, Barbeau suggests, the French language itself most decidedly is not.

This strongly felt sense of linguistic inferiority is undoubtedly one of the major factors creating dissonance in terms of French ethnic identity, as one is often embarrassed at the quality of the very essence of the identity. It is not unusual for French Canadians to openly discuss the "quality" of their language in comparison with the Parisian yardstick and find it sorely lacking: "Sometimes I really can't see the use in going on. . . . All we have is a language no one understands mixed with English" (male French instructor, 35).

It is important, Barbeau maintains, for French Canadians to realize that bilingualism is degrading because it directs French Canadians toward English, a language which is the "result of a compounding of heterogeneous linguistic materials, an amalgam of linguistic debris," (40) rather than French, which is "the most perfect instrument of humanization and communication which man has ever invented" (13).

French Canadians—usually those who speak broken or no English—frequently maintain that English, in contrast to French, is such a simple language that anyone can learn it in at most a period of a few months. In one radio "talk show," the commentator took exception to this point casually uttered by his caller as if universally accepted:

De comprendre l'anglais Américain avec un vocabulaire de trois cents mots c'est facile, mais de comprendre le bon anglais d'Angleterre avec un vocabulaire assez grand ce n'est pas facile non plus.

To understand American English with its three-hundred-word vocabulary is easy, but to understand good British English with its rather large vocabulary is not easy either.

Many French Canadian intellectuals have argued that their people suffer from an inferiority complex. They often appear "to have the mentality of a colonized people.... [which] would explain the ambivalence apparent in their struggles for French survival" (Landry, 1968:58). Curiously enough, Landry, who himself has argued persuasively for assimilation, denies that this complex exists. On the contrary, he says, French Canadians have developed a "superiority complex" arising from an ability to operate within both linguistic spheres:

Think of a group of French Canadians chatting together, in French naturally. An English-speaker has just joined the group. Immediately, without even seeming to notice, everyone switches to English, whether the new arrival be a boss, an equal, or an employee. Is this a reaction of colonized peoples, an example of a complex? This would be true if the French Canadians of the group felt ashamed to speak French among themselves as if they feared reprisals on the part of the new arrival. Ask them, however, why they changed languages. Because of politeness and pride. *We, we can speak both languages. We, we can switch from one language to the other without even noticing it. We, we condescend to speak to the poorly-equipped arrival in the only language he understands.* In any case, cowardice is so little a factor that if the arrival has the misfortune to slip and suggest that they "Speak white!" they will take out their placards demanding retaliation.

If the arrival insists, as often happens, that we continue to speak in French, a rare occasion for him to practice our language, we'll go along in as circumspect a fashion as possible, translating difficult words to help him, very paternally, but will soon switch back to English to simplify things. *If the other ventures a few words in French, we'll bite our lips to avoid laughing.* (Landry, 1969:59; emphasis mine)

While it is doubtful that a "superiority complex" has been the result of the necessity of French Canadians to learn two languages, there can be no doubt but that dual language capacity has provided major compensatory benefits which deserve further discussion.

Primary among these benefits is that in being able to speak two languages the French Canadian, who has himself vividly experienced in most cases a sense of linguistic inadequacy, is able to transmit—if only for a fleeting moment—the same sensation to his English interlocutor. Thus, even when it is quite obvious that an individual is English, and in heavily English areas, many supermarket checkers will address him in French first to force him to admit his incapacity to understand. If he attempts to respond in French it must be with fluency or he will be tossed to the ground by even so lowly an individual as a checker, as his efforts to speak French are ignored with a yawn—or worse, a smile—and English takes over.[36]

I, myself, have engaged in this form of interaction, which oftentimes has the air of a judo match with each player at the other's lapel waiting for an opportune moment to cast him down. It was not unusual in the beginning of my fieldwork to be addressed in French and then, as I persisted in speaking French, to engage in conversations in which I, the English partner, spoke French while the French partner spoke English. One conversation of this type with a young French owner of a "head" shop lasted for at least fifteen minutes, with neither of us yielding except finally to the smile of a game brought to the surface by my failure to play by the rules.

An interesting variation upon this theme occurred just after the October crisis, when I went to a radical French bookstore where I had been told I might be able to purchase a copy of *Nègres blancs d'Amérique,* which was banned at the time. After buying the book from the shopgirl in attendance, a monolingual from the lower St. Lawrence,[37] we had a long, casual conversation about the future of Québec and especially of the English in the province. After a time, we were joined by a middle-aged French Canadian labor organizer, who entered into our conversation assuming I was French. After several minutes, he asked me where

I was from and I told him that I was American. Immediately, he switched from French to a broken English. The shopgirl made matters worse by saying: "Même s'il est américain, il parle français mieux que nous deux," and, after several minutes of a conversation which she and I carried on in French and he in English,[38] he switched to rapid *joual*,[39] filling his conversation with slang. As his initial conversation, although heavily accented, had been in more or less structurally good French, this shift caught me off guard, but with strain I was able to follow it and respond to his frequent questions directed at me. His shift at this point was clearly an effort to find a level on which he could retrieve his lost linguistic dominance, a conclusion which the shopgirl wholly agreed with in our dissection of the incident upon his departure.

Incidents of this sort abound. While there is continual complaint among French Canadians that the English do not bother to learn to speak their language, it is clear that their attitude on this point is much more ambivalent than their publicly made claims would admit, and an English Canadian who embarks on an effort to learn French needs a very thick skin. Prime Minister Diefenbaker, for example, was the butt of numerous jokes as he strove to express himself in French. In his attempt to do so, he actually probably reduced his stature in Québec as, rather than remaining in his own language, which few *québécois* actually have mastered to a sufficient degree to be critical of its improper use, he exposed himself as an object of ridicule.[40]

Ridiculing English who attempt to learn French, while usually not so blatant as that encountered by Mr. Sharp, is a favorite pastime of the French. The only evidence most English will see is a smile. English Canadians, on the other hand, are not that interested in ridiculing the French. One frequently encountered television commercial showed an American and a *québécoise* strolling a beach as young lovers, with a voice-over in Texas-accented French recounting the joys of a past summer and concluding: "Je vous aime." Situation comedy shows often utilize an actor in the role of an anglophone attempting French to draw an easy laugh, and it is common to have short English phrases injected into ordinary conversation for their ironic humor value, a favorite phrase being: "Yes, Sir!"

It is evident that, having been forced to learn English in such massive numbers, the French have made the best of it in terms of self-evaluation. The fluent use of French by an English-speaker on the one hand brings pleasure and an effort to discern whether he really is English, and on the other, a sense that the ante has been cruelly raised, that no longer is something reserved to the French which the English cannot touch. In a very real sense, it is as if the anglophone has, in learning French, incorporated the heart of a French Canadian's ethnic self.

On occasion, this reservation of language will be used to maximum benefit, and the English-speaker will be insulted in his own presence in French. One particularly interesting incident of this sort occurred at a "mixed" party which I attended. While I was engaged in conversation (in French) with a French Canadian professional woman, she was approached by an intoxicated Britisher, who asked her (in English) to dance. Pretending not to realize she was speaking in French, she turned to him and said: "Va-t'amuser chez les Grecs." ("Go enjoy yourself with the Greeks.") Then, as if catching herself, she explained that she was speaking with me and didn't wish to dance at the moment. He persisted, asking: "What's the matter with me?" She found herself unable to resist the opening and responded, again in French: "Ta gueule où je pisse là-dedans," (Your mouth [of an animal, similar to English "trap"], in which I am pissing [is what is the matter with you].") before explaining to him jokingly in English that nothing was the matter with him, she just didn't feel like dancing.

In encounters outside the sphere of language, French Canadians evidence an obvious pleasure in incidents, especially political, which evoke anxiety and fear among English. Opinion polls eliciting the attitudes of *québécois* toward the federal and provincial governments' handling of the October crisis belied the degree of support which the government originally received from the populace in its efforts to crush the revolutionaries. At the moment of the Cross kidnapping, the great majority of the French population seemed to support the act or, at least, derive pleasure from seeing the English squirm once again in the face of the FLQ. All conversation, all interest centered on the act and the view of the average French citizen toward the kidnapping appeared to be rather sympathetic. The aura of the crisis in the beginning was rather gay: the whole thing was a lark, with the French scoring one against the English. Even the presence of troops did nothing to dampen this feeling; in fact, to the contrary, it heightened the sense of importance. Only the garroting of an already starved and injured Laporte with the chain of his own crucifix brought the vicious potential of the situation home and ended the dalliance of the populace with the sweet fantasy of revolution.[41]

La Presse cartoon appearing during the October crisis: "Communiqué from the 'armchair' [literally, "slipper"] cell to the other cells: Michel Chartrand, Québec union leader: "Go to it lads! I'm with you all the way, we're going to win." (Jean-Pierre Girerd; *la Presse,* 15 octobre 1970:A4)

The English of Québec, and especially of Westmount, seem to be very uncertain of their future. Many apparently have resigned themselves to an unpleasant future in Québec, and, tired of being outsiders, are leaving. "For Sale" signs dot Westmount and English areas in general, and, although an actual significant emigration is difficult to document at this point, the supposed departure of Québec English from the province is a common topic of conversation. The degree of uncertainty of the English population manifests itself in what can only be considered to be a touchiness, a heightened sensitivity, toward French–English issues.[42] Conversations on the subject, especially those initiated by Americans, have to be entered into with circumlocutions which indicate: "I know the French are being silly . . ." or "This problem is certainly nothing like the racial problem in the United States, but. . . ."

The governments of Québec and the City of Montréal appear to play, perhaps not consciously, on these fears in their frequent assurances that English will remain an official language despite the fact that French must become the language of work. Paradoxically, these assurances have the opposite effect as their very utterance places in question something which had always been taken for granted among the English population and suggests that their linguistic "rights" are merely privileges held at the sufferance of French Quebekers. This shift from "right" to "privilege" is doubtlessly the intention of at least some officials, who appear to see in this shift the possibility of holding the linguistic rights of English Quebekers in question in exchange for the guarantee of French rights outside of Québec.

As if the expressive victory on the level of daily linguistic encounters and that of provincial politics were not enough to counter the relative economic deprivation of the French and their anger at being left alone on the continent, a final attack upon the self-image of English Canadians and a corresponding boost of their own can be seen in the frequently encountered charge of "English racism." Ignoring the all-too-obvious fact that ethnic prejudice is quite strong on both sides, French Canadians, even those who are otherwise quite perceptive, tend to cast the charge of racism wholly in the direction of the English. The 1973 federal elections in which Prime Minister Trudeau's "French-Canadianism"[43] was a major issue thus once again was to reveal, according to the editors of *Le Devoir,* "the racism and intolerance which sleeps [very lightly] in the depths of the English Canadian conscience"

(2 mars 1972:4), and Marcel Chaput, the author of *Pourquoi je suis séparatiste,* found incredible:

> ... this attitude of English to speak constantly of the racism of others while in the entire history of the world, including the present epoch, no people on earth have ever been more racist than the English people.... We believe we know something about this racism. (Chaput in *Point de Mire,* 28 mai 1971:27)

French, Québécois, or Joual?

> Our students speak *joual,* write *joual* and don't wish to speak or write in any other fashion. *Joual* is their language. Things have deteriorated to such a degree that they are no longer able to recognize a mistake which is pointed out to them at the end of a pencil and corrected at their desks. "The man what I spoke," "We are going to undress themselves," etc., don't bother them at all. They even seem elegant to them. For spelling errors, things are a little different; if one points out an error of agreement to them or the omission of an "s" they can still understand that error. The vice is deeper: it is at the level of syntax. It is also at the level of pronunciation—of twenty students whose names you ask at the beginning of school, there won't be more than two or three which you will catch the first time. You will have to ask the rest to repeat their names as they utter them as one admits an impurity. (trans. from Desbiens, 1960:24)

With the appearance of *Les Insolences du Frère Untel,*[44] the province of Québec shook with the debate of an issue of which all were aware but few had dared to make public: a major segment, in fact the majority, of the province's population spoke a language so heavily accented, structurally altered and blended with English expressions, that it was incomprehensible to a speaker of "real" French and, what is more, the schools of the province were either unable or unwilling to remedy the situation.

It is generally conceded that three levels or dialects of French are spoken in Québec: (1) "Parisian" or "real" French; (2) *québécois;* and (3) *joual.*[45] While there is some variation to the rule, the three forms of French can be seen to delineate the boundaries of the major classes within *québécois* society. Thus, the French

spoken by most of those of the upper classes is structurally correct and accented in the "international French" fashion. The
middle classes, as a rule, speak what is widely known as *québécois,* or structurally correct French accented in the pleasant
twang of Québec, while members of Québec's lower classes, on the
other hand, virtually all speak *joual.*

The consciousness of level of language is quite high and is
clearly a major symbolic indicator of class status.[46] While it is
possible to obtain the wealth of a member of the upper-middle
or upper classes and continue to speak *joual,* it is inconceivable
that one could obtain the necessary educational validation to fully
enter and continue to do so. In any event, the appropriate language level is so fully a part of the collective class symbols which
must be demonstrated that one could not possibly violate class
language level in everyday speech and be fully accepted.

An individual of the upper class speaking a language which
approximates Parisian French finds himself somewhat protected
by the trappings of his class, which serve to provide him a degree
of isolation, although in interacting with his fellow citizens of
lower rank he may choose to adopt a more *québécois* accent. For
the "real" French, who are likely to be solidly middle class, the
effect of bearing the wrong accent in the wrong class is frightful,
and is seen as a "putting on of airs." Many, disgusted with their
reception, with the education of their children in parochial
schools, and with *joual,* actually choose to assimilate to English:

> And the *salauds,* not being conditioned to a reflex demanding
> of French rights, anglicize as if there was nothing to it. With this
> they steal our jobs. For the damned Frenchman this is only one
> of the things he must suffer for once assimilated he is nothing
> more than a damned "bloke."
>
> It's even worse for those who decide to remain French, as
> fifteen years after their arrival they'll always be strangers.
> (Landry, 1969:31)

Even at the level of *québécois,* spoken, for example, by most of
the province's professionals, there is some sense of linguistic
inadequacy. While this feeling is usually not sufficiently strong to
induce one to cut against the grain of his fellows, it was enough so

that I, quite obviously an interested but removed party, was frequently asked by *québécois* speakers: "Do you think my French is bad? You don't have any trouble understanding me, do you?"[47]

Although it is obviously an impossible task to delineate a sharp division between international French and *québécois,* since the structure is not a major point of variation and all manner of gradations of accent may be found, it can be said with some certainty that *québécois* has become the official language of the province. Most of the radio and television stations of the province use it—especially in the all-important newscast which indicates the desired standard—although the national network, *Radio-Canada,* aims at a level intermediate between Parisian and *québécois* and certain commercial stations, as Montréal's channel 10, feature programs which are unabashedly *joual.*

Joual, as Desbiens notes, is difficult to adequately describe. As the term is generally used, it refers to the popular French of the province and vies strongly with *québécois* for priority. Generally, it is considered to include structurally incorrect French, English loan-words which have not been accepted into common French usage, as: "le bosse," "le fun," and "le bébé burger." Old French terms which have been retained as a form of marginal survival and whose meanings have been extended to a modern context, such as *char,* formerly meaning exclusively "wagon" and today used in Québec for "car," are in a doubtful category, as are terms such as *piastre* and *sou,* which are the preferred terms for "dollar" and "cent." While most media will use older French forms, use of certain English loan words is considered to be poor form. A recent provincial communication, in fact, published in newspapers to alert the citizens to their new right to nullify a contract made with an itinerant salesman within a specified period of time, as well as other recently passed consumer-protection statutes, concluded with the slogan: "Un pia$tre, c'est un pia$tre!"

Formerly, use of *joual* appeared to cause little anxiety, and Maurice Duplessis, for one, seemed to relish it as a means of contact with the population and for the shock value its use had among the "snobs."[48] The continued presence of "bon français" movements and the clear association of language quality with national pride has somewhat alleviated the indifference to its use which Desbiens found so discouraging:

> [In reading Laurendeau's article on *joual*, at the moment of its appearance, to my students, they] recognized that they spoke *joual*. One of them, nearly proudly, even told me: "We've invented a new language!" They don't see any reason to change. "Everyone speaks like that," they argued. Or again: "We would be laughed at if we spoke differently from everyone else." Of all the objections to change, however, the most difficult to counter was: "Why force ourselves to speak differently when everyone understands us. . . ." (1960:25)[49]

Today, however, a sense of anxiety, of dis-ease, over language appears to have penetrated into the hearts of most *joual* speakers. In speaking with individuals who spoke *joual*, I was frequently told that one should speak better "but I can't." The province currently provides courses leading to eighth grade equivalency certificates for certain farmers and chronically unemployed individuals. Of several farmers and unemployed workers taking these courses with whom I spoke there appeared to be a genuine pride in learning to speak good French (which, for them, largely meant purging their vocabulary of English words and certain structural usages) and even some tendency to themselves be critical of those who spoke "really bad" French. One of these students, indeed, took a pleasure in teaching me French words which he had obviously just learned himself; an example: *indiscret,* which he used to label one of his fellow students who, having failed to have been shamed by the emphasis placed in the class on *bon français,* continued to speak *joual* boisterously during class recesses. Ironically, at a moment in which a real desire to speak "proper" French seems to be gaining ground, radical students, singers, and artists have begun to affect, in many cases, *joual* to indicate their solidarity with "the people."

The felt severity of the problem can be seen in the fact that in *Les Insolences,* which sold well over one hundred thousand copies, Jean-Paul Desbiens felt constrained to suggest radical, only slightly facetious, solutions. What should be done to eliminate *joual* and save French in Québec?

We must work with the axe and gain

a) Absolute control of Radio and Television. It must be forbidden to write or speak *joual* under pain of death;

b) Destruction, in a single night, by the provincial police of all commercial signs in English or *joual;*

c) Authorization, for a period of two years, to summarily execute any government minister, teacher, priest, who speaks *joual* (28)

One of the most deep-seated aspects of the *joual* problem is the realization that *they* know. The English guard as comforting knowledge that Québec's French don't speak "real French" and do not hesitate to let this knowledge surface. Nothing is more likely to invoke the anger of a blow cruelly applied, striking the heart, as is a reference to Québec French as a *patois* or, since the English come well armed, *joual.*[50] It was probably this fact, as much as any anger over his disclosure of the failures of Québec's schools, which led to a short, and yet incredibly revealing encounter with a Church superior before his true identity was generally known:

[In taking a bus with a brother of the same order, the two were separated by a failure to find adjoining seats. While his companion sat with a Canon, Desbiens found a seat two rows in front. Normally in this situation no conversation of any significance would take place, but the Canon had something on his mind. Finally, he asked if the brother knew Frère Untel:] "He's sitting in front of you," my colleague responded like a good "stool-pigeon." The Canon then had a great deal to say about my intemperate language and theological errors. My friend defended me valiantly. . . .

Upon leaving the bus, the Canon extended his hand to me. I asked his name and he refused to tell me. I insisted, he refused; I insisted and finally discovered it. . . .

After telling me his name he cautioned me to be prudent and patted me paternally on the forearm. "Be careful," he told me, "be careful, or you'll never advance." "Careful with whom?" I asked. "Be careful," was all he said.

In thirty seconds of conversation with this stranger we had exhausted the tactics of certain Québec clergy: a paternal tap on the forearm and an unctuous threat. (145-146)

CAN AN ACCEPTABLE IDENTITY BE FORGED? 6

La Dernière Frontière

Every being, individually or collectively, protects his identity in diverse fashions. Some do it with a rind, others with shell, bark, fur or schools. Indeed, the business of identity protection is what frontiers are all about.

Our identity has long been protected by at least three frontiers; geography, religion and language. All three have now been breached, and that is the root of our illness.

The geographic frontier hardly exists any more because of the mobility of individuals and radio and television waves, which know no boundary. The religious frontier no longer has any serious effect upon our collective life. As for the linguistic frontier, it continues to suffer the effect of an internal devitalization, while at the same time it is weakened by the simple fact that its boundary is maintained by relatively fewer and fewer people.

In the face of the disappearance or weakening of these three traditional pillars of our collective being, it would be fatal for us to look to the political level for the symbol, guarantee and absolute refuge of our identity.

Whether we speak of immigration, of electoral and educational reform, of the economy, or of the constitution, we are always brought back to the linguistic question because it is the central one. It is the last frontier. It is important to realize that whatever the political solutions are to this question, there will always be a price to pay, which will be a very real and reasonable one if the solution is to be real and not merely rhetorical.

There has always been a price to pay and there will always be one. This is the cost of being French in violation of our geographic situation. This price for a long time took the form of isolation. Today isolation is no longer possible, and it seems very likely that the price is going to have to be one of austerity and economic discipline. (Jean-Paul Desbiens in *La Presse*, 24 mars 1971:44)

The traditional means of coping with threats to the maintenance of French Canadian identity—isolation—has been destroyed. In the world of the twentieth century, a Québec already industrialized and in the process of becoming more fully so has lost the option to turn inward. The reality of economic survival in the modern world has seemingly eliminated withdrawal as a response and seriously placed in question the possibility of continued ethnic survival. In conflict with an ethnic group armed with continental and, to some degree, world dominance, this *petit peuple* finds itself forced to interact with the dominant group as underlings to retain its identity. What residuals of withdrawal are retained must be left to one's leisure hours and maintained with effort on an individual level in the face of a cultural and linguistic bombardment from a group long accustomed to incorporate other peoples.

In the face of potential loss of the only certain means of ethnic maintenance, is the effort required to retain ethnicity worth it? As Desbiens reminds all *québécois,* today, more than ever, "il faut payer un prix pour être soi." Are *québécois* willing to pay the price? Can an acceptable identity, one that will be on balance attractive and resistant to all challenges to its integrity, be forged?

Today, more than ever, the challenge to *québécois* is one that must be met with action, for this time it is truly a matter of survival. In contrast to the present challenge, previous talk of the struggle of *québécois* to maintain their identity dwindles to ludicrousness. Despite all of the claims advanced by the Church for its central role in fighting for French survival in North America, the simple fact is that in Québec there was no challenge. From the moment tens of thousands of *québécois* turned inward to the rural farm life, survival was a *fait accompli*. It is no longer.

If the reality of waking to realize that the barriers had been rent by modern English technology, such that henceforth every *québécois*, individually, had to fight the ethnic struggle within himself was not sufficient to do so, the discovery of the presence of a third uncontrollable force within Québec society has resulted in panic. That third force is the body of *néo-québécois:* immigrants who have entered Québec and settled in Montréal since the close of World War II. These non-English-, non-French-speaking immigrants, coming for the most part from the countries of southern and eastern Europe, choose to adopt English rather than French to make their way in Montréal in a proportion of *at the very least* three to one (Arès, Richard; *Le Devoir,* 8 mars 1969:5).[1] While at present 64.2 percent of the population of greater Montréal is French and the entire body of immigrants represents exactly the same percentage of the population as do those of British origin, being 17.9 percent each, the continued influx of immigrants and their high birth rate promises a rapid decrease in the proportionate number of those whose maternal language is French in the city.[2] Claude Gravel, in the lead editorial of *La Presse,* March 11, 1971, warned that at present in Québec a problem is growing which all had thought forgotten:

> If French Canadians think of themselves as in the majority in their own province, they are not less worried because of this fact for their collective future. This is because their birth-rate has continued to diminish for the past fifteen years and the immigrants enter the English population at an ever-increasing rate.
>
> At the current rhythm, Montréal will be a city with an English majority in ten years. Since 40 percent of Québec's citizens live in the metropolitan area, what will happen to Québec's French once this landmark is passed? This is the agonizing question of the decade for the "urbanized" French-speakers who can no longer count on their traditional reflexes to survive. (Gravel, 11 mars 1971:A4)

It is this potential loss of Montréal—*the second-largest French-speaking city in the world*—which has given the present period all the urgency and tension of a ticking time bomb—it is certain to go off if left untouched, but the question is: How can it be defused?

The first question which must be approached in order to reverse the trend of immigrant assimilation to English is why immigrants select English. What factors give it such an advantage over French in gaining the allegiance of immigrants? Chief among all factors motivating immigrants to adopt English is that which brought most of them to Canada: desire for economic gain, for a better life.

Over and over upon their arrival immigrants assess the division of Montréal society and reach the conclusion given me by a young Yugoslav pharmacist:

> The French have nothing. They're poor and they all have to learn English to get jobs. Why should I learn French? The bosses are English and they like to hire an immigrant rather than a French Canadian because they don't make much trouble.[3]

Additional factors directing immigrants toward English are greater attractiveness of English culture and the fact that full assimilation to the English population is achieved with greater ease than to French society. Immigrants, especially the more youthful ones, view English as the international language of popular culture. As such, it is seen as the key to an exciting world of motion pictures, popular music, and television. The learning of French, for all except the most sophisticated who partake in international French culture, on the other hand, leads to a cultural vacuum.

Most immigrants are also aware of the fact that their acceptance in the English world is much more easily accomplished than in that of the rather closed French society of Québec. The *québécois'* xenophobic attitudes are successfully transmitted to the degree that most immigrants are well aware of a generalized French Canadian hostility toward them. General xenophobia aside, French hostility is quite rationally based, as the immigrants are seen as a group in direct conflict with the French: they are stealing their jobs and their city. In neither of these areas do they represent any real threat to the English, and in the latter the immigrants represent a sweet promise.

French resentment of *néo-québécois* is grounded not only in a feeling that their province is being overrun by them but in day-to-day experience. Many immigrants, especially in the central city, have opened small restaurants or shops. Invariably, in a city in which two thirds of the population is French, the language of preference, maximal competence, and, often, the *only* language of these shops, is English. Thus, in an immigrant establishment,

" . . . and every nine months after every nine months the English language made progress in *La Belle Province!*" (Jean-Pierre Girerd; *La Presse*, 16 mars 1971:A4)

it is not unusual to find a French Canadian's request made in French responded with: "What did you say?" forcing him to place his order in English. Sometimes a *québécois* will make a futile attempt to stand his ground. In one incident I witnessed in a Greek pastry shop, located in a region populated primarily by French Canadians and immigrants, a middle-aged *québécoise* ordered pastry in French, only to be responded with: "Which one?" Unyieldingly, she continued in French, pointing and using her fingers to further the immigrant's education, until the end of the transaction, in which the shopkeeper asked: "Is that all?" Visibly angry at this point, she snapped: "C'EST TOUT!" and another xenophobe left the shop.[4]

In view of the fact that immigrants assimilate to the English population in overwhelming proportions, many French Montrealers are convinced that Federal encouragement of immigration to the province is part of an English plot to gain control of it and negate the possibility of separatism, *that Canada's immigration policy has as its primary goal the drowning of French Canada and the crushing of the threat of the formation of an independent French nation in North America.*[5]

In view of the urgency of the problem and the fact that all odds are weighed against the French in gaining the hearts and tongues of the immigrants, what can be done? One of the most logical responses, that of requiring immigrants to educate their children in the language of the province's majority and thus perhaps capture the next generation, was removed in the passage of Provincial Bill 63 (1969), recently approved by the lame-duck (pre-*Parti Québécois*) *Union Nationale*-dominated assembly. Bill 63, ironically titled: "loi pour promouvoir la langue française au Québec,"[6] guaranteed parents the right to educate their children in the language of their choice and was the result of a crisis provoked when the municipality of Saint-Léonard-de-Port-Maurice in the Montréal suburbs passed an ordinance instituting French as the required language of all its primary schools.

The consideration of the bill by the Assembly resulted in general strikes in French secondary schools, C.E.G.E.P.'s, and universities, as well as protests from numerous private organizations under *le Front du Québec français,* all of which opposed its passage as representing only one more step toward assimilation.

A final factor weighing upon the future of French in Canada as a whole is what René Lévesque has called "L'assimilation galopant," outside of Québec. Over 34 percent of those of French origin in the rest of Canada today speak English as their native language, with the percentage of assimilation ranging from 9.3 percent in neighboring New Brunswick to 81.6 percent in Newfoundland:

	Population of French Origin	French Still Maternal Language	Assimilated	Percent Assimilated[7]
New Brunswick	232,127	210,530	21,597	9.3 (12.1)
Manitoba	83,936	60,899	23,087	27.4 (30.3)
Ontario	647,941	425,302	222,639	34.3 (37.7)
Saskatchewan	59,824	36,163	23,661	39.5 (43.2)
Yukon and N.W.T.				40.0 (46.6)
Alberta	83,319	42,276	41,043	49.2 (49.7)
Prince Edward I.	17,418	7,958	9,460	54.3 (55.1)
Nova Scotia	87,883	39,568	48,315	54.9 (56.9)
British Columbia	66,970	26,179	40,791	60.8 (64.7)
Newfoundland	17,171	3,150	14,021	81.6 (85.2)
Total	1,298,992	853,462	445,539	34.3

(Arès quoted by Lévesque 1968:115-116)

Faced with an ethnicity devalued in the economic sphere, apparently increasingly unmaintainable outside Québec and under serious threat there, what does one do? What coping responses have been adopted by *québécois* today to replace that of withdrawal lost in the last half-century?

Patterns of Coping with French Ethnicity Today

Assimilation.

One obvious means of coping with a devalued ethnic identity is to attempt to cast it aside and assimilate to one which provides an easier accommodation to everyday life. While it is perhaps the most obvious response, it is also almost certainly the most difficult.

For French Canadians, the path of assimilation has been rendered particularly difficult, as rejection of French for English is one of the most socially disapproved acts that one can commit and one which rends most previously held interpersonal bonds. Intermarriage, the major route of assimilation, has been traditionally viewed in Québec as "a treason on the part of a French Canadian to his race and to the language of his fathers" (Carisse, 1969:39).

Yet, statistics of language retention outside Québec reveal that more than one third of all Canadians of French Canadian origin no longer speak French as their maternal language.[8] Assimilation is obviously taking place, but how? How frequently is the act of assimilation a conscious decision marked by a decisive act such as an individual rejection of French as his language of communication?

Evidence indicates that "passing," a difficult phenomenon to achieve in any case, is also a marginal one. Few individuals consciously decide and succeed in wholly casting off their identity—a process which requires an accentless English and a change or re-pronunciation of name in addition to the severance of family ties. And few even attempt to pass, as the negative aspects of French identity rarely so clearly outweigh the positive that the trauma associated with passing is worth it.

When the phenomenon does occur, it is primarily situational. The identity is secreted, or better, understressed, in situations in which its presence is undervalued. Thus, outside of Québec, in Ontario, Manitoba, and New Brunswick, where there are large French communities, many children of French Canadian parents learn to speak unaccented English, and, while known as French within their communities, find situational passing a relatively easy phenomenon.[9] Within Québec, "passing," whether situational or permanent, seems to be a particularly deviant act. Of two instances in Montréal which came to my attention, one of the individuals, a woman in her early sixties who had left Catholicism for a fundamentalist English sect, was clearly psychotic.[10]

Much more interesting than "passing"—especially realizing that, as mentioned above, a perception of French identity as so unacceptable is likely only to be held by very disturbed individuals—are those patterns followed by individuals entering the process of assimilation for themselves or their progeny often *without apparent conscious decision to do so*. It is rare for an individual to openly embrace assimilation as did Yves Landry in his letter to *La Presse* quoted at the beginning of Chapter 5. In most instances leading to assimilation the basic decisions leading in that direction fall far short of a clear and perhaps conscious delineation of the consequences of the decision.

Decisions which in all likelihood will lead to assimilation may be arranged according to the clarity with which the probable result is perceived at the time of decision. In doing so, five major assimilation decision categories may be delineated in increasing order of French social acceptance of the initial decision: (1) intermarriage with English spouse with assimilation as stated intent; (2) intermarriage with English spouse with intent to raise bilingual children; (3) intermarriage with immigrant with use of English as a common language; (4) emigration to the United States; (5) emigration to the rest of Canada.[11]

The first of these decisions, that of intermarriage with an English-speaking individual with intent to raise children only in English, represents the extreme of the assimilation decision, and, while encountered frequently in the United States and the rest of Canada, is relatively rare in Québec. Most interethnic marriages within the province appear to be entered into in anticipation of the rearing of bilingual progeny with an understanding in most cases that English will be the primary language. In her study of cultural orientations of French-English intermarriage in Montréal, Carisse found that the results of the marriages could best be seen in terms of a bargaining over which aspects of each group's culture would be stressed. As can be guessed from previous discussion of relative ethnic strength of instrumental and expressive sectors of Montréal society, usage of the English language is dominant, whereas expressive aspects of French society dominate interpersonal relationships.[12]

Aellen, in a detailed questionnaire administered to French, English, and mixed high school students in Montréal, found that the English students apparently more openly expressed their desire for French intermarriage than did French students, possibly indicating a stronger taboo against admission of a desire for assimilation to the English population among French students (see chart, page 125).

Interestingly, almost one third of the French Canadians ex-

Expressed Preference for Intermarriage

Marital Preference	English Students	French Students
French	6 (12%)	40 (67%)
English	37 (73%)	1 (2%)
Preference not given	8 (16%)	19 (32%)

(After Aellen, 1967:70)

pressed no preference. Aellen interprets this to indicate that many of the French Canadian students "may sometimes feel that it would be exciting to marry a stranger, but [are] unwilling to admit it openly" (71).

Intermarriage with an immigrant and use of English as the dominant common language is apparently one available avenue of assimilation carrying less negative cathexis than marriage to an English spouse. While it is impossible to be certain what proportion of Québec marriages which involve non-French, non-English partners are of this type, my own experience leads me to believe that the arrangement is not at all uncommon. An implicit assimilation decision in many of these marriages may partially account for the observed fact that non-French, non-English intermarriage is almost twice as frequent among French females as among French males, as it may be seen as providing a more socially and personally acceptable vehicle through which to provide one's children the advantages of primary English upbringing.[13]

The decision to leave Québec for the United States, while perhaps initially expressed as a temporary one, is certain to lead to eventual assimilation if maintained.[14] Beaulieu, in his study, "Le Québec d'en bas: . . . ou la fin d'un beau rêve en Nouvelle-Angleterre," appearing in the December 5, 1970 magazine supplement to La Presse, chronicles the rapidly approaching conclusion of the massive French immigration to New England in total assimilation. "The reality is," he says, "that in the cities of New England, one seldom meets young people who speak French." In an experiment to test the depth of French retention in a city with a large population of French Canadian origin, he attempted to obtain directions from young individuals. He found that those he approached either used English in their response or attempted to reply in a French which he found "absolutely incomprehensible, in which the word order [was] a literal translation of . . . English into French" (1970:6).

The final, and most innocuous, of the various decisions leading toward assimilation is that of leaving Québec to settle somewhere in the rest of Canada. Innocuous as it may be, however, Lévesque's chart cited above indicates that fully one third of the French stock outside of Québec speaks English as their maternal language, and this number is constantly being augmented by new losses from the French population. Today, many *québécois* separatists, like Lévesque, appear to have resigned themselves to the loss of French outside of Québec—with the exception perhaps of New Brunswick's Acadians—and turned the whole of their efforts toward salvation of the French language to Québec itself.[15]

Integration

Canada, more so than the United States, views itself as a nation which values the ethnic mosaic which necessity has thrust upon it. While a favorite pastime of liberal Canadians is to laud themselves for their recognition and supposed appreciation of ethnic diversity, in contrast to an America which is seen to pour its peoples from the melting pot into a single mold, Canada has never had one ethnic group so totally dominant that all felt it necessary to assimilate to that group: the French retaining their identity made it much easier for the Ukrainians, Greeks, and other immigrant groups to do the same.

The French fact cannot be eliminated—not, at least, in the foreseeable future—and the English one is as secure as is humanity. The adding of additional ethnic "facts" from the need to encourage immigration in the settlement of this vast, empty country has only reinforced the apparent necessity to recognize, to institutionalize Canada as an "ethnic mosaic" if it is to remain a nation. In a very real sense the philosophy of respecting each group's language and institutions, of working together in the fashion which has been known as "integration" in the United States, is the "official" Canadian method of coping with ethnic diversity.

No man so personifies the concept of ethnic coexistence as does

Pierre Trudeau; born in Montréal, graduate of *l'Université de Montréal* and Harvard, student of *l'Université de Paris* and the London School of Economics, *absolutely* bilingual, and married to an English Canadian.[16] In his compilation of articles devoted to the defense of Federalism, *Le fédéralisme et la société canadienne française,* Trudeau, without denying the difficulty of being French within the Canadian unity, insists that coexistence of French and English in the confederation is the only reasonable solution. Following the theories of separatism, he argues, *québécois* have been led to "believe that the state of Québec could give more to French Canadians than they possess collectively." It would result, separatist economists have argued, in theory

> where anything is possible . . . in an independent Québec in which the entrepreneurs and technocrats of other lands will bring their capital and inventions to us at an ever accelerated rhythm. (But, incidentally, what a funny way to retake possession of our economy!) (Trudeau, 1967:cover, 26)

Not only have efforts been made to convince *québécois* that the ethnic conflicts of the province would evaporate in the face of separatism but that there would be economic benefit. Absurd, says Trudeau:

> the truth is that separatism is a counter revolutionary goal of a minority of an impotent *petite-bourgeoisie* afraid of being held to account by the twentieth century revolution: Rather than create a niche for oneself on the basis of excellence it wants to force the entire tribe to return to its wigwams by declaring independence. That will of course not prevent the outside world from marching along with giant steps and it won't change the laws of history or the real balance of power in North America. . . . Separatism, a revolution? *mon oeil*. It's only a counter-revolution: the national socialist counter-revolution. (Trudeau, 1967:226–27).[17]

Critics of Trudeau and the federalist-integration response argue that *his* solution is itself a chimera. Invariably losing sight of the fact that federalism in a bilingual country does not mean that all individuals are expected to be bilingual[18] —and of the fact that even among Québec's French population, home of Canadian bilingualism, 60 percent of all individuals are monolingual French-speakers—its critics argue that biculturalism and bilingualism *per se* means eventual unilingualism—English unilingualism.

> Total bilingualism is a utopian concept and represents a grave threat to a weak, minority people without sufficient cultural defense. Practical bilingualism, alone, in Québec has long placed the entire French civilization of North America in danger. Practical bilingualism can only be temporary in a conquered country like Québec. When we become sufficiently bilingual, when our language becomes sufficiently eaten away by anglicisms, when we demonstrate sufficient decline on the economic and demographic levels, we will cease to be French–English bilinguals and become monolingual English-speakers. *Bilingualism will have served to totally assimilate us. Bilingualism is nothing but a step towards unilingualism in the direction of the most powerful language.* (Barbeau, 1965:90; emphasis mine)

The spread of these beliefs—that bilingualism, as a natural coping response for French economic inferiority, leads to unilingualism and that federalism is only a camouflage for a bilingualism in *sens unique* eventually leading to assimilation—have served more than any others to erode confidence in the integrationists' position and in Trudeau's position as a "reasonable man" operating with the only "reasonable" solution: coexistence. Coexistence, more and more *québécois* maintain, can only mean, and is intended only to mean, eventual assimilation.

Trudeau's own marriage to the young English Canadian Margaret Sinclair, added as much to the spectre of assimilation in Québec as it did to *bonne entente,* as the following pungent dialogue from a radio short produced by a Montréal French station the day after their marriage suggests:

> "Margaret?"
> "Yes, Pierre."
> "Je t'aime."
> "What Pierre?"
> "Je t'aime beaucoup."
> "Damn it Pierre, *Speak White!*"

Separatism

Ten Canadians travelled through the country for months, met thousands of their fellow citizens, heard and read what they had to say. The ten do not now claim that they are relying on this as a scientific investigation, nor do they have solutions to propose at this stage. All they say is this: here is what we saw and heard, and here is the preliminary—but unanimous—conclusion we have drawn.

The members of the Commission feel the need to share with their fellow citizens the experience they have been through, and the lessons they have so far taken from it. This experience may be summarized very simply. The Commissioners, like all Canadians who read newspapers, fully expected to find themselves confronted by tensions and conflicts. They knew that there have been strains throughout the history of Confederation; and that difficulties can be expected in a country where cultures exist side by side. What the Commissioners have discovered little by little, however, is very different: they have been driven to the conclusion that Canada, without being fully conscious of the fact, is passing through the greatest crisis in its history.

The source of the crisis lies in the Province of Quebec; that fact could be established without an extensive inquiry. There are other secondary sources in the French-speaking minorities of the other provinces and in the "ethnic minorities"—although this does not mean in any way that to us such problems are in themselves secondary. But, although a provincial crisis at the outset, it has become a Canadian crisis, because of the size and strategic importance of Quebec, and because it has inevitably set off a series of chain reactions elsewhere.

What does the crisis spring from? Our inquiry is not far enough advanced to enable us to establish exactly its underlying causes and its extent. All we can do is describe it as it is now: *it would appear from what is happening that the state of affairs established in 1867, and never since seriously challenged, is now for the first time being rejected by the French Canadians of Quebec.* (RCBB, Preliminary Report, 1965:13; emphasis theirs)

The decade of the 1960s was one which saw a deep erosion of support for the position of ethnic coexistence in Québec. Integration within the Canadian unity has lost much of its appeal due to its inability to resolve *"the* problem"—the social and economic chasm which separates the two peoples—and because of the fact that more and more French Canadians are convinced that integration can only result in their total absorption by the English.

The Problem, the French-English problem in Canada, as we have previously discussed, has its roots in both the expressive and instrumental aspects of the society, although it is the economic facet which dominates virtually all discussion. Within the Canadian union, separatists maintain, Québec will always be doomed to economic disadvantage, condemned to the crumbs from English Canada's table. As Rodrique Tremblay in his *Indépendance et marché commun Québec-Etats-Unis* notes:

> The level of per capita personal income of Quebekers (85 percent French-speaking, 15 percent English-speaking) is, in effect, approximately 11 percent less than the Canadian average; it is 27 percent less than that of Ontario, 50 percent inferior to that of the entire United States, and 75 percent inferior to that of the American west coast—the position of the French-speaking *québécois* is even worse in this respect, since the Royal Commission on Bilingualism and Biculturalism has established that the English-speaking minority of Québec has the highest level of income in Canada. (In Québec, the average income of the French-speaking citizen is 35 percent less than that of the English-speaking citizen.) (1970:9-10)

A recent analysis by Professor Paul Harvey of l'Ecole des Hautes Etudes Commerciales confirms separatists' suspicions that the reasons for this inequity lie deep within Canada's economic structure and are perhaps too firmly entrenched to be resolved short of separation. Efforts to reduce Québec's permanently high level of unemployment and, in the process, to increase wages for those employed are always guaranteed a foredetermined failure due to the fact that meaningful economic improvement in Québec results in unacceptable economic imbalance in English-speaking Canada. Keeping in mind that 3 percent is the absolutely minimal level of unemployment which can be accepted without major inflationary pressures, Lemelin, in his analysis of Harvey's study, states that one can quite readily see why any serious attempt to approach full employment in Québec will result in serious damage to Ontario's economy:

> If Ottawa wishes to reduce the average Canadian level of unemployment to 3 percent then that of Québec will reach a yearly level of 4.6 percent per year with a winter level of 6.9 percent. In return, the level of unemployment in Ontario

would fall below the 3 percent level so that the economy of the area will be disturbed by strong inflationary pressures.

On the other hand, if it is the level of Ontario unemployment which Ottawa wishes to maintain at 3 percent then Québec will have around 6.1 percent unemployment with a winter level of 8 percent; and the Canadian average will probably be above 4 percent.

Finally, it follows from Professor Harvey's analysis that, if the central government wishes to reduce unemployment in Québec to 3 percent, then unemployment in Ontario would fall to around 1 percent of the total labor force while the Canadian average would stay at around 2 percent—all of which would produce unacceptable inflationary pressures in the entire country. (Lemelin, Claude, *Le Devoir*, 1 mai 1972:A4)

The conclusion that Lemelin draws? Either Ottawa must begin serious and sustained efforts directed toward the economic development of Québec or "*Québécois* will realize once and for all that they will never know full employment within the present political system" (A4).

The spectre of assimilation, of an end to Québec's French destiny in America, has always haunted French Canadians. They have never had to search deeply to discover English intentions in this direction. As early as Lord Durham's report following the revolution of 1837–38, assimilation was clearly advanced as the only solution acceptable to Canada:

A plan by which it is proposed to ensure the tranquil government of Lower Canada, must include in itself the means of putting an end to the agitation of national disputes in the legislature, by settling, at once and forever, the national character of the Province. *I entertain no doubts as to the national character which must be given to lower Canada; it must be that of the British Empire; that of the majority of the population of British America; that of the great race which must, in the lapse of no long period of time, be predominant over the whole North American Continent.* Without effecting the change so rapidly or so roughly as to shock the feelings and trample on the welfare of the existing generation, it must henceforth be the first and steady purpose of the British Government to establish an English population, with English laws and language, in this Province, and to trust its government to none but a decidedly English legislature. (Craig, ed. 1963:146; emphasis mine) [19]

Headlines: "Québec's independence threatened by our financial impotence"
—F.-A. Angers. Bum: "And you know that he found that out all by himself!"
(Jean-Pierre Girerd; *La Presse,* 13 mars 1971:A4)

Following the assumption that the ultimate goal of the English
is to eliminate linguistic dissonance in Canada, it is frequently
assumed that official encouragement of bilingualism—which is
sens unique in any case—is only a cloak for darker intentions. *Le
livre noir de l'impossibilité (presque totale) d'enseigner le français
au Québec,* compiled by the Association Québécoise des professeurs de français (1970), argued that the passage of Bill 63, which
permitted parental choice of the language in which their children
would receive instruction, "legally opens a door to English unilingualism in Québec" (48):

> the Québécois of average education is gradually losing his
> French identity. Bilingualism always works in favor of the
> strongest, it abolishes the minority language. It kills slowly, it
> eats the weakest. (77; emphasis theirs)

Evidence of the aid to assimilative pressures provided by Bill 63 before its revocation may be seen in the fact that in the province's Québec region as much as 50 percent of the attendance at English schools was comprised of students whose maternal language was French. In an English Catholic high school of Québec City, for example, 553 of the 1,121 students enrolled were French while in a recently established English secondary school in suburban Sainte-Foy 90 percent of the students were French-speaking. In at least one school district, that of Sillery, the English-speaking population would not have been able to provide the necessary minimum level of attendance to sustain their school were it not for a disproportionate enrollment of French students (*Le Devoir,* 23 mars 1972:11).

A recent Federal commission recommended that Québec and numerous other areas throughout Canada be officially declared bilingual districts. Since all of Québec—even areas where the English population is virtually nonexistent—was to be declared bilingual while only a portion of Ontario would meet the same fate, the *Parti Québécois* insisted that the goal of the government was to tacitly reject nationwide bilingualism and set up a series of bilingual reservations while waiting for assimilation to work its course. The result of this policy would be to place English on an equal footing in all of Québec and "check all the efforts that the Québec government might be able to make in according the French language priority status in Québec" (*La Presse,* 8 mai 1971:A12).[20]

The *Parti Québécois* has accused the provincial liberals of "treason" in their failure to immediately follow through with their pre-election promises to make *le français-langue-de-travail au Québec.* In its rejection of an amendment to a bill creating a Society of Industrial Development in Québec which would have required investors seeking aid from the Society to commit themselves to hire Québec residents as administrators and to use French as the language of work, Guy Jaron, a "péquiste" deputy, accused the government of undermining its own program and treasoning the populace (*La Presse,* 8 avril 1971:A2).

Additional impetus for the separatist cause has come in recent years from a fear that the Federal government's alienation of

Labrador, a former Québec territory now part of Newfoundland, might be repeated in Québec's northern territories. Recently, the Federal government has renewed its economic hold on Québec's northern territory today known as Nouveau-Québec (formerly Ungava), as provincial interest in gaining full sovereignty over it seems to have waned under the liberals. Naud, in an analysis of recent developments on the northern front, questions whether Ottawa's recent trebling of the budget for the area is a result of a sudden burst of concern for the region's Indians and Eskimos or of

> a correct analysis by Ottawa of the amplitude of the Québec separatist movement? Is the Federal Government increasing its budget in Nouveau Québec with the intention of retaining control of the territory in the event of the province's separation? (Naud, Leonce; *Le Devoir*, 11 février 1972:5)

As Michel Brochu in his *Le Défi du Nouveau-Québec* has commented:

> The most striking thing in landing at outposts of Nouveau-Québec is that one feels oneself to be in another province: nothing recalls that we are in Québec territory. . . . [One finds that] : (a) Québec is absent at the administrative level, (b) the lot of the Eskimos there differs not at all from that of those living in the Northwest Territories, especially in the schools, where not a word of Eskimo or of French is taught, (c) the French language, with the possible exception of Fort Chimo, enjoys no official use. (Brochu, 1962:43)

In view of the inability of the integrationists to solve Québec's severe economic woes and the widespread belief that this policy will eventually lead to assimilation, separatism, directed toward the creation of a separate French nation in North America, has gained numerous adherents in recent years. Today, it perhaps enjoys the support of a majority of French Quebekers as the only way in which French survival, if not the *épanouissement,* or flowering, of French culture can be achieved. With the vitality and powerful intellectual support of the *Parti Québécois* the separatist response is today *very* thinkable and *very* popular. More and more it is casting off its former aura of lunacy and becoming a reasonable response.

Separatism, the modern face of withdrawal, seeks to solve the problem of *québécois* simply by terminating the present relationship with Canada and making the new system wholly French.[21] This response, while enjoying widespread support in all classes of Québec society, has its primary roots in the *petit-bourgeoisie* and the new managerial class created by the industrialization of the province.

The psychological barriers to the separatist response lie principally in the fear of many *québécois* that their economy, bad as it is, would wholly collapse with separation. One factor often advanced by *québécois* for this possibility is that there is too much intragroup jealousy within the French population to permit successful separation, or, in the words of one woman: "We are ambivalent when one of us makes it . . . we are happy but then begin to wonder how he did it." An additional factor often appears to be that in "making it" an individual places an additonal psychic burden on his fellows to do the same and surmount the ethnic excuse for failure.

Other than this economic barrier, there are few ties between the French of Québec and the rest of Canada felt sufficiently strongly to maintain the bond. It is relatively rare to see emotional outbursts—as one which I witnessed in the Carré Saint-Louis, a separatist stronghold in Montréal, in which a middle-aged French woman defiantly walked from park bench to park bench singing "O Canada" in French, to the amusement and derision of the Park's occupants—supporting Canadian unity, while it is quite common to see defiant symbols of Québec independence as the tri-colored flag of the patriots of 1837-38. Many argue that Québec is today isolated in a remote *cul-de-sac* of the world in any event. Why not formalize it? Who wants to remain with English Canada anyway? As René Lévesque argued in a 1963 interview:

> [Lévesque presented the interviewer with that day's copy of *La Presse* in which an article appeared noting that the president of the Central Housing and Mortgage Corporation had boasted that he had successfully resisted pressures to appoint any French Canadians to the board.] "How would you feel," asked the minister, "if the president of a crown corporation could make that boast with respect to your people? . . .

"They talk about our educational system. Yet often we have many men available with the same academic background as many highly placed English Canadians. Look at the lawyers— I don't know how many lawyers we've got. As to quality, brains, and achievement, we don't notice that English Canadians are exactly world-beaters!" (Lévesque, interview with Myers, 1956:16-17)[22]

Again and again, separatists turn to the most persuasive argument of all: separatism is not something which must be wrought from unity but is already a *de facto* entity—Canada is composed of two peoples, of *two nations,* and separatism would merely be an acquiescence to reality rather than an almost revolutionary achievement. As a recent minority report—whose filing was rejected by the Trudeau government—written by two Québec members of a recent commission on constitutional reform argued:

Each of Canada's provinces certainly contains a population which serves to distinguish it from all other provinces, *but in Québec one finds a nation,* using the term in its sociological sense. Whether one likes it or not this population considers itself *Québécois* before being Canadian. (Debané, Pierre et Martial Asselin; *Le Devoir,* 17 mars 1972:5; emphasis mine)

La Révolution Tranquille: The Rebirth of Separatism

It would be impossible to understand the turmoil of Québec today without a realization that the present openness of Québec society is itself a very recent phenomenon. Prior to 1959, the year which marked the death of Maurice Duplessis, Québec society was dominated by the Church, the provincial government, and fear of innovation. The first half of the decade of the 1960s, known today as "la révolution tranquille" or "the quiet revolution," represented the *printemps* of Québec, in which the pressures which had long brewed in Québec's industrialized middle class broke through and gained expression.

In Québec today one often hears this rapid change expressed in such phrases as: "You wouldn't recognize this place ten years ago." Evidently the changes have been profound; and pre-"quiet revolution" days often carry descriptions of Québec's French population which can only be labeled as defeatist. For in the years before the death of Maurice Duplessis the province seemed to have slept for generations under the complacency of isolation, only to find itself rudely awakened at the bottom of a new order, weighed down with graft-ridden municipal and provincial governments, a Church and school system of the past, and an image as a folkloric relic. André Laurendeau, in his *Le Devoir* editorial of June 22, 1963, outlined the progress of the quiet revolution:

> the new epoch began in September, 1959, with the death of Somebody. The historian will be better able to show us the causes and connections. But it is necessary to record that rupture—the explosion. . . .
>
> . . . the psychological revolution begins with Paul Sauvé. In three weeks he made it clear that his government did not resemble that of his predecessor and ex-chief. From now on, intelligent suggestions would not be automatically dismissed, nor their authors insulted. It was under him that education began to be looked on with real interest. Thanks to statutory grants, arbitrary methods of aid received a setback. The province, stiff-jointed, undertook to unfold and stretch itself: what joy and what hope, yet in an element still calm. (Laurendeau, *Le Devoir*, 22 juin 1963, quoted in Myers, 1963:xxi)

Although Québec's springtime is dated from 1959 with the death of "Somebody" (Maurice Duplessis), cracks in its winter had slowly developed during the previous decade. Not surprisingly, one of the major architects of the quiet revolution was Pierre Trudeau. His editing of *La grève de l'amiante* (1956) detailed the interconnection between the provincial government and Johns-Manville to the detriment of Québec's workers and was one of the earliest texts to openly put in question whether or not Duplessis' economic stance was in fact directed toward the amelioration of the French Canadian's lot. His direction of *Cité Libre*, with Gérard Pelletier, formerly Canada's secretary of state, engaged him in a continuing effort to counter Duplessis and open Québec society. For his efforts, which seemed vitriolic in their contrast to the surrounding silence, he became known as a radical —so much so, in fact, that the future Prime Minister was denied teaching privileges at the *Université de Montréal* as a "Communist" and an "anti-cleric" (Trudeau, 1967:vii).

Also during the 1950s, Jacques Hébert, today president of

la *Ligue des droits de l'Homme* and *Editions du Jour,* published
Coffin était innocent (1958) in which he argued that the English
Quebeker Wilbert Coffin, executed for the murder of three American hunters, was presented as a sacrificial offering by Duplessis
to American tourists. In 1958 the book was largely ignored. Also
in 1958, *Le Devoir* made a major effort to unseat members of
Duplessis' government, accusing various ministers of having
profited from a manipulation of the sale of the province's Natural
Gas Corporation. For days the paper carried banner headlines
attempting to interest the public in the scandal with only marginal
success. Duplessis was still alive.

Hébert's publication of *J'accuse les assassins de Coffin* (1963),
however, met a wholly different fate. As Myers states, the attitudes of the province had so greatly changed that, whereas five
years before a previous book on the same subject by the same
author was ignored as were charges of corruption directed against
the provincial government, in 1963 the public:

> . . . IS READY TO BELIEVE A MAN WHO ACCUSES PRO-
> VINCIAL AUTHORITIES OF LEGAL MURDER. . . .
>
> In 1958, *Le Devoir* threw everything into an attack on the
> government, it represented some ministers as swindlers. It
> never really got the public with it, not for a year or two
> anyway. Now ONE MAN calls down some of our mighty
> judges and policemen, saying they're just a lot of assassins,
> and receives such a wave of instant, spontaneous support that
> in less than a month (the book appeared on December 11)
> the government has to do just what he says it should do, that
> is, set up a Royal Commission to investigate the conduct of
> the Coffin trial and the behavior of all concerned. . . . (1964:
> xvii-xviii)[23]

Duplessis died September 7, 1959, at Schefferville in what was
formerly the Ungava territory (today Nouveau-Québec) at the site
of Québec's massive iron lode, which he had encouraged American
investors to develop—encouraged to the extent that, as Rioux
declared, "[he gave] to the American capitalists for almost
nothing the resources of his country" (1971:101). At the very
least, he wasn't a hard bargainer—exploitation of the site near
Labrador was offered under an arrangement in which Québec
received one cent per ton while at the same period Newfoundland

negotiated a similar contract receiving royalty payments of 23 cents per ton (Rioux, 1971:101; Bergeron, 1971:206). As Laporte offered in *Le Vrai Visage de Duplessis,* published shortly after his death:

> Even in death he illustrated the passions which he aroused in the hearts of men. His friends declared that he died in the heart of the "empire" he had opened to civilization and progress. His opponents whispered that through some twist of fate, he had died on the scene of his worst treason. (1960:26)[24]

A profound awakening of French Canadians began the very year of Duplessis' death. Among the first issues to impress upon French Canadians how impotent they were was the strike of Radio-Canada, the national French language network. The strike, which lasted from December 29, 1958 until March 7, 1959, was begun by the Radio-Canada producers, whose right to form a union was rejected by the CBC and supported by three thousand fellow workers. At the end of the strike, which lasted through the coldest days of the winter, the French had separated from The Canadian Conference of Authors and Artists and formed *La Fédération des auteurs et des artistes du Canada,* and bitterness ran deep. The March 3 issue of *Le Devoir* carried two pictures of René Lévesque—then a commentator on Radio-Canada, later the most important force in Quebec's first reform liberal cabinet after the fall of Duplessis' *Union Nationale* and today head of the *Parti Québécois*—one picture showed Lévesque being arrested and entering a police wagon, the other his release. March 7, the day the strike ended in victory for the producers, Lévesque responded in an article appearing on page 2 of *Le Devoir:*

> Radio-Canada is a fiction; the reality is called "C.B.C."
>
> ... [throughout the strike something has existed which is] nearly intangible and at the same time monstrous, which refuses obstinately to show its true face. Moreover, it's a face that would try desperately to grimace a smile if perchance one managed to unmask it. The rest of this article is written in the language that this face speaks.
>
> ... [The rest of the article is written in English and is composed of a list of those who have prolonged and exacerbated the strike.] Some of us, and maybe many, came out of this

> with a tired and unworthy feeling that if such a strike had
> happened on the English CBC, it would—as the Hon. George
> Nowland said, on this occasion not erroneously—have lasted
> no more than half an hour. To this day, ours has lasted sixty-
> eight days. Of such signal advantages is the privilege of being
> French made up on this country!
>
> And even at the risk of being termed "horrid nationalists," we
> feel that at least once before the conflict is over, we have to
> make plain our deep appreciation of such an enviable place in
> the great, bilingual, bicultural, and fraternal Canadian sun. . . .
> (Quoted in Myers, 1964:13-14)[25]

Then came Jean-Paul Desbiens's *Les insolences du Frère Untel,*
which shook the province with the assertion by the then-
anonymous teaching brother that the administration and teaching
system in Québec's schools was a fetid mess. His style and his
charges swept the province, and he knew controversy as none
before him had. If one had to form a triumvirate of man, action,
and the written word to date the beginning of Québec's revitalization, it would be: the death of Duplessis, the strike at Radio-
Canada, and the publication of *Les Insolences.*

Desbiens's incredible wit, apparent even in English translation
(although the original French is almost indescribably humorous),
caused the acidity of his comments to burn that much deeper.
His book sold well over one hundred thousand copies and reached,
at least partially, its goal of educational reform largely through the
stimulus of passages such as the following:

> We are good, fat fools, we public secondary teachers. On the
> faith of promises we convince ourselves that there is hope.
> We wait for *L'Instruction publique* each year. It arrives. (Here,
> if I weren't Frère Untel, pious, pure and Marist, I would write
> twice the word you all know to describe the manual). In the
> April, 1960 issues of *L'Instruction Publique,* M. Roland
> Vinette adds a surrealistic poem under the title "Information
> and Directives."
>
> He applies himself to the task of saying nothing, M. Roland
> Vinette. He beats around the bush and is mysterious, not by
> incompetence (we know he is competent, lucid and capable
> of writing in French), but by the *politics* imposed upon him.
> Everything happens as if the officers of the department wish

to confuse us. Apparently, it is not necessary for us to understand. . . .

I am soft-hearted, you understand. I cannot hurt anyone but
we must close the department. I am for giving all the members
of the Public Department of Instruction all of the medals
there are, including the one for Agriculture Merit, and even
creating some special ones such as a medal for Solemn Medi-
ocrity and assuring each of these men a comfortable retire-
ment before sending them back to their mommies. (Trans.
from 1960:41, 51–52)

The year 1961 saw the publication of Marcel Chaput's *Pourquoi
je suis séparatiste*, which thought and reasoned out the unthinkable: separation, an idea so radical at the time that he tells his
readers to either commit themselves to read the book with an
open mind or not at all. In it he develops four principal premises
which he feels are necessary to accept if *québécois* are ever to
thrive: (1) French Canadians already form a nation; (2) this nation
is a nation as much as any other; (3) the State of Québec is the
national state of French Canadians; (4) to progress, French Canadians must be the masters in their own territory (1961:11). In
noting Lionel Groulx's remarks that "a people who wishes to live
must know how to do something other than just how not to die"
(149), Chaput suggests that the epitaph for French Canadians
may soon be, if they don't act to separate themselves from
Canada, "Here lies a people who died on their *chemin* (way, road)
because they didn't know where it went" (142).

What action will permit *québécois* to cast off their sense of
inferiority and flower? What must be done, says Chaput, is simply:

1. Proclaim sovereignty so that a global approach may be
   taken.

2. Decree French the sole official language, and in so doing,

3. Make French necessary and profitable to know.

4. Supervise the correctness of everything that is printed and
   posted.

5. Rehabilitate France and its culture in our eyes.

6. Create a feeling of belonging to the great French family of
   twenty-five nations and 150 million persons.

7. Create a French news agency to free our magazines and newspapers from the need to utilize Anglo-American sources.

8. Maintain a balance between foreign cultural invasion and domestic contributions.

9. Re-francify our teaching institutions, commencing with the professors and textbooks.

10. Send technicians to the Black French language nations in exchange for French professors. (45-46)[26]

These proposals, which seemed radical in 1961, have all, except for the first, become rather tame, and attempts to implement most of them have been made. As early as 1962 the newly formed Liberal government—largely under the impetus of René Lévesque—deciding to proceed with the nationalization of Québec's electric power companies, took the matter to the electorate under the theme *Maîtres chez nous* ("Masters in our own house") and won handily. After their assumption of office, a policy of gradual erosion of federal jurisdiction in the province's favor was instituted which has continued until the present. Indeed, the actual effect of *la revolution tranquille* on the political arena can best be seen as engaging the province in a tug-of-war with the federal government for every possible degree of autonomy.

Recent examples of this struggle for authority within Québec can be seen in the province's unilateral decision to construct a massive hydroelectric installation at James Bay and Ottawa's attempt to gain greater control over the Province's social services. In the former instance, Québec has developed and is in the process of implementing plans for the hydroelectric exploitation of the province's portion of the James Bay— plans for which it did not seek federal approval despite the fact that the federal government has prime authority over all of Canada's navigable waterways. In the second instance, that as to who shall have the power of the purse over provincial welfare services, the federal government has acquiesced to provincial control over family allowances while retaining control of various unemployment programs.

In recent years, under the leadership of provincial Premier Robert Bourassa, however, there seems to have been a tendency to permit federal encroachment within the province rather than defending every bastion as if it were the last. The resignation of Claude Marin, who had served in the highest rank of the ministry of Intergovernmental Affairs (Quebec-Ottawa) under four Québec premiers brought this apparent failure of the Bourassa government to the fore. Marin, in lectures at *l'Université de Québec* under the theme "OTTAWA parmi nous," argued that it is the intention of the federal government to penetrate as deeply as possible into the everyday life of Québec; so deeply that in creating ever more widening contacts with Québec's citizens and institutions it would become impossible for Québec to modify the relationship, that is, to separate. The path upon which this process is being carried out is that of the gathering of federal revenues for direct redistribution to the populace such that the spectre of Québec "sous la Saint-Vincent-de-Paul fédérale" has been raised (Marin, Claude; *Le Devoir,* 13 mars 1972:5). The process is clear, Marin argued: the Federal government under Trudeau is attempting in every possible fashion to strip powers from Québec, render it a branch of Ottawa and leave it with no greater power than that held by a municipality. "When one is a municipality," Marin warns, "one doesn't negotiate independence . . . one is content just to hope that the superior governments will behave generously towards you" (4). As Laurent Laplante argues in a *Le Devoir* editorial, Québec is at a crossroads: "either we choose independence while Québec still has certain powers, or it's all over" (13 mars 1972:4).

What has been the English Canadian attitude toward Québec's revolution? In a discourse titled "The average English Canadian View," Douglas Fischer, a member of Parliament from Ontario, responded to a previous speech made by René Lévesque claiming that he thought English Canada needed French Canada more than the reverse:

> If I was speaking to my constituents or anybody from Sudbury westward, trying to explain what little I know about French Canadians, their reaction would be: "Well, what has the French Canadian to offer us, that we should be so excited about *bonne entente* and learning the French language and so on?" And I wonder what they would say about French-Canadian culture? I suppose for us the greatest impact of French-Canadian culture has been made by Maurice Richard and Lili St-Cyr. We did have Gisèle, of course, but she became Gisèle

McKenzie and went off to the United States. I wonder
whether we are to be fascinated by your marvelous police
tradition, the magnificence of your telegraphers, the ingenuity
that I witnessed when I was looking into the operation of the
Jacques-Cartier bridge in Montreal. . . . I wonder if we are to
be impressed with your tradition of literary censorship, or
whether your educational system has a great deal to offer us
in a society where technocracy is becoming so much more important. I cannot honestly say I believe that we need your
resources. You have lots of iron ore here, but so have we and
so has much of the rest of Canada. You have a lot of base
metals, but so have we. You have lots of water power, but so
has British Columbia; and we've got all kinds of natural gas,
oil, and coal in the rest of the country. (Myers, 1964:53)

An overview of the early 1960s in Québec makes it apparent
that it was a period of great ferment in several realms of Québec
society: the religious sphere, in which the Church progressively
lost its grip on the population, the political sphere, in which
demands for autonomy ranged from Premier Daniel Johnson's
(1965) demand for *Egalité ou indépendence* to Chaput's insistence that the chimera of federalism be buried once and for all,
and in the cultural sphere, in which questions of the linguistic
ability of French Quebekers in their own language as well as that
of the general value of French Canadian culture as a whole dominated. It was a heady period, in which options which previously
seemed unavailable suddenly became inevitable.

In the political arena, *la révolution tranquille* gave birth to a
succession of parties of independence, from the *Rassemblement
pour l'indépendence nationale,* the *Mouvement Souveraineté-
Association* (formed by René Lévesque after leaving the liberals
in 1967), to today's *Parti Québécois,* an independentist party
which draws its strength not only from Québec's intellectual and
middle class, but its industrial workers as well. René Lévesque,
in his eloquence and in his well-reasoned polemic for independence, *Option Québec* (1968), has gradually gained more and
more of the crucial political middle ground within the province's
electorate and is today viewed by many as a reasonable man with
a suddenly reasonable plan. Today, few observers doubt that
Lévesque's *Parti Québécois* will continue to gain support among
the electorate and may eventually be able to form a government.[27]

Québec's efforts to establish itself as a vital center of French culture in the eyes of English Canadians, Americans, French Canadians outside of Québec, and, most importantly, in the eyes of *québécois* themselves, have been largely successful. Literature, cinematography, the plastic arts, the popular songs have all been domains in which recent efforts have been marked above all by a sense of vitality. The old Québec, the folkloric relic of marginal survival, still survives, to be sure, but its image is today hidden by a people *en train d'épanouir.*

Within Canada, and even within all of North America, Québec has begun to take upon itself the responsiblity for French destiny in the hemisphere. Once considered by France to be an underdeveloped country in which a young man of military age could fulfill his obligation by teaching the province's natives, Québec has begun to reverse the role. Today Québec is not only in the process of assuming the role of the metropole for Canada, but has provided aid, primarily in the form of French teachers, to Louisiana to promote the French language and culture.

The FLQ and Revolutionary Separatism

Patriots,

Since the second world war many exploited peoples of the world have broken their chains to acquire the liberty which is their right. The great majority of these peoples have vanquished the oppressor and today live freely.

As so many others, the Québec people have had enough of submission to the arrogant domination of Anglo-Saxon colonialism.

In Québec as in all colonized countries, the oppressor furiously denies his imperialism and is supported by our so-called national elite, which is more interested in protecting its personal economic interests than those vital to the Québec nation. It continues to deny the evidence and to concern itself with the creation of numerous false problems in an effort to detour the subjected people from the sole essential goal:

Despite this, the eyes of the workers each day open a little more to reality: Québec is a colony! . . .

Our situation is a national emergency. We must remedy it now . . .

> But it is not enough to want independence, to work within existing independentist parties. The colonists will not let such a choice morsel go so easily. The independentist political parties will never be able to gain the necessary power to defeat the colonial economic and political power. More importantly, independence alone will solve nothing. It must be completed at any price by social revolution. The Québec patriots are not fighting for a title but for facts. Revolution doesn't take place in the parlour. Only a total revolution can have the necessary power to effect the vital changes which will force themselves upon an independent Québec. The national revolution, in its essence, can accept no compromise. There is only one way to overcome colonialism and that is to be stronger than it! Only the most aberrant polyannaism can believe the opposite. The time of slavery is over.
>
> PATRIOTS OF QUEBEC, TO ARMS! THE TIME FOR REVOLUTION HAS ARRIVED! INDEPENDENCE OR DEATH! (FLQ Manifesto; 16 April 1963, quoted in Savoie, 1963: 43-46)

On March 8, 1963, Molotov cocktails, filled with virtually incombustible fuel oil, were thrown at military garrisons in Montréal. Soon thereafter, the Wolfe monument was overturned, a railroad track over which Prime Minister Diefenbaker was to pass was dynamited, a night watchman was killed by a bomb at a Canadian Forces recruiting station, and mailboxes began to explode in Westmount. The quiet revolution, if not ended, was at least being drowned in the emotions of one practicing more violent means.

For those French Canadians beyond the pale of power, and especially the young among these, one of the most psychologically satisfying coping responses to the problems engendered by their ethnicity has been that of revolutionary separatism, which seeks not only to sever ties with English Canada but to raise a new socialist order in Québec. If Québec is a colony, if québécois are exploited, a glance at Westmount indicates whose colony it is. Yet, if the English control the uppermost levels of the current social regime it is also obvious that all québécois are not equally exploited; some are quite well-to-do. Obviously the English have their henchmen: French Canadians who have "sold out" their fellow countrymen for the privilege of being the intermediaries between the exploiters and those exploited. One must smash the English, but as importantly, if not even more so, it is necessary to destroy those *vendus,* the group the FLQ referred to as "notre soi-disante elite nationale," whose very cooperation, or collaboration, provides the basis of colonial survival.

Throughout its history, according to the dogma of radical separatists, the people of Québec have always been sold out by their own elite. During most of the nineteenth and early twentieth centuries it was the Church; while today the bourgeoisie has usurped the honor. Even René Lévesque and his *Parti Québécois* are viewed as primarily bourgeois opportunists operating under the cloak of an essentially reactionary nationalism who only wish to eliminate the English presence in Québec so that they may fill the vacuum.[28]

Today the *vendu* is epitomized in the person of Pierre Trudeau, who is often portrayed as a blatant collaborator whose intelligence and cunning make him a dangerous adversary of the people. Vallières, in his *Nègres blancs d'Amérique,* took pains to identify those politicians whose power and abilities rendered them most dangerous: Jean Drapeau, mayor of Montréal ("Will he someday become our Fuhrer?"), Daniel Johnson, formerly Premier of Québec, today replaced by Robert Bourassa, and Pierre Laporte (1968:328). Dwarfing even these men, however, are Trudeau and Gerard Pelletier, former editors of Cité Libre and later French Canada's leading public officials on the federal scene:

> Trudeau and Pelletier could not believe that the youths who they had influenced, from 1950 to 1960, had become separatist. It was as if they had given birth to a monster. And the young people, themselves, found it difficult to realize that their old idols had aged so quickly. One day separatists burned Pelletier in effigy in front of the *La Presse* building. During the first FLQ wave, in 1963, his life was threatened. Today, in Ottawa, Pelletier and Trudeau cannot understand that they are traitors or that they are serving the imperialist aims of the United States and English Canada. They are too intelligent, however, to be considered as irresponsible. That is why it is impossible not to see them as traitors. One day, they will have to assume all the consequences of this treason. (295)

Trudeau and Pelletier, men who provoked and led the silent

revolution when it was completely mute, are traitors to those of the next generation and "will have to assume all the consequences" of their treason!

More than any other group, the *Front de libération du Québec,* or *Front de libération Québécois,* as it is often known, stood as the symbol of the Québec awakening of the 1960s. Despite the fact that in its eschewing of electoral tactics for the rhetoric and action of violent revolutionary separatism it represented an isolated, extremist position, it was the bombs of the FLQ which notified the world, and many French Canadians as well, that the days of Québec as a scenic outpost of seventeenth-century France were gone.

The formation of the FLQ, which presumably took place in 1962 or the early part of 1963, arose from the sense of frustration of certain *québécois* that the "quiet revolution" was not proceeding far or fast enough and was being led by those with limited and largely personal goals. The organization was formed as a revolutionary vanguard with theoretical roots in the groups which led revolutionary struggles in Algeria, Cuba, Vietnam, and China. Its stated purpose was to "awaken" the workers and people of Québec to their position as a "colonized" people and to induce them to rise up and jettison the ties which held them in this state. Although initially the philosophy of the revolutionary group was thin, its essential demand—independence from Canada within a socialist framework—was quite clear.

The tactics of the new revolutionary movement were based on maximum use of publicity gained through the strategic deployment of explosive devices. Thus, while the FLQ maintained as its primary goal the complete destruction of the English colonial presence and, specifically, that of the Royal Canadian Mounted Police, the Canadian Forces, English radio, television, and newspapers, as well as all enterprises which discriminated against French Canadians, in actuality its attacks were limited to the painting of slogans (usually consisting solely of the letters "FLQ"), the destruction of mailboxes, and occasional bombings of public buildings.

Human victims, when claimed in the revolutionary bombings, were invariably workers, both French and English, and never directors. This loss of human lives in the wake of FLQ activity formed a serious contradiction to the professed love of the people proclaimed by revolutionary separatists. One of the first factors which the FLQ had to contend with was the fact that as long as its activities extended only to painting its insignia on walls, and its bombs exploded harmlessly, the sympathy of the population might rest with it or at least be neutral. But what would be its response to the first injury or death? Taking care to absolve itself from blame, the FLQ asserted in one of its earliest documents that there would never be attacks which jeopardize the lives of "innocents" and that if death did result, the responsibility, contrary to the wisdom of first glance, *"retombe entièrement sur le colonialisme anglo-saxon, cause du notre existence"* (Savoie, 1963:42).[29]

The structure of the FLQ was such that one or two individuals who were interested in undertaking revolutionary activity would form a cell having little or no contact with other cells and then seek to attract others to it. Although as apart of a bandwagon approach the FLQ claimed a large network in constant process of expansion, it is unlikely that it ever had more than a handful of adherents. Indeed, the very concept of a "Front," itself, fostered an inaccurate impression of the structure of the group. The fact that the bombings and other activities of the Front came in waves, each wave evidencing a distinct style, suggests each wave with its subsequent arrests and appeals for aid from other "patriotes" in carrying on the struggle served to wrest from the population its individuals inclined to seek a revolutionary solution rather than the pattern of orderly recruitment which the FLQ claimed to be in operation.

In many ways the structure of the FLQ can best be described as that of a revolutionary gang. Its members were bound by ties of friendship and camaraderie as much as by ideology, and, on the whole, one's contacts were limited to fellow members of each individual cell. There was no membership card, no dues, no regular publication. Lacking a central structure, membership in the FLQ was gained simply by claiming to be a member and conducting oneself in the proper fashion. Undoubtedly, the small group structure of the cells, given a *machismo* ethos, pushed many to action; it is very difficult for a man to speak of revolution day after day within a small group and not suffer a major loss of face if he shrinks from action.

The gang-like character of the FLQ gave each of its waves its own peculiar stamp—those who preferred the anonymous destruction of bombs chose them while those who preferred the life of bank robbers chose to style themselves as *patriotic* bank robbers. In the beginning, most FLQ activities demonstrated the air of a collection of patriotic Jean-Paul Belmondos engaged in a fascinating lark, an air which only shifted with the ideological adherence of Pierre Vallières, who sought to give the movement the respectability of a group of concerned, dedicated, socialist revolutionaries.

Due to the idiosyncratic cast given to Québec's revolutionary separatist movement by each of its *vagues,* an adequate analysis of it can only take place within the context of each individual wave.

The First Wave

Beginning of 1963

Bombing of federal buildings and mailboxes. Inscription of "FLQ" and of the slogan "Québec Libre" on the front door and on the walls of the residence of the Lieutenant-Governor in Québec.

Arson in several country train stations.

Molotov cocktails thrown at three military quarters in Montréal. No explosions as fuel oil used in lieu of gasoline.

Overturning of Wolfe monument in Québec.

April, 1963

Bomb explosion of the track of the Canadian National near Lemieux several hours before the passage of the campaign train of Prime Minister Diefenbaker.

Bomb found in corridor of Montréal Canada station and defused.

Bomb exploded without injuries in the Federal Revenue Building in Montréal.

Bomb explosion without injuries in the rear of the Westmount R.C.M.P. headquarters.

Bomb found and defused near an English radio station in Montréal.

Bomb exploded in the Canadian Forces recruitment center in Montréal killing Wilfrid O'Neil, a nightwatchman.

May, 1963

Bomb defused in la Prévoyance *building in Montréal.*

Bomb explosion without injuries in the Montréal headquarters of the Black Watch.

Bomb explosion without injuries in the technical service of the Royal Airforce in Montréal.

Explosion of five bombs in Westmount post office boxes and ten others defused, with one victim, Walter Leja, Sergeant-Major in the Canadian Army, rendered a mental and physical invalid for life.

False bomb threat in an Ottawa Federal Building leads to the death of Louis Ducette, 26, who was killed in attempting to escape from a stalled elevator.

Bomb explosion without injuries in front of the R.C.M.P. building in Montréal.

July, 1963

Bomb explosion on the Queen Victoria monument in Québec.

(Pelletier, 1971:225-226; Morf, 1970:9-11)

The initial attacks of the FLQ, while attracting widespread interest and even alarm, were apparently not regarded very seriously by the Québec government. Until April, 1963, the attacks consisted of paint raids in which slogans were smeared on the walls of buildings. Even the March 8 attack on three military quarters in Montréal was made with Molotov cocktails filled with heating oil. According to Savoie the *felquistes* substituted the oil for gasoline to avoid any damage and yet still create some noise (1963:26).

It was the death of the sixty-five-year-old nightwatchman, Wilfrid O'Neil, in an April 20 attack upon the Montréal Canadian Forces recruiting center that mobilized the government of Jean Lesage to offer a reward of ten thousand dollars and to undertake an intensive effort to capture its revolutionary opposition. The May 17 maiming of the Canadian Army bomb defusing specialist Walter Leja added to the ire of the police and boosted the reward to fifty thousand dollars for information leading to the arrest and conviction of those responsible. At this time, in an effort to shore their moral stance in relation to death and injuries resulting from bomb attacks, which was based solely on the thesis that, since the colonialists had forced them to take revolutionary action, all responsibility for resultant deaths was to be assumed by the establishment, the FLQ issued a manifesto declaring that it recognized only two classes of individuals: "revolutionary-patriots and collaborator-traitors" (Morf, 1970:11).

The body of the first wave ended on June 2, 1963, with the arrest of eight individuals. On June 14, 1963, George Schoeters, Raymond Villeneuve, Gabriel Hudon, Jacques Giroux, and Yves Labonte were accused of conspiracy in the murder of O'Neil. Four others were charged with the injuries sustained by Sgt. Major Leja and six more with material damages. With the exception of one individual who fled to Algeria and two against whom evidence was deemed insufficient, all were convicted and sentenced to prison terms of up to fifteen years; the maximum sentence served, however, was four years.

The individual credited with the founding of the FLQ, George Schoeters, was not *québécois* or even French Canadian, but Belgian. Born in Anvers in 1930, the son of a wealthy individual and his mistress, he was raised as an orphan until the Nazi occupation of his country, when he found a place in the resistance. In spite of his asthma, and perhaps because of his youth, he was apparently a useful messenger and spy. In 1944, he was captured by the Germans and held until released by the advancing American army. Apparently life as a post-war adolescent was pale in relation to his memories of the war and induced him to immigrate to Canada in 1951. Upon his arrival in Canada he was unable to find anything other than menial employment, even with his quatrilingualism and obvious intelligence. Eventually he enrolled at a classical college and later at *l'Université de Montréal,* where he gained his B.A. in Sociology.

In 1957, Schoeters married a French Canadian hospital technician who continued to work after their marriage to help support herself and their two children. In 1958, at the expense of a student organization, he travelled to Algeria to study the *Front de libération nationale* and afterwards spent a year in Cuba at the expense of the new revolutionary government before returning to Canada.

Upon his return, Schoeters became a member of the separatist *Rassemblement pour l'indépendance nationale* (R.I.N.), which he soon left to join a group known as the *Réseau de Résistance* (RR), which differed from the former primarily in its degree of radicalism and willingness to use force. Although radical, the RR limited itself to the plastering of slogans, and shortly after its founding changed its title to the *Front de libération québécois,* holding meetings of its fifteen members in Schoeter's house or in a restaurant.

Soon the group began to take advantage of unguarded *Métro* construction shacks to steal dynamite. Pushed largely by their personal inability to withdraw from the logical extension of their group rhetoric into violence, the group launched its attacks against the colonial establishment and were eventually brought to trial— not as the political prisoners which they claimed to be, but as murderers and vandals (one of the group, Mario Bachand, refused to testify before a court nominally under the Queen, claiming: ". . . mon pays ce n'est pas le Canada, c'est le Québec" (Savoie, 1963: 115).[30]

The second of the founders of the FLQ, Raymond Villeneuve, was born in September, 1943, the eldest son of a French Canadian artisan. After failing a high school chemistry course, which prevented his acceptance to a university, he worked in his father's shop. Gradually he began to devote more and more of his time to politics. Morf (1970) describes him as a young man of superior intelligence and athletic build for whom an idea demanded action. At his trial he conducted himself with arrogance and he refused to testify. In prison he did well in his studies and was able to pass his entrance exams to the School of Advanced Commercial Studies and was given a conditional release to attend *l'Université de Montréal.* Soon, however, he began to concentrate more and more in sociology, and, suffering a revolutionary relapse, left Canada for Cuba.

The Second Wave

September, 1963

Holdup at the Royal Bank of Canada netting $6,929.

October, 1963

Publication of La Cognée *("The Hatchet"), clandestine organ of the FLQ.*

November, 1963

Burglary of radio station CHEF in Granby; booty: radio transmitters and equipment valued at $4,000.

January, 1964

Holdup at headquarters of the Fusiliers Mont-Royal. Theft of equipment (arms, telescopes, munitions), with value of $20,000.

Holdup of a military establishment, with a booty of $1,640.

February, 1964

Theft at the quarters of the 62nd regiment of the Canadian artillery at Shawnigan of $21,000 worth of arms and munitions.

March, 1964

Holdup at La Banque Provinciale of Rosèmere, netting $3,000.

April, 1964

Holdup at the Banque Canadienne Nationale in Mont-Rolland, netting $5,000.

(Pelletier, 1971:226-227; Morf, 1970:27-28)

The leader of the second wave was none other than the younger brother of Gabriel Hudon, one of the original members of the FLQ, who began serving a twelve year sentence October 7, 1963. The oldest member of Robert Hudon's group of six was twenty-three, and most of the members were nearer to his own age of nineteen. Although the group had stolen forty thousand dollars in cash and fifty-five thousand dollars in arms and equipment, at the time of their capture only the equipment was found in its entirety, while the money had apparently been spent to provide for the army's needs. Hudon, himself, had been provided with two trucks and an automobile from the army's slush funds. At his trial Robert professed himself to be insulted at being tried as a thief, explaining that the money and equipment were only stolen for the purpose of establishing *l'Armée de libération*. Morf concludes that:

> The six conspirators had lived a life of adventure like that of 16th and 17th century pirates of the high seas. The liberation of Québec was only a pretext to give them the liberty to follow their criminal tendencies and thirst for adventure and independence. (1970:28)

The Third Wave

June, 1964

Robbery at construction site at Saint-Jacques-de-Windsor of 700 sticks of dynamite.

Robbery at construction site at Estérel of 150 sticks of dynamite.

August, 1964

Creation of training camps for the Armée révolutionnaire du Québec *at Saint-Boniface.*

Robbery of several cases of arms at Port of Montréal.

Holdup at International Firearms in Montréal killing two employees.

October, 1964

Robbery of Hydro-Québec truck in Baie-Comeau of several cases of dynamite.

January, 1965

Arsonous attack on L. G. Power Sawmills, Ltd. at Gifford, Québec.

April, 1965

Robbery at an Expo-67 construction site at Caughnawaga with theft of several cases of dynamite and detonators.

May, 1965

Robbery of one thousand sticks of dynamite from Alma construction site.

June, 1965

Derailment of two trains of the Canadian National and the tossing of a Molotov cocktail in a third.

Robbery at Sainte-Anasthasie of arms and munitions.

Robbery of several cases of dynamite in Milan.

August, 1965

Bomb disarmed before explosion on railroad track near Sainte-Madeleine.

Bomb without detonator placed on a railroad bridge near Bordeaux.

(Pelletier, 1971:227-228)

The third wave of the FLQ was primarily the result of action by a group calling itself *l'Armée révolutionnaire du Québec,* founded by François Schirm, a Hungarian immigrant who had spent much of his life in the French Foreign Legion and had seen action on several fronts in the French colonial wars of the 1950s. Schirm was born in 1932 in Budapest and raised as the only child of a cabinetmaker. As a child in World War II he was witness to atrocities committed by both Russians and Americans. Later, he joined the French Foreign Legion and served in Vietnam and Algeria before immigrating to Canada to marry a Hungarian woman he had met through correspondence. After a series of personal misfortunes and low-paying jobs he gravitated toward the Québec independence movement. Initially, he joined the *Rassemblement pour l'Indépendance Nationale,* but soon found the organization insufficiently revolutionary and, with his experience in the Foreign Legion as his guide, decided to form an army of liberation for *québécois.* He established the first of what was to be a network of training camps for the revolution at Saint-Boniface and began to recruit *felquiste* sympathizers. After several weeks of frustration waiting for promised supplies from the FLQ, he and his men organized and executed the holdup at International Firearms which resulted in the deaths of two of its employees. One, the vice-president, was killed as he advanced toward a member of the holdup party, a slightly built French Canadian twenty-year-old whom he apparently thought was a child feigning a robbery. The other death was caused by police who mistook an International Firearms employee for one of the robbers. Several days later the members of the Armée were surprised at their camp and arrested.[31]

The Fourth Wave

October, 1965

Breaking and entry into headquarters of Parti national democratique *in Montréal in which mimeograph machines and office supplies were stolen.*

1965-1966

Regular publication of the underground journal La Cognée, *containing information on acts of violence and thefts of dynamite, instructions on the fabrication of bombs, bank robberies, arson, use of Molotov cocktails, etc.*

April, 1966

Robbery at South Stukely, south of Montréal, and theft of dynamite.

Burglary at Collège du Mont-Saint-Louis of rifles, ammunition, telescopes and other military equipment.

May, 1966

Location of a base at Saint-Alphonse at Joliette to use as a base for a new revolutionary army. Storage of dynamite, detonators and stolen arms. [32]

Holdup at Cinéma Elysée in Montréal netting $2,400.

Bomb in the shoe manufacturing firm La Grenade, killing one (Mlle. Thérèse Morin) and injuring three others.

Bomb explosion at Dominion Textile in Drummondville.

June, 1966

Bomb explosion at Centre Paul-Sauvé in Montréal at assembly of the provincial Liberal Party.

Armed robbery in Outremont at private residence of five hundred dollars and a bottle of liquor.

July, 1966

Bomb at Dominion Textile in Montréal resulting in one death, that of Jean Corbo, member of the FLQ, who was ripped apart by the premature explosion of a bomb he was in the process of deploying.

August, 1966

Holdup at Cinéma Jean-Talon in Montréal.

October and November, 1966

Writing of Nègres blancs d'Amérique *by Pierre Vallières in "Tombs" prison in New York City.*

December 1967

Theft of arms and ammunition at Cap-de-la-Madeleine valued at $9,000.

(Pelletier, 1971:228–229 and Morf, 1970:77–80)

The fourth wave of the FLQ was characterized by the careful mixing of revolutionary thought with the bombs and holdups which had already been adopted as tactics toward the revolution. Significantly, it began not with a bomb or a bank holdup but with the burglary of a mimeograph machine and office supplies at the headquarters of the leftist *Parti National Démocratique,* or NDP, as it is known to English Canadians. The acquisitions were quickly put to use in the publication of the underground journal *La Cognée,* published by André Lavoie, then twenty-four years old. The journal appeared twice each month with a circulation of approximately two hundred copies passed from hand to hand among members of the radical left. Its articles outlined revolutionary ideology and explained the fabrication of bombs. Although the authors of its essays were cloaked in pseudonyms, many of the articles bore the style of Pierre Vallières and Charles Gagnon.

After five months of concentration upon the publication of the journal, the group began the series of robberies and bombings which ended in the death of a secretary in her employer's office during a strike at La Grenade shoe company, a bombing of the provincial Liberal Party convention in Montréal, and the death of one of the FLQ's own members, nineteen-year-old Jean Corbo, killed while planting a bomb at Dominion Textile in Montréal. In late August and early September, the police gradually encircled the cell and made a number of arrests, but Pierre Vallières and Charles Gagnon, the apparent leaders of the group, eluded the police and escaped into hiding. On September 26 they both resurfaced at the United Nations, where they began a hunger strike to attract world attention to Québec. Shortly after beginning the strike they were arrested and held by New York authorities pending deportation proceedings. As both were already known by the intellectual elite of Québec for their work with *Cité Libre,* their association with the FLQ lent it a respectability which it had not previously enjoyed and provoked the following message of support:

> We firmly support the hunger strike undertaken by Pierre Vallières and Charles Gagnon in New York September 26, 1966. In this sense: we are fighting for the liberation of the workers of Québec, fighting against all form of exploitation of man by man and are trying to promote a more just and fraternal society through socialism. That Pierre Vallières and Charles Gagnon have believed it necessary to use VIOLENCE in organizing the new terrorist network of the FLQ was not without reason. One can question the realism of a world that the *bien-pensants* believe peaceful when VIOLENCE is perpetrated each day on the weakest.... (Morf: 1970:81)

On the thirteenth of June, 1967, six of the members of the fourth wave were sentenced to terms of from three and a half to nine and a half years for their activities. The individual who fabricated the bomb which exploded in the shoe factory killing Mlle. Morin received eight years and ten months in prison.

Pierre Vallières was charged with "meutre non qualifié" in Mlle. Morin's death for having inspired the attack which led to her death by his writings, actions, and attitude, and was sentenced to life imprisonment. Charles Gagnon, charged with the same crime, was declared not guilty. He, however, remained in prison to serve an earlier sentence for his part in the holdup of the Jean-Talon theater. After the announcement of the sentences, demonstrations protesting political repression in Québec were held in Montréal and Paris, and from his prison cell Gagnon appealed to the people of Québec to rise in revolt:

> The Québec people are angry. Their apparent indifference only masks a supressed furor. All that is needed is a spark to start the fire. This is precisely the role of the revolutionary avant garde; our role is to create that spark. We must spread its fire throughout Québec. (Morf, 1970:84)

Pierre Vallières

Pierre Vallières stands apart from all others in Québec's revolutionary separatist movement, both as a result of his forceful personality and his text, *Nègres blancs d'Amérique: Autobiographie précoce d'un "terroriste" québécois,* which serves as the bible of Québec's revolutionary left.

Nègres blancs d'Amérique is not only a revolutionary document in a traditional polemical sense, but, more importantly, an autobiographical documentation of the degradation felt by an individual bearing a devalued ethnicity. As always in any document which purports to join one's own traumatic childhood with that of his countrymen, it is difficult to separate trauma specific to his family from that general to the society. Evidently, Vallières's personal history strikes strong chords with many young French Canadians, revolutionary separatists or not, as *Nègres blancs* is often presented as a capsule response to one wishing to know "what being a French Canadian is really like." In the words of one Québec revolutionary: *"Nègres blancs* is what we've all lived." In the mixing of Vallières's personal history with the social history of Québec, the text draws its great power and merits detailed discussion.

> It was a funny marriage, that between the disenchantment of my mother and the timid yet tenacious hope of my father. I do not know if it was a happy marriage. But I don't remember having seen in my parents the *joie de vivre* that one can see among those who know security, who have confidence in themselves and can believe easily in life.

> I always saw my parents worried, uncertain, anxious . . . even when they laughed. Those condemned to death also are sometimes overcome with foolish laughter. . . .

> My parents lived continually in fear of tomorrow, which meant possible unemployment, sickness, hunger, and a myriad of other potential miseries. . . . Escape from this fear through a little tossing aside of daily cares, of a little recreation, was never permitted. No. One always had to economize. Economize on everything . . . even on affection. The budget had to be balanced before beginning to think about living.

> My mother lived in constant insecurity and her agony shut
> out the outside world. My father could only find freedom at
> the factory with his camarades.[33]

> My brother and myself could free ourselves by playing with
> our friends or going to school. We were thus able to escape the
> "family" hell. But my mother never left ... Nothing excited
> her. Nothing appealed to her ... but her *devoir d'état:* mean-
> ing, in her mind, the obligation to always guard against an
> "accident"...

> In several years, she transformed herself into the "boss" of
> our little family, of which she was (supposedly) the first
> servant. She became a slave to her fear and tried to subject
> my father, my brothers and myself to her need for security ...
> (1968:104-106)

As a child, Vallières felt himself condemned to a hell with no
exit and as an adolescent stood with a "back already bent with too
much effort." After childhoods like these, with mothers constantly proclaiming the need for security and that one is "born for
un petit pain," is it any wonder, asks Vallières, why it requires
so much effort, so much willpower to lift oneself up and purge
oneself of the "nigger" within him, "of the man who was born
defeated?" (113).

Vallières spent the first seven years of his life in an East-end
area of Montréal known as Frontenac Park, in a neighborhood
filled with rival gangs and public family brawls. The streets offered
the only place to play, and soon he found himself part of a gang
whose principal source of amusement was the turning in of false-
alarms, setting of fires, and the terrorizing of little girls. Gang life
was rampant with sadism and Vallières recalls one instance in
which a girl was punished for "stooling" by being swung from a
braid until it ripped off, leaving her screaming and covered with
blood.

When Pierre was seven his father bought a house, or rather, a
shack, in Longueil-Annex across the river from Montréal so that
the family could escape the city—escape to a shantytown without
without sewage or running water. The house which to his father
was the answer to his dreams, and upon which he devoted week-
ends making additions and repairs to its three-room structure,
Pierre found to be a slum. Enrolled in a Catholic grammar school,

he felt the oppressiveness of the teaching sisters and recalls that: "I don't remember having learned anything at the school other than to be ashamed of my, our condition" (138).

> To pass the time, I would draw faces on my desk and amuse myself in making the others laugh, in letting out, in the middle of a lecture on religion or grammar, a fart which made as much noise as a firecracker. I would act "puzzled," while the others collapsed with laughter and the teacher or nun waved her witch's wand over our heads. (104)

Pierre grew up in an environment dominated by the teaching sisters, and later, when he entered collège on a scholarship, by teaching brothers and, above all, always by his mother. As his father worked evenings in the city he was rarely home.

> On weekends, I could talk a little with him but he was so rushed to expand and improve his little shack that he could only think of that. I contented myself with participating in his projects for the future, of playing the favorite game of workers in our shantytown: castles in Spain. Each weekend he spent long hours talking with the neighbors of a hypothetical happiness. I would have liked to have gotten from my father the certainty that in this world we would not always be *losers*. But my father had no certainty. He had the faith, the obscure belief of the poor in some kind of justice. No one ever dreamed of *making* that justice. We all waited for someone to give it to us as a reward. We all believed in Santa Claus. (141–42)

After a series of newspaper exposés which revealed the state of life in Longueil-annex, a huge sewage project was undertaken to raise to a minimum the level of sanitation. Vallières describes the construction as beginning with lightning promises and a flurry of dynamiting and construction activity. Gradually, however, the machines fell silent, and except for a few public fountains and sewage connections in the petty-bourgeois neighborhoods, the only indication of millions of dollars expended on the project were gaping holes and huge piles of mud. As the months and years dragged by it seemed as if once again the underworld—which has always been very, very strong in the Montréal area and especially in Jacques-Cartier, which this area was later to become known as— had entered into the project, and that the pie had been divided between them and the politicans. Most families in the area were forced to buy water from a vendor who had been granted the monopoly on water sales. With water at five cents a pail, families went without bathing and doing laundry whenever possible. The situation lasted for years:

> The Americans made millions from our iron, Duplessis made millions from the Americans, the *Union Nationale* machine passed out millions to its supporters and "henchmen" . . . and we, who were starving, we had to buy water! (152)

As time passed people began to visit the fountains of the streets that had water to avoid the cost of buying from the vendor. As Vallières's family lived only about two thousand feet from one of these more well-to-do neighborhoods with a public outlet, they tried to get

> *permission* to take the water we needed from the fountains in their quarter, whose streets were already asphalted. They treated us with an unbelievable contempt (and they weren't English). Several weeks after they had spit their contempt in our faces, the *petits bourgeois* of new Longueil erected a high fence so that they wouldn't have to face the thirsty look of "the dirty people" every day. (152-53)

But nothing ever happened to change the lot of the people in Jacques-Cartier; they never organized, as: "Everyone came and went too fast; people did not have time to know each other. . . . *In the deepest sense, everyone was alone*" (160; emphasis mine).

Vallières's introduction to secondary school was equally as alienating as that to primary school. In order to gain admission to the then more limited realm of the *collège,* he was forced to fake a vocation—pretending that he was studying for the clergy—to gain the necessary scholarship. Although he did well there and had some rapport with his instructors, he felt that the preoccupation with Latin fundamentals and syntax which formed the core of the curriculum had little relevance to the life around him. Rather than serving as an entrance into the indolent clerical élite of Québec, he used the leisure provided by his education to read voraciously.

Home became more and more of a hell. His father was absent constantly, not perhaps absent in the pattern of so many

Québécois fathers of the lower class with their habits of spending long hours in the sacred territory of the corner tavern, but absent nonetheless, and his mother's presence and insistence that he do something practical ("Leave this day school! When you have finished studying there where are you going to work, especially if you don't know how to speak English?" (175)) became more and more unbearable.

> *For reasons which I did not clearly perceive, my mother wanted to force me to return to the passivity, the docility, the resignation, the humiliation, which I had just freed myself from, once and for all* [emphasis mine]. (175)

At the age of sixteen he took a summer job at a bank and decided to stay there for a time after the *collège* began in the Fall. Soon he became tired of the bank and applied for readmittance, which he succeeded in gaining without penalty. Upon his return to school and the death of his mentor, Father Vary, he found that he was no longer able to tolerate the atmosphere of the religious school and permitted himself the luxury of dropping his cloak of deceit and telling off the faculty, after which he took his year-end exams and ended his formal academic training.

With the aid of a friend he found a job on the Rue Saint-Jacques with the French-Canadian brokerage house of L. G. Beaubien and Co. as an account clerk.[34]

> The great majority of my fellow workers were poor men, poor women, whose salaries ranged between $25 and $60 per week. Some had worked for the Beaubien family for more than twenty years. These were the most exploited, the most poorly paid and alienated of all. They justified their slavery according to a simple formula: they had lived through the crisis of the 30's; at a time when most workers were unemployed, the Beaubiens could have tossed them into the street because business was not good but kept them in their service, nevertheless. Since then, they believed themselves to be obliged to be eternally grateful to the Beaubiens and accepted as a *gift* their little salary of $50 or $60 a week ... after 20, 25 and, sometimes, even 30 years of "loyal service"! (194-95)[35]

Here in the financial district of Montréal, Vallières realized that alienation was not a commodity monopolized by Québec's lower classes but that the white collar workers of Québec also belonged "to the *Québécois* nation of 'cheap labor' and that they were even *more alienated* than the factory workers and the farmers" (195).

At New Years the elderly wife of the proprietor of the brokerage house would take time from her philanthropic activities to attend the annual party for the employees:

> When we had swallowed Madam's chocolate and her hideous smile, the "Big Party" began. It was our annual bonus: as much Scotch, whisky, gin and beer as we wanted together with a gift of a few ten-dollar bills. After this night of grotesque, paternalistic debauchery, the routine brought us back to our basic dependence, to *the reality* of our daily servitude....

Each night Pierre would leave the job he detested for the comfort of his room—which his father had built so that he could study in peace—reading and writing abortive novels. All of his friends from the *collège* seemed to feel the same malaise as he—the sense that there was nothing in Québec. A trip to New York gave him the sense of freedom and possiblity but he was alien there and his return to Montréal and Ville Jacques-Cartier only added to his frustration.

In the autumn of 1958 Vallières sought sanctuary from a sense of total disorientation in a Montréal Franciscan monastery. For several years he sought God as his solution until he finally fled from the oppressive life of the order. He was disgusted by the avarice he found in the financial dealings of the order—an order which prided itself on its poverty—and by the epicurean eating habits of the community while the poor were offered sandwiches of canned meat-paste.

> I was door-keeper one day, just one, and the "chief porter" reproached me for putting a little too much "paris-patê" in the sandwiches. "After all," he told me, "we're not rich!" I never worked at the door again because I think I would have given revolvers to the poor instead of those disgusting sandwiches. (238)

As to the debt which the Church is constantly reminding *québécois* that they owe it for their survival, Vallières responds:

> *Québécois* owe nothing to the Church except three centuries

of obscurantism. But the Church owes to our ignorance and passivity the fact that it has become the largest French Canadian financial institution, the only one which the Americans respect. (238)

He left the monastery at the time of the first bloom of the "Quiet Revolution" when Trudeau and Pelletier were editing the "radical" review *Cité Libre* and René Lévesque was frightening English Canada with threats of nationalization and separation. He authored several articles for *Cité Libre* and was offered a chance to air his views on separatism in an issue devoted to the subject— views which he believes were rejected for publication because of his tolerant attitude toward this aberrant option.

He found a job as a sales clerk in a campus bookstore near the *Université de Montréal* but found that "the book trade made me sick" and that he constantly had to show his gratitude to his employers for his job. After a few months he "told off the manager of the shop and offered my resignation" (247).

Disgusted with the book business and "disappointed by the intransigent attitude of Pelletier and Trudeau concerning separatism, disillusioned, unemployed," he decided "to become a simple worker, a day laborer like my father and to abandon my philosophical search" (247). After several months of work on a construction job he decided to go to France to seek renewal:

> France, of which I had so often dreamed. Land of our ancestors. Fatherland, it is said, of free men, of great thinkers. . . .
>
> The France I knew was a sad, disillusioned country, profoundly torn apart by the Algerian war. . . .
>
> [Without] *québécois* friends—and two or three French ones— I would have died of hunger on one of the docks of the Seine where thousands of wretched humans lay extended each day like abandoned corpses or moved around slowly like large, tired insects, with no work to attend to, no longer living except to savor among themselves the profound contempt which the "universalist" France of the American tourists inspired in them. (252; 256-57)

It was in France, in the fields of the Côte d'or (Burgundy) that Vallières came upon Marxism as his truth. "I understood," he writes, "that revolution was not a choice made from one's free will but a vital necessity for all workers . . . for *conscious* workers it was a *responsibility*" (254; emphasis his).

But Vallières was unable to relate to the France of the day. For him, as for many *québécois,* the "return" to France was a bitter one: there no one who really cared about Québec, all a *québécois* really represented was an individual who spoke a marginal, humorous French. Soon feelings of despair and suicide began to re-envelop him:

> I had nothing to do here. Like in Québec. Like in Algeria. No one needed me or my services. Men were satisfied with their shit. Why "bother" them with ideas which they didn't know what to do with. All countries, all peoples were alike. Why travel? There was nothing to do anywhere. . . . (263)

Vallières fled from France to a Québec where there was still little hope or place for him. However, at almost the very moment of his arrival the Wolfe monument was overturned in Québec City (March, 1963) and the first wave of the FLQ was underway.

Upon his arrival in Montréal, Gerard Pelletier gave him a job at *La Presse.* Apparently satisfied with his work, Pelletier soon offered him a position as co-editor of *Cité Libre,* which Vallières sought to use to gradually turn the review into a revolutionary socialist journal. As it became apparent that he was attempting to define a political stance for the publication which was clearly at variance with the beliefs of Trudeau and Pelletier, he was asked to resign, which he did, leaving it "clearly a review of the 'center left' and an ideological nonentity" (295).

Upon leaving *Cité Libre* he joined with members of its staff and other interested journalists to found *Révolution québécoise.* At this same time (June, 1964–January, 1965) the staff of *La Presse,* of which he was still a part, struck and failed in its demands, which Vallières felt was attributable to the policy of "negotiating 'a coups de mouchoirs' and with respect for bourgeois legality" (229), rather than rejecting the techniques of gentlemanly negotiation—tactics *par excellence* of the bourgeoisie. After the strike at *La Presse* he began to organize anti-American, pro-Vietcong demonstrations in front of the U.S. Consulate. It was at this time that he joined the FLQ.

We found it useless to work within the traditional parties, including the leftist parties and the R.I.N. We were convinced (and we still are) that the electoral battle is always lost for the wage earners, meaning lost for the great majority of the nation. As Duverger would say, each election, organized with millions of dollars, expresses less the real participation of the masses than the ways in which they are legally excluded from power. . . .

The FLQ was concerned and is still concerned, among other objectives, with accelerating this awakening of consciousness, of bringing to awareness the need to struggle *to the death* against the despotism of the capitalist system, despotism experienced daily in the factories, forests, mines, farms, schools and universities of Québec. The sooner that the *Québécois* unite to sweep away the rottenness that poisons their existence, the sooner they will be able to build in solidarity with other exploited peoples a new society for a new man, a humane society for all men, just for all men, in the service of all men. A fraternal society.

It is not by adding up little reforms that we will realize this ideal. (306)

Nègres blancs d'Amérique is, and was obviously intended to be, an odyssey for all *québécois*. In it the process of education to acceptance of a foreign-dominated society is thrown in harsh contrast by one who could not accept that dominance. The book represents the fruit of a long and tortured route through disgust with his fellow French Canadians, through a period in which his well of hatred lost external cathexis and turned inward until, finally, he found " 'ma' verite" in the love of his fellows and hatred of their domination from above. Regardless of the respect Vallières calls forth, of all the esteem in which he is held by many genuinely sensitive and intelligent young French Canadians, one is forced to the conclusion that his personal revolution comes back home in a belated attempt to devour a hated mother. Trite as it may be, passages such as the following, which dominate the discussion of his personal life, leave little choice but to choose the obvious: Vallières's hatred for a mother perceived as constraining, degrading, suffocating, later found itself locked in battle against an enemy to which he had generalized all of her attributes. In contrast there is a deep identity between father and son—which indeed seems almost a requisite for an ethnic revolutionary—which arose, not so much from early closeness between them, as from a realization that they were both to be claimed victims of the same woman: that their manhood was to be destroyed in an unholy alliance between a mother and wife and the foreign exploiter:

> "I don't know when we will be able to relax a little and enjoy life without worrying about tomorrow?" my father often asked. And my mother always replied with a bitterness mixed with resignation: "When one is born for a little loaf, you can't expect..."
>
> My father kept quiet, repressing his hopes as one holds back sobs. I would look at his gentle, deep eyes, where I could see an immense kindness, silent suffering and perhaps also anguish. Sometimes he would smile just long enough to tell me, without opening his mouth, that his dreams were realizable, that one had to believe that. My mother complained of headaches, of the dullness of the radio shows, of the slovenliness of some neighbor . . . while, forcing myself to hear nothing around me, I listened to the revolt that mounted inside me and heated my blood. (81)

Vallières felt trapped, bound, asphyxiated by his mother, just as many French Canadians feel themselves caught by their ethnicity. Pierre Trudeau's cry: "Open up the frontiers, *this people is suffocating*" (quoted in Chaput, 1961:13; emphasis mine),[36] while meant for the French Canadian nation as a whole, captures Vallières's own personal dilemma. Interestingly enough, it seems that rebellion against a group seen as denigrating your ethnicity is aided through an identification of pathos with the father and of conflict with the mother, while revolution within one's own ethnic surroundings may be furthered by the reverse constellation. One wonders what it must be like to be the mother of an ethnic revolutionary. Are they, as Morf (1970:94) has maintained, only the "first victims of the Revolution," or the fomenters themselves?

After his return from the Manhattan House of Detention for men ("the Tombs"), when he hastily wrote *Nègres blancs* in apparent concern that there would not be adequate stationery supplies awaiting him in Québec, Vallières was charged with conspiracy resulting in the homicide of Thérèse Morin and condemned to life. In 1969, the conviction was overturned by an appeals court and he was bound over for a new trial. Upon his second conviction he was sentenced to thirty months in prison but released pending appeal in early 1970. During the October, 1970 crisis, Vallières was among the first arrested and, tiring of incarceration, went into hiding shortly after his release.[37]

On December 13, 1971, *Le Devoir* headlined its edition with a bombshell: "Pierre Vallières rompt avec le FLQ." Still in hiding, Vallières had sent a twenty-seven page text entitled: "Le FLQ et les grand leçons d'octobre 1970," with an accompanying letter to *Le Devoir*.

> Participant in the 1966 FLQ wave, prisoner for more than four years, political writer, favorite scapegoat of many governments, revolutionary symbol, still sought by police . . . the most prestigious leader of Québec's revolutionary movement,

as *Le Devoir* referred to him in struggling to sum up the man in a single paragraph, has arrived "in general at the same conclusions as M. Claude Ryan[38] (*Le Devoir et la crise d'octobre 1970*) and M. René Lévesque (in the last manifesto of the PQ)" (*Le Devoir:* 13 décembre 1971:9). The October crisis, Vallières argued, indicated that the FLQ, far from aiding Québec's independence, had come to represent one of its greatest threats as the Federal, provincial and municipal (Montréal) governments attempted to confuse the distinction between the FLQ and the separatist movement as such in order to crush the latter. The FLQ had become, he argued, the pretext which permitted the government to attempt to crush the genuine movements of liberation: the central unions, the citizens committees, and above all, the *Parti Québécois*.[39]

Shortly after the appearance of his article in *Le Devoir*, Vallières turned himself over to authorities and was released on bail to engage in (peaceful) social action in the Ottawa Valley region west of Montréal. Later, the Québec court of appeals overturned his manslaughter conviction in the death of Thérèse Morin and he was given a four month suspended sentence for his activities during the October Crisis. Most indicative of his emergence from an existence in a revolutionary twilight has been his willingness to present the separatist case to any individual or group willing to listen. As he told one reporter:

> Two weeks ago I was invited to speak to a group of business executives in a fashionable restaurant in Old Montréal. While they were enjoying their after-dinner cigars and liqueurs, I sat wondering what I was doing there. Not so long ago I couldn't have imagined myself at this kind of function. But now I'll talk to anybody and listen to everybody to see if we can find common solutions, or whether our differences are irreconcilable. (Charney 1973:57)

Vallières's decision to leave the FLQ and his reasoned argument for doing so has given the separatist solution a tremendous boost as it no longer faces a serious threat from its left and, since the FLQ has been effectively eliminated as a threat to public order, government efforts to confuse the separatists with the terrorists can no longer have any effect.[40]

The Fifth Wave

September, 1968 to December 1969

Thirty-five bomb explosions, the most serious a "super-bomb" which exploded in the Montréal Stock Exchange wounding twenty-seven people in February, 1969. A dozen more bombs were discovered and disarmed before they exploded, including two bombs which had been placed in Montréal's Eaton's department store during the Christmas shopping season.

February, 1970

Charles Gagnon, in leaving prison, announces that he is going to relaunch the FLQ and to make it the most representative movement of the revolutionary forces of Québec.

Pierre Vallières, in leaving prison, announces that he is still a militant of the FLQ and that he believes in revolutionary violence properly placed in a precise strategy of action.

Plan to kidnap the Israeli consul in Montréal. Arrest of two presumed members of the FLQ.

June, 1970

Sentencing of Marc-André Gagné for seventeen armed robberies presumedly perpetrated for the FLQ.

Plan to kidnap the Consul of the United States in Montréal and arrest of six presumed members of the FLQ at Prevost. Seizure of arms and dynamite.

Bomb explosion, one death (Mlle. Saint-Germain), two wounded in the headquarters of the Ministry of Defense in Ottawa.

August, 1970

Training of Québec terrorists in guerilla training camp in Jordan with Palestinian commandos. The terrorists state that selective assassination will soon be added to the list of FLQ tactics.

September, 1970

Car laden with explosives not equipped with detonator found behind the offices of the Bank of Montréal in Montréal.

October, 1970

Kidnapping of British diplomat James Richard Cross.

Kidnapping and assassination of Québec minister of labor and immigration, Pierre Laporte.

(Pelletier, 1971:229-33); Morf, 1970:123-44)

The lengthy extension of the fifth wave of the FLQ is an arbitrary one and can well be divided into a fifth and sixth wave with the line of demarcation being the arrest of Pierre-Paul Geoffrey during the night of March 4 and 5, 1969. Although Geoffrey was undoubtedly only a part of a larger network, he pleaded guilty to the majority of the acts of the wave of bombing, claiming that, while he had acted on the orders of his particular cell, he had done all the manufacturing and placement of the bombs. For his testimony he was sentenced to life imprisonment on April 5, 1969 (Morf, 1970:133).

The October Crisis

On October 5, 1970, James Richard Cross, British trade minister in Montréal, was kidnapped from his elegant Redpath Crescent home near McGill University. At 8:15 A.M. a taxi approached the

house and two men carrying a gift-wrapped package, ostensibly
delivering a gift for Cross's recent birthday, rang the doorbell.
When the maid answered, the men entered and abducted Cross as
he was dressing. Three hours later a phone call to the police indicated that a communiqué had been placed in a mailbox on the
campus of the *Université de Québec*. The communiqué demanded
the immediate release of twenty FLQ political prisioners to either
Cuba or Algeria and five hundred thousand dollars in gold bullion
to aid in their period of adjustment. In addition, the police were
to cease all search operations, the manifesto which they included
was to be published throughout the province, and the "Gars de
Lapalme" were to be hired by the federal government on their
own terms.[41]

October 7

Publication of the FLQ Communiqué:[42]

> The *Front de Libération du Québec* is not a messiah or a
> modern Robin Hood. It is a group of Québec workers who
> have decided definitely to take in hands their own destiny.
> The *Front de Libération du Québec* seeks the total independ-
> ence of *Québécois*, reunited in a free society and purged
> forever of its clique of ravenous sharks, the "big boss" patrons
> and their lackeys who have made Québec their hunting reserve
> of cheap labor and scrupleless exploitation. . . .
>
> We believed for a while that it was worth the effort to channel
> our energies, our impatiences, as René Lévesque said it so well,
> in the *Parti Québécois,* but the liberal victory really shows that
> what one calls democracy in Québec is always only the
> "democracy" of the rich. . . .
>
> Yes, there are reasons why in the poverty, in the unemploy-
> ment, in the slums, in the fact that you, M. Bergeron of
> Visitation Street, and you also, M. Legendre of the Ville de
> Laval, who earn $10,000 a year don't feel free in our country
> of Québec. . . .
>
> Yes, there are reasons why you, M. Tremblay, of Panet Street
> and you, M. Cloutier who work in construction in Saint-
> Jerôme, can't pay for "ships of gold"[43] as Drapeau did, one
> who is so concerned with slums that he had colored panels
> put up in front of them so that the rich tourists couldn't see
> our misery. . . .[44]

Yes, there are reasons why you, M. Lachance of Sainte-Marguerite Street drown your despair, your rancor and your anger in the beer of the dog Molson. And you, Lachance *fils* with your marijuana cigarettes. . . .

We live in a society of terrorized slaves, terrorized by the huge bosses Steinberg, Clark, Smith . . . terrorized by the Roman Catholic Church, even if it seems less and less so (who owns the stock exchange?), terrorized by the loan payments to Household Finance. . . .

Production, mine and forest workers; service workers, teachers and students, you who are unemployed, take what belongs to you: your work, your determination and your liberty; and you, workers of General Electric, it is you who run your factories, your machines, your hotels, your universities, your unions; don't wait for miracle organizations! Make your revolutions yourselves in your own quarters in your own work milieux. . . .

We are Québec workers and will stop at nothing. We want to replace this society of slaves with a free society for everyone, functioning of itself and for itself, a society open to the world.

Our struggles can only be victorious, one cannot long hold an awakening people in misery and scorn.

Vive le Québec libre!
Vive les camarades prisonniers politiques!
Vive le révolution québécoise!
Vive le Front de Libération du Québec!

(*Trait, 1970:55-60*)

October 8

Sharp, federal minister of external affairs, asks the FLQ to name a negotiator.

Cross asks government to meet the FLQ demands in a letter released by the cellule de libération.

Radio-Canada broadcasts the manifesto of the FLQ.

October 10

Québec Justice Minister Jérôme Choquette rejects the demands of the FLQ, saying that "no society can expect that the decisions of

*its governments, or of the courts of law, can be erased by the use
of blackmail, because this signifies the end of all social order.*

Seventeen minutes after Choquette's rejection of the FLQ
demands, a blue Chevrolet with four occupants approached the
suburban Saint-Lambert home of Pierre Laporte, Québec's congenial minister of labor and immigration and the number two man
in the province's Liberal party. Approaching Laporte, who after
listening to Choquette's speech was tossing a football with his son
and nephew on the lawn, the masked men, armed with machine
guns, forced him into their automobile and drove away.[45]

October 11

*First communiqué of "la cellule de financement Chénier": "Faced
with the stubbornness of governmental authorities in not comply-
ing with the requirements of the FLQ and conforming with plan
3 previously established in the event of such a refusal, the finance
cell Chénier has just kidnapped the Québec minister of unemployment and assimilation, Pierre Laporte. The minister will be executed tonight at ten o'clock if before that time the authorities*
en place *have not responded favorably to the seven demands
sent out in the wake of M. Cross's kidnapping" (Trait, 1970:84).*

Later that evening:

> FLQ
> Chénier finance cell
> Communiqué 2 (the last)
>
> This is the last communication between the finance cell
> Chénier and the authorities *en place. . . .*
>
> We repeat: if before ten o'clock tonight, the two governments
> have not responded favorably to the seven conditions of the
> FLQ, the minister Pierre Laporte will be executed.
>
> Pierre Laporte will be released within twenty-four hours
> following the complete realization (meaning the seven condi-
> tions) of the *Opération Libération.* The slightest hesitation
> of the authorities *en place* will be fatal to the minister. It is
> already a very great concession for us to be obligated to re-
> turn him alive and well. Do not ask too much of us.
>
> *Front de Libération du Québec*
> *Nous vaincrons. . . ."*

Later that day another communiqué containing a number of Laporte's credit cards as well as a letter to Premier Bourassa was sent to authenticate the second communiqué, which had been handwritten. The letter to Bourassa was obviously designed to evoke the maximum degree of concern for Laporte's condition and to place Bourassa in the mold of a cold-blooded dismisser of intimates if he should refuse the FLQ demands:

> My dear Robert,
>
> 1. I feel I am writing the most important letter in my life;
>
> 2. For the moment, I am in perfect health and am well, even courteously treated.
>
> 3. I insist that the police cease all efforts to find me. If the search should succeed, it will result in a bloody gun battle from which I will certainly not emerge alive. This is really a matter of life and death.
>
> 4. In sum, you have the power to decide my fate ["Tu as le pouvoir en somme de décider de ma vie"]; if it were possible that some good could come from my sacrifice I could understand it. But we are in the presence of a well-organized escalade which will only end with the liberation of the political prisoners.
>
> 5. You know my personal circumstances which should be kept in mind. I have two brothers who are both dead. I am the only one remaining as the head of a large family comprising my mother, my sisters, my own wife and children as well as Rolland's children of whom I am the guardian. My departure would result in an insurmountable mourning because you know the strength of the ties which bind together the members of my family. . . .
>
> 7. . . . Decide on my life or my death, *je compte sur toi et t'en remercie.*
>
> Amitiés,
Pierre Laporte

(1970:88–89)

October 12

Letter from Laporte: "I hope to be free in 24 hours."

FRAP subscribes to the objectives of the FLQ while taking issue with its approach.

The Liberation cell verifies that Cross is still alive.

October 13

Government and FLQ reported to be taking the first steps toward an agreement.

The Parti Québécois *hopes that Bourassa's gesture toward negotiating has not been taken only to stall for time.*

The negotiations are broken off as Robert Lemieux waits for a new mandate from the FLQ.

October 14

Cellule Chénier *issues a communiqué accusing the government of illegal arrests and lack of good faith.*

The ministers study the proposals for the liberation of Cross and Laporte.

Assembly at l'Université de Montréal.

A massive student strike begins in sympathy with the demands of the FLQ.

October 15

Assembly at Centre Paul-Sauvé. Assembled professors vote for a resolution acknowledging support for FLQ manifesto and the demands made upon the government. Three thousand persons cheer Robert Lemieux, Pierre Vallières and Charles Gagnon and shout "FLQ! FLQ!" at the top of their throats. Vallières "was magnificent as usual . . . using all his efforts to calm the crowd and prevent it from falling into the trap of repression set by Trudeau" (Piotte, 1971:23).

The Société Saint-Jean-Baptiste issues a communiqué declaring that our governments are reduced to negotiating with terrorists because they ignored more moderate groups.

October 16

Invocation of the War Measures Act and the placement of troops throughout the city.

The FLQ declared "hors de la loi," with those belonging to the organization or aiding its members subject to penalties of as much as five years in prison.

Massive arrests begin, with a first day total of approximately 250. The detainees are questioned concerning any possible FLQ involvement and are held under the War Measures Act if the police entertain any suspicion concerning their activities.

War Measures Act justified by the alleged formation of a "Provisional Government" in Québec, supposedly composed of some of its most respected leaders including, apparently, Claude Ryan, editor of Le Devoir, *and by the wish to "break at the roots the birth of a parallel power which had the pretension to wish to negotiate with the authorities" (Beauchamp;* La Presse, *16 octobre 1970:1).*

October 17

Trudeau announces that the government will not yield to a blackmail which would only have the effect of encouraging future terrorism as each kidnapping would be used to release all prisoners and thus to nullify previous police and legal efforts to eliminate terrorism.

Pierre Laporte garroted with the chain holding his crucifix, and his body dumped in the trunk of an automobile.

October 18

Québec students in Paris occupy "la maison du Canada" in support of the FLQ.

Suddenly the popular support for the FLQ is hushed. There is a panic on the left and massive desertion by those who cannot accept explanations blaming Trudeau or Bourassa for Laporte's death. The bubble of revolution has exploded in the midst of a general feeling that: "I never thought they would go that far." One FLQ sympathizer of my acquaintance now wants to kill "the murderers of Laporte for what they have done to the movement's image."

Claude Ryan, René Lévesque, the directors of the major labor unions in Québec and other individuals issue an appeal to the government and the FLQ to save Cross's life.

Demonstrators gather at Parliament in Ottawa to support Trudeau's invocation of the War Measures Act.

Police announce search for Paul Rose and Marc Carbonneau in connection with Laporte's death.

October 19

Jean-Paul Desbiens publishes Appel aux Québécois *in* Le Devoir:

1. No society is possible without some form of authority. . .

2. For a society as complex as ours to function thousands of decisions must be taken every hour of every day.

3. Now an incredible idea forces itself upon us! Imagine for a minute that all those responsible for the functioning of our country: ministers, deputies, civil servants, heads of enterprises, school directors, mayors, etc. resigned immediately and left their offices unoccupied. Who would be able to replace them?

4. It has come to the point where we would welcome this so that each citizen will understand once and for all what anarchy is.

5. Who would like to be governed by the members of the FLQ? Because, in the end, there are no other choices than that between the government and the FLQ. . . .

9. If Québec does not gain control of itself immediately it is lost. We speak French *comme langue de travail.* We would really like to know how many immigrants henceforth are going to come settle among us and how many among those who do will have the stomach to attach themselves to a society whose youth, for example, declares its solidarity with the FLQ. Our power of attraction has become a power of repulsion. . . .

10. Who loves this people. Those who assassinate a minister? Those who agree with the FLQ?

11. Some *Québécois* have killed another *Québécois* in cold blood for the love of *Québécois* they say.

12. Let us repeat that if responsible citizens, those who work for a living, do not find the means, beginning today, to

demonstrate their support to the government, Québec risks not making it through the winter. In any event, the winter will not be easy.

13. The people must be with the government or it will be felled by the FLQ.

14. This is not the moment to listen to the intellectuals who debate the sex of liberty (*la* liberté), and rouse the children. There again these people are not in the majority. And there again responsible intellectuals must stand up."

(Jean-Paul Desbiens, *La Presse*, 19 octobre 1970:A4)

October 20

Revelation that the major suspect in the assassination of Laporte, Paul Rose, twenty-seven, has been until this fall a substitute instructor in classes for maladjusted children.

Publication of a poll taken October 17, after the promulgation of the War Measures Act but before the assassination of Laporte. "Frankly, do you have the feeling that the governments of Ottawa and Québec have been tough and intransigent in their stance toward the FLQ kidnappers up to now, or not tough enough? . . .

	Too Tough	Not Tough Enough	Just Right	Undecided
Canada	4%	37%	51%	8%
Québec	5	32	54	9
Rest of Canada	4	40	49	7

Denial of a rumor which had swept Québec that the FLQ had captured a woman in Hull and carved FLQ on her stomach with a knife. The Hull police in their investigation found the story without foundation.

Student calm in Québec seems to be more or less complete.

1,627 interrogations, 341 arrests made under the War Measures Act to date.

October 22

The Federal Minister of Regional Expansion, Jean Marchand, in an

An illustration of the level of paranoia in Québec during the October Crisis:
An individual wearing a helmet sporting the emblem of Hydro-Québec—
whose current commerical slogan is: "On est douze mille douze pour assurer
votre confort" (There are 12,012 of us working to assure your comfort")—
which has obviously been mistaken for the similar emblem of the Parti
Québécois is being brought into camp for questioning. Soldier: "Captian, we
surprised this *péquiste* (member of the Parti Québécois) on a telephone pole
in the camp." Captain: "How many are there in your network?" "*Péquiste*":
"12,012, *mon Capitaine!*" (Jean-Paul Girerd; *La Presse*, 27 mars 1971:A1).

interview over a Vancouver radio station revealed that FRAP (Front d'Action Politique) was a "cover" for the FLQ. La Presse carries "Jean Marchand: le FRAP est une couverture pour le FLQ" in a large two-column headline which spans the paper's six columns. This announcement, coming only three days before the baptismal test of FRAP (an organization of radical-liberals in Montréal) against Jean Drapeau's Parti Civique is seen by the supporters of Frap as a planned coordination between the federal and municipal governments to destroy the radical electoral movement in Montréal. It is particularly galling because Drapeau is regarded by leftists as the leading fascist in Québec.

Québec's justice minister reportedly agrees to notify the relatives of all detained under the War Measures Act.

Drapeau's response to the revelation of Marchand was to announce on an English radio station that "blood will flow in the streets" if FRAP is brought to power in the upcoming elections.

October 23

La Presse *reports the charge by the leaders of FRAP that Drapeau is trying to seed terrorism in his efforts, along with those of Marchand, to identify FRAP with the FLQ. FRAP announces a suit of $3,500,000 has been filed against Drapeau.*

Marchand announces that his trouble with English made him translate "couverture" as "cover," not being aware of the English connotation of the word. Although the damage is done, under an article entitled "Les malheurs linguistiques de Jean Marchand," Pierre C. O'Neil, of La Presse, *argues that although Marchand cannot be forgiven for the damage his error has caused, that it is only one of a string of errors brought by bilingualism. He recalls the earlier political quarrel caused by the translation of the words "lousy French" by "le français de pouilleux" ("the French of the scum" would be an accurate relation of this erroneous translation—a translation which obviously evoked tremendous anger among French Canadians).*

October 25

Publication by the police of a supposed FLQ communiqué which identifies Vallières, Gagnon, Lemieux, and Chartrand as the heads of the FLQ and threatens to "make Montréal jump" if they are not released. The form of the note, written with an electric typewriter and without letterhead, as well as its provocative nature, made its authenticity suspect, but it was released nonetheless, and the headlines of the Sunday Express carried its threats just in time for a last minute election push as if Drapeau needed more than the death of Laporte and the association of FRAP with the FLQ.

Montréal goes to the polls in record numbers and gives Drapeau and his hand-picked civic party councilmen 91.7 percent of the vote, fifty-two seats of fifty-two in the city council and even a majority of the votes in all 3,309 arrondissements.

The election results were clear beyond all possibility of misinterpretation. The FLQ had indeed succeeded in "awakening the people" but they had gotten up on the wrong side of the bed.
Drapeau's vote in the past four elections:

	Jean Drapeau	Percent	Others	Percent	Total Votes
1960	75,455	52.6	67,330	47.4	142,785
1962	130,207	87.1	18,069	12.9	148,276
1966	117,490	94.4	6,971	5.6	124,461
1970	314,609	91.7	29,261	8.3	348,870

Considering the fact that Drapeau had come under heavy criticism from much of the news media for the authoritarian manner in which he conducted the affairs of Montréal as well as a supposed preoccupation with events such as Expo-67 and the 1976 Summer Olympics rather than with the poverty of many of the city's residents, it was anticipated that he would lose ground in this election. His conduct during the campaign suggested he feared the same. Under these circumstances, his reaction to the events of October must have been mixed, as they provided Drapeau with the finest stage of fear upon which to perform his law and order drama; and there can be little doubt that the people of Montréal—including those from the city's most impoverished areas, where he had supposedly lost support—turned to Drapeau in the anxiety of the crisis.

On election eve, with the crushing victory in hand, Drapeau entered the chamber in which he was to deliver his victory speech with a tight, drawn, seemingly angry expression. His speech was delivered in the tone of a man on the defensive and was interminable, dragging on and on, full of recriminations against his opponents and the news media, until one thought it could go on no longer—but it did. Then, without a pause, Drapeau switched into English and continued.[46]

> I am extremely happy about this very clear testimony in the workers' quarters where the idea of opposition to *l'hôtel de ville*, an idea which is so widespread among those who believe they dominate public opinion, was totally rejected. . . . I am certain that these commentators will draw lessons from this verdict in the days which are ahead, but I will permit myself, too, to draw some lessons tonight. . . . (*La Presse;* 26 octobre 1970:A1).

October 27

Louis Robichaud, forty-five, French Prime Minister of New Brunswick since 1960, is defeated by English liberal opponent Richard Hatfield. While it is difficult to attribute his defeat directly to the crisis, there can be little doubt that the anti-French feelings engendered by it did not aid him with the English half of the province's electorate.

Parti Québécois announces that it is ready to join with the Liberal Party of Bourassa to put an end to the crisis and "to retake the power which he (Bourassa) had abandoned to the Federal government.

Mrs James Cross broadcasts a message to her husband's kidnappers begging his release as a "victim des circonstances."

October 28

Teach-in by the Comité de Défense des Libertés Civiques *at* l'Université de Montréal.

Bourassa states that the rumor of a "Provisional government" formed during the crisis by the unions, the Parti Québécois *and the editor of* Le Devoir, *Claude Ryan, was only a rumor.*

Rose signs a communiqué of the FLQ with his fingerprint.

Trudeau indicates that Québec will be expected to pay the cost occasioned by the military presence in the province required by the October crisis.

October 29

Choquette reveals that it was on his order that the publication of the content of the latest communiqué of the FLQ (the one with Rose's fingerprint) was prohibited. He has decided to eliminate the FLQ's news management, in which reporters blessed with a phone call from a felquiste *scrambled to obtain the latest communiqué and publish it.*

October 30

Lemieux, being held incommunicado, attempts to gain his release on a writ of habeas corpus.

November 2

Lemieux request rejected.

George McIlraith, solicitor general of Canada, admits that Paul Rose, the major suspect in the Laporte kidnapping, was under surveillance prior to Laporte's death. The police chose not to make an arrest, however, in hopes that he would lead them to Laporte, but Rose eluded them.

November 4

Editorial of Pellerin in La Presse *accusing those who have participated in sit-ins during the crisis of being anarchists and/or terrorists.*

November 5

Twenty-one men and three women, arrested under the War Measures Act, appear in court to respond to various accusations. Among those appearing in court are Michel Chartrand, Pierre Vallières, Jacques Larue-Langlois, Charles Gagnon, and Robert Lemieux, all charged with seditious conspiracy and association with the FLQ.

Canadian Justice Minister Turner accuses the New Democratic Party (NDP) of being hysterical in its attacks against the War Measures Act.

November 6

Arrest of Bernard Lortie, nineteen, one of those suspected of having taken part in the kidnapping of Laporte, discovered hiding in the closet of an apartment.

November 7

Inquest into Laporte's death. Lortie testifies that Laporte had been bound, gagged, and transported to a house in suburban Saint Hubert, where he was held, handcuffed to a bed for the most part, until he was garroted. Using the house as a headquarters, members frequently left to place the latest communiqués in Montréal. Laporte, in the midst of a raid at a neighboring house (which may have been scheduled for the house in which he was secreted and made in the other by error), attempted to escape by throwing himself through a window. Unsuccessful in his attempt and bleeding profusely, he was pulled back into the house by his kidnappers.

Québec's Justice Minister, Choquette, proposes the obligatory carrying of an identity card containing photograph and fingerprints for all Quebeckers and assures the population that honest men will have nothing to fear. The idea of having more plastic in one's wallet is popular enough that a private company begins brisk sales of identity cards.

Release of photograph of James Cross showing him playing solitaire on a small table on which Vallières's Nègres blancs d'Amérique had been placed as if it were a bible.

November 11

The Union Nationale opposition leader, Jean-Jacques Bertrand, questions whether or not Québec abdicated its responsibility in favor of control by Ottawa during the crisis.

The abbé Charles Bonville, priest of the parish of Saint-Paul-de-Matane in the Gaspésie and an area where the level of unemployment is as high as 50 percent of the total work force, stated: "The great majority of the population and priests of the counties of Matane and Matapédia are fundamentally in agreement with the claims made in the FLQ manifesto."

November 14

Appearance of a communiqué from the combined "Information-Viger" and "Financement Chénier" cells to counter the impression that Lortie has traitored his camarades and adding of his name to the twenty-three political prisoners whose liberty the FLQ has already demanded. At the time of the raid in which Lortie was captured, the communiqué continues, there were three other members of the cell in the apartment as well as two women. As the police were battering down the door, the other males had a chance to hide in a false closet within a closet. After twenty-four hours, the two policemen guarding the apartment left to have dinner and the three hidden in the apartment (Paul and Jacques Rose and Francis Simard) left. This claim was later confirmed by authorities.

November 21

Receipt of another FLQ communiqué addressed to Québécois "who still have a minimum of dignity and desire to struggle" and "non pas aux racistes anglo-saxons, non pas aux petits dictateurs de toutes sortes, non pas aux apprentis fascistes à la Trudeau-Choquette" and to the demand of U Thant that the FLQ liberate

Cross. "If Thant really wants to save this man's life and to conform to the humanitarian principles he defends then he will take a stand towards the liberation struggle of the people of Québec, of the Latin peoples of America, of the peoples of Asia, Africa as well as the black people of Amerikkka . . ." Attached to the communiqué were two letters written by James Cross, one to be made public, the other written to his wife.

November 28

La Presse reports the results of a poll of Québec citizens indicating tht 83.1 percent of Quebekers are in favor of an obligatory identity card, 72.8 percent of Quebekers approve of the federal government decision to invoke the War Measures Act and 53.8 percent of the citizens are satisfied with the Bourassa government.

Choquette confirms that some of those arrested have been beaten by police in their cells and promises an investigation.

December 1

Paul Rose's sister is sentenced to six months in prison for her refusal to testify at the coroner's inquest into Laporte's death.

December 3

Several hundred troops surround a house in Montréal-Nord where it has been discovered that Cross and his kidnappers are in hiding. After negotiations between the cell and the police through a radical lawyer, an agreement is reached whereby Cross will be released in return for safe passage for the group to Cuba.

December 28

Jacques and Paul Rose and Francis Simard discovered hiding in an underground tunnel situated in the basement of a Saint-Luc farmhouse.

The kidnapping of Cross by the FLQ had several motives: to awaken the population against the domination of the Anglo-Saxons—as if the Québécois were not already sufficiently aware of it,[48] to gain access to the news media for the FLQ manifesto and its interpretation of history—although a very similar interpretation could be seen in Bergeron's *Petit manuel d'histoire du Québec,* which had already enjoyed phenomenal sales, and to gain the release of the various *felquistes* still in prison for their activities as well as to discover the identity of an informer whose information had been used to aid the police in their convictions of a number of members of the FLQ. Of the various demands, the latter were without doubt the demands of major importance: if the FLQ could, through the act of a kidnapping, free its prisoners and even discourage their arrest by placing the life of a potential informer in jeopardy, then clearly the FLQ would be a revolutionary organization operating with a *carte blanche* from its opposition.

The initial response of the population was rather like that of a people on holiday from humdrum existence. Indeed, in the beginning, the FLQ seemed to enjoy massive—if not majority—support in its action—not so much because the population approved of the act but because the frustrations which it represented touched home for the majority of the people. The radio talk shows faced an onslaught of people demonstrating themselves receptive to the *felquiste* manifesto. In speaking with individual *Québécois,* one gained the opinion that, while few would really identify themselves with the FLQ, their opposition to the kidnapping of the Englishman was not very heartfelt. In the short run—during which the government was being urged from all sides to negotiate with the FLQ, large support rallies were being held, and radio stations actually seemed proud to be able to broadcast the latest communiqués—the FLQ had definitely gained a certain curious respectability.

At the time of Cross' kidnapping, Paul Rose and his brother Jacques, members of an FLQ finance cell, were en route to a vacation in Texas. When they heard the news of the kidnapping they rushed to return to Québec. The day of liberation seemed at hand. Undoubtedly influenced by the massive public show of support which the kidnapping had gained and the carnival atmosphere of the left, they decided to "aid" the other cell by adding Laporte's kidnapping as an inducement for the government to negotiate. The choice of Laporte, one of those referred to by Vallières as most dangerous to the cause of Québec's liberation, the second-ranking member of Bourassa's government and his recent opponent for control of the party, was a logical one. Their need to share the limelight, however, was the undoing of the FLQ's propaganda effort.

After Laporte's kidnapping the pressures upon the government to yield to the terrorists' demands came from all quarters: from the leaders of the Province's labor unions, professors, students, as well as from figures as respected as René Lévesque and Claude Ryan. Already the government had entered a kind of semi-official negotiation with Robert Lemieux,[49] a lawyer acting as an intermediary between the government and the kidnappers of Cross who had previously represented Gagnon, Vallières and other members of the FLQ. Daily, Lemieux appeared with Vallières, Gagnon, and other radical leaders of Québec in televised news conferences to accuse the government of bad faith in the negotiations. Soon the government realized that it was fast approaching a position in which the pressures to release the FLQ prisoners might be irresistible. Adding to the government's dilemma were the *créditistes* and other rightists in the population who were replete with suggestions that the government release these prisoners by means of one execution a day until the FLQ yielded or that ten "of theirs" be executed for every one "of ours" executed.[50] The population was truly polarized and there was very little middle ground in which the government was able to move. Added to this was the very real dilemma the government faced: the lives of two men were at stake. For Bourassa, the dilemma was even worse: the man taken by the Chénier cell represented his only serious opposition within his own party and had been the individual whom he had edged out the previous year to become leader of the Liberal Party. Bourassa offered to release five *felquistes* who were eligible for parole, an offer which was rejected out of hand by Lemieux as "a joke." After Lemieux broke off the negotiations in rejection of the government's "definitive" offer, he joined Vallières, Gagnon, and Chartrand at the Centre Paul Sauvé, where three thousand cheering students awaited them. The sympathies of the crowd were with the FLQ, and no attempt was made to hide them.

At this point in the crisis the government had had two public officials kidnapped and was virtually without leads to their whereabouts, the leaders of the FLQ were strutting across the television sets of the province and the nation proclaiming their support for the demands of the FLQ and for revolution with impunity, the police were exhausted from days of round-the-clock investigations, the newspapers and other media seemed to be lending a sympathetic ear to the kidnappers, and the students were threatening massive demonstrations. As if this were not enough, the medical specialists of the province were preparing to strike against the institution of provincial health insurance. As Gérard Pelletier, in recounting his approach to the Crisis as a member of the federal cabinet, recalled:

> One of the major gains of the *felquiste* propaganda (aided in this task by complacent commentators) was to spread the belief that, thanks to violence, the FLQ had finally succeeded in raising the real priorities, whereas in reality it had distracted public opinion from these priorities. . . . Worse, it *detoured* the reformist energies of a government which had scarcely come to power. (1971:35)

Faced with a society seemingly on the verge of anarchy, the government invoked the War Measures Act, which gave the government the power, *in the event of an apprehended insurrection,* to place Canada under martial law and withdraw constitutional guarantees such as the right to *habeas corpus* and freedom from summary search.

The Federal Government, while admitting that the War Measures Act was a clumsy tool for the purpose and might well be considered a measure too strong to gain the government's major goal—that of preventing the "pantoufle"[51] cell, that large group of French Canadians sympathetic to the FLQ but unwilling to risk the potential dangers of such tactics themselves, from disrupting Québec society through strikes and massive demonstrations—chose to invoke it to impress on all Canadian citizens that things were deadly serious that October in Québec.

The government's invocation of the War Measures Act only served to provoke a more massive opposition—all basically centered upon the questions: Had the government over-reacted? Was there or was there not an apprehended insurrection? If so, where was the evidence to prove the revolt was at hand?[52]

As it soon became evident that there was no real threat of an insurrection in the usual sense of the term but merely of escalating disorder and perhaps loss of governmental control, the government began a process of dissimulation, implying without proof, for example, that a parallel government had been formed.

At this point, just as opposition to the War Measures Act began to reach a crescendo, the cell which held Laporte found itself "Faced with the arrogance of the Federal Government and its lackey Bourassa . . . [and] with their obvious bad faith" forced to execute Laporte. With the discovery of Laporte's body the next day in the trunk of a taxi, strangled with the chain of his crucifix, the government no longer needed to seriously concern itself with accounting for its actions. For the first time since the beginning of the crisis, the government was in control and those who, like René Lévesque, had used the crisis to jockey to their best advantage, suddenly found themselves on the defensive.

Why did the FLQ execute Laporte? Were the *felquistes* unaware of the backlash effect such an execution was to have? Were they unaware of the effect that the means of garroting would have on the still very Catholic province, or was it their very intent to demonstrate a connection between Laporte and the leading "roi-nègre" of Québec history?

While the "official" reasons given for the execution were that Laporte was a traitor to the Québec people, it is most probable that the major factors were a sense that the War Measures Act had caused them to lose face, that the FLQ was no longer in charge of the situation, and that the group had to prove that they were tough enough to live up to their word.

Who, then, was responsible for the death of Laporte? Was it simply the FLQ, as a band of murderous would-be revolutionaries, or was it the government? Although his death eliminated much of the polarization of the society, as those who had sided with the government from the beginning comforted themselves with an "I told you so" and most of those that had sympathized with the FLQ either rapidly changed positions or ran for the cover of silence, there was still a significant and vocal portion of the population which insisted that all blame lay with the government. Essentially their reasoning was that since the FLQ had indicated to the government all along that it was going to execute its captives unless its demands were met the government's refusal to negotiate was tantamount to the issuing of a death warrant.

As one of my *québécois* radical separatist informants indicated in his opinion of where the guilt for Laporte's death lay, many found no difficulty in accepting the *felquiste* logic and casting all blame on the government:

> It's too bad Laporte had to die but it was necessary to show the people how little concern for life the government has. They were willing to sacrifice one of their own to keep from giving in.

Piotte, while favoring the FLQ, wholly exonerates neither party in this matter, placing responsibility on each:

> Laporte was executed. Who is "morally" responsible for his death?
>
> Laporte ended his last letter to Bourassa with these words: "Decide . . . on my life or my death. I am counting on you and thank you for it."
>
> Ottawa—as Québec only submitted—decided on the death of Laporte as much as the FLQ. The FLQ in the name of the Revolution and Ottawa in the name of the right of the state, both decided to sacrifice the life of an individual.
>
> *One can readily see that the question is not a moral but a political one.* (1971:26-27; emphasis mine)

For Pelletier the attempt of revolutionary separatists to cast blame on the government represented a desperate attempt to render the act of the FLQ rational: *"il faut contrebalancer l'absurde"* (1971:25; emphasis his):

> The FLQ offered the necessary explanation: the unemployed, the poor, the exploited, the colonized, etc. The weight of all these social injustices didn't they compensate for some bombs and useless deaths? In any event, this seemed to be enough justification to permit many people to accept the idea that one could coldly assassinate a defenseless hostage. . . .
>
> . . . [among various other rumors seeking to explain his death

> which swept the universities were efforts] to dirty the repu-
> tation of the minister Pierre Laporte and to demonstrate that
> his death was "accidental," and really was not such a great
> loss for the society. (1971:27, 143)

At the end of the crisis, with the safe recovery of Cross, it was apparent that the FLQ and the revolutionary separatist option had suffered a tremendous defeat. In a Gallup Poll taken in early November it was revealed that 87 percent of the population supported the invoking of the War Measures Act. As importantly, the support given Bourassa and Trudeau was essentially the same within both major ethnic groups. At least in the short run the Federalist option had come out of the crisis stronger than ever.[53]

Perhaps the major damage inflicted in the short run was assumed by the *Parti Québécois* which, while not supporting the FLQ, showed solidarity with many of its demands and was identified with it among a large portion of the population largely as a result of its own reluctance to take a clear stance against the FLQ in the beginning and thus risk alienating student and intellectual support. While the option of political separation may have been given a temporary setback, however, it may well have provided it long-range support as Québec showed itself vulnerable as always to *the* crisis, always essentially the same French and English crisis, which could only be eliminated through separation. Perhaps as important as re-emphasis of French-English tensions was the fact that the crisis served to force both the radical separatists and integrationists to take unreasonable stances permitting the separatists, especially after the immediate effect of Laporte's death had subsided, to assume much of the middle, reasonable ground.

The radical separatist solution certainly suffered a serious loss of respectability during the crisis—a loss rendered even more marked by the fact that the Liberation cell had been so successful in gaining support before the Chénier cell entered the scene. In the aftermath of the events of October, its adherents sought in the main to extricate themselves from an association with terrorism *per se* and either to speak of revolution through the ballot box or of a vague armed revolution. The loss of support for terrorist means reached its apogee with the defection of Pierre Vallières to the *Parti Québécois,* a party whose long-range gain from the crisis may be substantial.

At their headquarters on rue Marie-Anne, in Montréal, the members of the general staff of *la Milice de la République du Québec* (MRQ) and several collaborating militiamen armed with 303 carbines (unloaded); Christine Lavoie, division commander, Claude Longtin, chief of the PMR (*Parti Militaire Républicain*); General André Maheu and Colonel "Jos" (*Le Devoir*, 2 décembre 1971:8). The poster in the upper left is that of Paul Rose, leader of the FLQ cell charged with the murder of Pierre Laporte.

La Milice a déjà fait une victime:
Eusèbe est mort de rire

La Milice has already claimed a victim: Eusébe has died of laughter. (*Le Devoir*, 4 décembre 1971:4)

A French State in North America

> We recommend that the Québec Government set itself the general goal of making French the common language of Québecers, that is, a language known by everyone which can thus serve as an instrument of communication in contact situation between French-speaking people and Québecers of other language groups. . . .
>
> We recommend that the Québec Government take the necessary steps to make French the language of internal communication in the Québec work milieus . . .
>
> We recommend that the Government of Québec amend the Law governing professional corporations to make a working knowledge of French a requirement for entering and practicing a profession. (Report of the Gendron Commission, 1972, Vol. 1:291, 297).

On July 31, 1974, French became the only official language in Québec. Among the provisions of the Official Language Act (Bill 22): most immigrant and French-speaking families are prohibited from sending their children to English schools, firms which use French as the language of work will be given special preference in the granting of government contracts, and consumer goods must carry French labels with lettering at least as prominent as that in any other language. The goal of the Language Act is to make it possible, if not mandatory, for Québec citizens to live, work, and thrive within a wholly French milieu.

Opposition to the act has predictably been strong. English-speaking quebekers have argued that the act violates Canadian law by failing to properly recognize both French and English as official languages. Immigrant groups have protested that they must bear the major cost of "francization" as they are required to send their children to French schools unless the children themselves can pass pre-enrollment English exams.[54] Bill 22's intent with respect to Québec's immigrants is quite clear: to prevent them from adding their numbers to the surrounding English-speaking world. Unfortunately, immigrants feel they will be penalized by being deprived of the opportunity for English educations without gaining real acceptance into what seems a closed and xenophobic French society.

Opposition to Québec's Official Language Act has not, however, been limited to immigrants and English-speakers. Sensing that Robert Bourassa's Liberal Party sponsorship of the Act was an attempt to undercut their nationalist support among *québécois,* many members of the *Parti Québécois* have argued that Bill 22 does not go far enough in promoting the French language. Members of this group feel with some reason that it will still be possible for Québec's English-speaking business and professional elite to operate within wholly English milieus, and thus mastery of English will continue to be mandatory for upwardly mobile immigrants and *québécois.*

The controversy surrounding the 1976 strike of Air Canada pilots against the use of French by flight controllers at Québec airports is typical of the apparent increase in French-English polarization which has followed the declaration of Québec as a French state. Declaring that the use of French created an "unsafe" flying situation, members of the Canadian Airline Pilots Association and the Canadian Air Traffic Controllers Association shut down most Canadian air service for nine days. To end the strike the government was forced to establish a panel of three judges to study the situation and agree that all three must certify bilingual communications to be safe before French could be used in air traffic control communications. Additionally, members of Parliament were to be given the opportunity of voting on the question without being bound to vote along party lines. In effect the agreement seemed to directly conflict with Canada's bilingual policies and to be a "sellout" of French Canada. Certainly French Canadians saw it as such: Jean Marchand, the Minister of the Environment, resigned from Prime Minister Trudeau's cabinet in protest at the government's concessions to the pilots, and Québec once again fumed over what most *québécois* seemed to feel was a clear violation of French rights.

Although it would be unfair to judge the Official Language Act's success or lack of it so soon after its implementation, the first few years have not been particularly auspicious ones. The strong opposition of non-French-speaking quebekers to Bill 22 has further convinced many *québécois* that as long as they remain in Canada English "racism" will seek to thwart their ambitions. On the other hand, non-French-speaking Quebekers have tended to view the passage of Bill 22 as merely one more illustration of French Canadian xenophobia and as evidence that the long standing sensitivity toward minority rights in Canada does not hold when the situation is reversed.

THE MINORITY POLITICIAN:
PRAGMATIST OR ROI-NÈGRE?

7

The politician who attempts to bridge the differences between his own and other ethnicities in a plural society is one of its most important, yet most vulnerable figures. For the society to function smoothly; meeting the aspirations of its peoples, individuals willing to transcend a parochial commitment to their ethnicity must be found. For an ethnic minority, politicians who can gain the trust and support of the majority group have a value beyond price, as they can articulate and seek to achieve the concerns of their group on the largest of social scales. Yet the minority politician, if he is to become more than a spokesman for his ethnicity, must commit the cardinal sin of all ethnic purists: he must compromise, he must lift the screen of his own ethnicity and accommodate the horizons of others, thus becoming vulnerable to the charge of "sell-out" from his own group.

The role of the minority politician in Québec can best be understood by approaching him in his two clearest manifestations: the national leader, i.e., the individual who represents the society as a whole, and the ethnic spokesman, who concerns himself solely with the interests of his group. In five of its politicans in particular—Sir Wilfrid Laurier, Henri Bourassa, Maurice Duplessis, Pierre

Trudeau, and René Lévesque—the province offers an ideal ground upon which to view the dilemma of the minority politician: to cling close to his ethnicity and perhaps attempt to create a nation with it as the base or to accommodate oneself to the reality of a plural society and attempt to function on a larger scale. Four of this group of five, joined in the pairs of Laurier/Bourassa and Trudeau/Lévesque, will be discussed in terms of the clear national/ ethnic politician polarity which they present, while the fifth, Maurice Duplessis, primarily considered to be an ethnic politican yet exhibiting much of the behavior of a national one, will be discussed as a not altogether favorable resolution of the opposition.

Laurier and Bourassa
The relationship between Wilfrid Laurier, the first French Canadian to become Prime Minister of Canada, and Henri Bourassa, a younger colleague later to become an ardent French Canadian nationalist, represents the prototype of the conflict between the national and the ethnic politician.

Laurier, the Prime Minister of Canada from 1896 to 1911, gained support from English Canada and was brought to power largely through his frequent indications that French Canadians owed their religious and cultural existence to British institutions, surviving under the British flag, which

> floats tonight over our heads without a single English soldier in the country to defend it, its sole defense resting in the grati- tude which we owe it for our freedom and the security which we have found under its folds. (Barthe 1890:79)

Only rarely did Laurier waver in his affirmation of the need for coexistence of the two peoples, as when in a speech immediately after Riel's execution he cried that: "If I had been on the banks of the Saskatchewan, I, too, would have shouldered my musket" (Wade 1968:417).[1] Far more typical of his orientation as that of a man devoted to unhyphenated Canadianism was the following address:

> We are French Canadians, but our country is not confined to the territory overshadowed by the citadel of Quebec; our country is Canada, it is the whole of what is covered by the British flag on the American continent. . . . Our fellow-coun-

> trymen are not only those in whose veins runs the blood of
> France. They are all those, whatever their race or whatever
> their language, whom the fortunes of war, the chances of fate,
> or their own choice have brought among us, and who acknowl-
> edge the sovereignty of the British Crown. (Barthe 1890:
> 527-528)

In 1896, Laurier was elected Canada's first French Canadian
Prime Minister. The same elections saw the coming to office of a
young Québec journalist, Henri Bourassa. Only twenty-eight at
the time of his election to Parliament, Bourassa, who had already
demonstrated his brilliance as the scion of an aristocratic family,[2]
had been urged to enter the race for national office by Laurier
himself.

Upon his arrival in Ottawa he encountered the scrutiny of older
politicians, one of whom, Senator L-O David, a close friend of
Laurier, saw in him

> the air of a gentleman, rapid words and gestures, energetic, a
> quick military step, the allure of a French officer. In sum, the
> exterior of a man who is not common, of a personality which
> draws looks and attention. (Quoted in Morrow, 1968:16)

Laurier quickly realized that Bourassa was a man to be reckoned
with in the future. Addressing Bourassa as, "Mon cher ami,"
Laurier implored him to, "speak to me honestly, my dear Henri,
as you do when surrounded by your close friends," concluding
this letter with a prescient "I pray you to think of your future"
(17). Almost immediately, it seemed as if Bourassa was being
groomed for greater things, perhaps eventually even as a replacement for Laurier.

The Boer War, however, was at hand, and Laurier found himself
under great pressure to strengthen Canada's ties with Britain. It
appeared as if Britain were going to war and if that were the case
then most English Canadians assumed Canada would naturally
follows. French Canadians, many identifying more with the Boers
than the British, sought on the whole to avoid any involvement in
the imminent conflict. Laurier, trapped in the middle, attempted
to forestall any engagement.

After Britain's declaration of war, an article, planted by military
officers who wished to prod Laurier, appeared in the *Canadian*

Military Gazette announcing that troops would be sent to South Africa. Upon reading the article Laurier hastily returned to Ottawa from a trip to Toronto to find out the article's source. As his train reached the Ottawa station he discovered Bourassa awaiting him demanding to know why the government had forsaken its anti-imperialist position.

The Prime Minister immediately issued a denial of the government's supposed intention to send troops. The denial, cabled in code to British Prime Minister Chamberlain, brought word of Britain's irritation with Laurier's stance. Lord Minto, the Governor-General of Canada, sought to reverse his position in a series of lengthy meetings with Laurier followed by a letter regretting

> . . . the impression that may be produced in the old country by a decision on the part of Canada not to offer troops. It may be taken perhaps to indicate a certain want of loyalty here, which would be all the more unfortunate at a time when we are relying a good deal upon Imperial support in the Alaska question and in view also of Canada always having to rely to a great extent in any foreign complication on the sympathies and support of the British public. (23)

In the face of Imperial prodding and growing support in the English press for the dispatch of troops to South Africa, Laurier capitulated to a temporary acceptance of Empire. Considering English Canadian sympathies in the matter, this capitulation with the hope of eventually gaining greater independence for Canada seemed to be the only practical course for a politician not ready to forsake power.

Bourassa, however, was incensed. For him this was a time for a stand against all empires. In August, 1897, he spoke in the Commons against the spirit of jingoism then enveloping the country. Later, at a meeting in which Laurier presented the draft of an Order-in-Council which would permit the sending of a Canadian contingent, the thirty-two-year-old Bourassa began to examine the party leader. After a series of pointed questions, Laurier responded: "My dear Henri—the circumstances are difficult," only to be met with: "It is because they are difficult that I ask you to remain faithful to your word. To govern is to have the courage, at a given moment, to risk power to save a principle" (25). Bourassa's stinging criticism came as a great shock to Laurier, as he had indicated only the night before that he would go along with the troop commitment. His open reversal of this agreement and his attack represented a forsaking of Laurier, and a future career in the Liberal Party, for principle.

On October 18, 1899, only five days after his open confrontation with Laurier, Bourassa sent Laurier a letter of resignation from Parliament questioning whether Canada's aid was really needed or if this was only an act designed to lead Canada back to the status of a Crown colony. A week later, having received no response, Bourassa penned a second letter indicating admiration for the Prime Minister mixed with the information that

> I will always regret what I consider to be an act of feebleness on your part. . . . I will use all my force to protest the present *unreasoned* imperialism. . . . *Au revoir cher M. Laurier.* (29)

To this second letter Laurier responded, indicating the pain he felt at Bourassa's spurning was more than political:

> Tell me what attitude should the French take in the Confederation? They must isolate themselves, as a separate body or march at the head of the Confederation. It is necessary that we choose between English Imperialism and American imperialism. I see no other alternative. If there is one I wish you would indicate it to me. . . .
>
> But it is a personal chagrin, more than just chagrin, to be separated from you. I had hoped for other things. (29-30)

The next year Bourassa stood election as an independent and, Laurier having made certain he faced no opposition, was reelected by acclamation. But Laurier was by no means unaware of the threat which Bourassa's defection posed for the future: "When the trouble comes from our enemies, it is not a great surprise," he wrote a colleague; "It is certainly more disagreeable when it comes from our close friends, but it is inevitable" (31). However, for the time, Laurier was able to comfort himself with the knowledge that the war was going well.

Suddenly, however, in the worst of all possible moments for success, Bourassa attacked Laurier for illegal use of executive power and asked that Parliament pass a resolution explicitly recognizing that the government's act in sending troops was not to represent a precedent for future colonial wars. Laurier immediately challenged Bourassa, first noting his youth and inexperience, and then adding:

> It is only too true, Sir, that if we had refused at that time to do what was in my judgment our imperative duty, a most dangerous agitation would have arisen—an agitation which, according to all human probability would have ended in a cleavage in the population of this country upon racial lines. A greater calamity could never take place in Canada. (35)

While Laurier's speech placed his dilemma in clear light, his condescending reference to Bourassa was an error. Already the affect which Bourassa displayed indicated that much of his effort may well have been the result of a need to have all or nothing of Laurier's affection, of a need to contrive total rejection rather than accept half a loaf. In any event, shortly thereafter Bourassa allied himself with Goldwin Smith, a Toronto anti-imperialist, with the intent of forming a French-English pact to push the cause of Canadian nationalism. In June of 1900, Bourassa accused Britain, in a speech before Parliament, of waging an unjust war against the Boers—a situation which reminded him of French-English relations in Canada. A member called for three cheers for the Queen in response, and the House rose to sing "God Save the Queen" as if to ward off a demon.

During this period Bourassa continued to write inflammatory letters to Laurier reminding him of his "capitulation" and suggesting that he was a servant of the British Prime Minister. In August, Laurier responded to Bourassa that:

> if instead of conducting as I have during recent events, I had adopted your manner of seeing things, the result would have been absolutely disastrous and if I were to tell you all my thoughts, I would express my surprise to you that such a logical spirit as yours would not see this truth. . . . (41)

Unable to accept Bourassa's abuse without response, he added a handwritten postscript:

> Your letter gives the appearance of a declaration of war that you are holding in reserve to introduce at an opportune time. There will always be a time to respond if it comes to that! (41)

Shortly thereafter, however, Laurier sent Bourassa a copy of *Vie de Gladstone,* a man whom Bourassa admired greatly, and followed it with a letter imploring him not to come to town "without giving me the pleasure of chatting with you for a moment. . . . We can agree to disagree." Laurier's shrewd conciliation, heartfelt or no, placed Bourassa in a bind, rendering him unable to complete the break with Laurier and seek to end the latter's political career.

During the following eight years until his resignation from Parliament in 1908 to run for a seat in the Québec assembly, Bourassa began to withdraw more and more into the French world of Québec, evidencing a distrust of things English. With the passage of time he began to make more speeches praising the Church and the old values of the province. Laurier, not sensing that Bourassa was giving up the last vestiges of his role as a national politician to retreat to one—that of the minority politician— which he found more congenial, remarked to a friend that Bourassa was hurting himself nationally.

When Bourassa did take leave from Parliament, Laurier wrote him, "I regret your going. . . . We need a man like you at Ottawa, though I should not want two" (54).

After Bourassa's leavetaking, Laurier found himself once again under imperial pressure to aid Britain. In the years before the onset of World War I, Germany began to make serious inroads against British naval superiority, and pressure arose both from Britain and within Canada for Canada to build several battleships for use by the Royal Navy. Again Bourassa's nationalism— French at heart but willing to ally itself with like-minded English Canadian nationalists in a common Canadian bond against the Empire—was offended and again he responded. This time, however, he decided to found an organ which would report events to French Canadians in a strong, nationalist light. On January 10, 1910, Bourassa launched *Le Devoir,* dedicated to "political liberty for his French Canadian compatriots and for his country, Canada," to "a socio-economic order less deceitful in the benefits it bestowed on the strong and more favorable to the aspirations of the weak," and, of course, to the propagation "of the principles and doctrine of Christianity as manifested in the Catholic Church"

(Ryan; *Le Devoir;* 10 janvier 1970:4). As if its title were not enough to indicate its sense of purpose, a subtitle, "Fais ce que dois," "Do your duty," was added.

Armed with a personal organ and a gifted tongue, Bourassa immediately launched into Laurier, writing editorials and making speeches against military aid to Britain with a passion that was to bring him down. When several months later Laurier's "masterful compromise" passed the House of Commons, establishing a small Canadian navy of eleven ships which could only be placed under imperial directive by an act of Parliament or an order-in-council if Parliament was not in session, Bourassa responded to a friend:

> Laurier has now driven not one nail in his coffin but many. On Sunday I speak at the church door at Sorel. The next Sunday I speak at another church, and it will go on till he is finished. (67)

Bourassa toured the province making speeches against Laurier in various parishes and describing him in *Le Devoir* as a man who ". . . despises the confidence and love which a people has given him" (67). His voice, long limited to Québec, began to have more and more of a national influence as he sought to promote the cause of Canadian independence. When Laurier dissolved Parliament in July of 1911, announcing elections for the following September, Bourassa allied himself with the Conservatives, led by Robert Borden, to defeat him. The election was a hard fought one, primarily contested over the nationalist issues, with Bourassa leading the day in Québec. When the ballots were counted, the fifteen-year reign of Laurier was over, primarily as a result of losses in his home province. Again and again, during the campaign, Bourassa had succeeded in firing the people of Québec with ethnic rhetoric as did his English counterparts in the rest of Canada. Laurier, having to straddle two peoples, had compromised himself beyond fervor and fallen.

What was Québec's reward for having turned against its own as a *vendu?* On September, 1912, its harvest became apparent: the conservative Robert Borden, who after his election had asked Bourassa to serve in his cabinet, announced that there would be an emergency naval bill granting $35 million for the building of three ships, an amount several times that which Laurier had authorized. Québec, and Bourassa, awoke to find that they had aided the election of a man who only represented an amplification of the policies that they had found distasteful in Laurier.

Five years later, during a war in which his attacks upon the Borden government had gained him universal hatred in English Canada, in which riots prevented an attempt on his part to speak in Ottawa, in which Laurier wrote a friend, "Bourassa is playing with fire. If he thinks that he will be able to extinguish it he may have a rude awakening" (89), and in which the Borden government introduced conscription, Bourassa himself capitulated.

> Arriving in Ottawa, Bourassa rode the streetcar out to Laurier Avenue to talk with the aging leader. The meeting between Bourassa and Laurier on October 18, 1917 was the end of an era. Laurier, who had fought Bourassa for eighteen years in his effort to sustain and foster unity in Canada, had been forced to realize that in this election Quebec would probably be his only stronghold and that short of a miracle the results of the December balloting across Canada would reflect a clear English Canadian–French Canadian split. Laurier did not want overt Nationalist support, but he and Bourassa shared many of the same goals that year—the defeat of conscription, a somewhat more limited war effort, and harmony between the peoples of Canada. The Leader of the Opposition could not refuse Bourassa's endorsement as the two men sat in the privacy of the home on Laurier Avenue. (Murrow, 1968:99)

Maurice Duplessis

In Maurice Duplessis Québec found its ethnic politician *par excellence*. A man who seemed to pride himself in his use of *joual*, he took pains—if indeed any were needed—to always identify with the farmer, the worker, the average Québécois against those with intellectual and linguistic pretense. A man who prided himself on being an idealist or an intellectual was dismissed as a "poète" or publicly insulted. A minister whose French was without flaw was likely to be cut short in the middle of a speech with a stern "toé, tais-toé!"[3] And he did.

Any relation of the life of Maurice Duplessis always turns again and again to the myriad tales clustered around him. Even with the careful news screen which he insisted upon, enough of the man slipped through to regale the province. Events such as the throwing of objects at opponents in the National Assembly, Duplessis' reprimands toward Ministers who were not repeating the words he wanted to hear -he would interrupt them in the midst of an address, call them to his desk, and inform them what the text of their speech was to be before sending them back to their place to continue[4] -a public investigation in which he summoned the Lieutenant-Governor—the Queen's representative—by his first name ("Quick, quick get Gaspard over here"), and the transfer of the Great Seal of Québec, in the midst of which he publicly announced: "The little *sôt* brings the Great *Sceau*" ("The little *fool* brings the Great *Seal*"), all were papered over in the press. As Pierre Laporte, a former reporter for *Le Devoir*, complained:

> Duplessis would have cried Foul! if the press had ever reported the goings-on as they actually occurred. There did exist at least the common sense to maintain a minimum of parliamentary dignity . . . in the newspapers. (1960:49)

Two short anecdotes will serve to capture the flavor of the man—a man who ruled Québec with a jest and a fist for nearly two decades.

Onésime Gagnon, a former adversary for the direction of the pre-*Union Nationale, Parti Conservateur:*

> . . . was giving an excellent, well ordered speech, divided into three parts in the classical style, with beginning and peroration. He embellished his text with literary and historical recollections. He was well acquainted with the history of Canada. Moreover, he recalled with pleasure, when the occasion lent itself, the memory of celebrated painters or musicians. This oratorical elegance was sometimes expressed with humor and often very pleasant to listen to. One can imagine that these qualities irritated Duplessis, especially when they manifested themselves in extended speech. One day "Onésime" as he was known had launched into a moving conclusion. He invoked the memory of Richard Wagner, recalling the glory of Tristan and Isolde as well as Percivale. Caught up in his eloquence and virtuosity, all listened with interest, all except Duplessis, who was becoming more and more exasperated. Suddenly, he approached Onésime, gave a strong pull to the tails of his coat and told him loud enough for several others to hear: "C't-assez, Nésime, c't-assez." The spell was broken. The

deputy from Matane, used to these kinds of affronts, sputtered
for a second then hurried to sit down. (Chaloult, 1969:33–34)

René Chaloult, a former *Union Nationale* deputy who broke
with Duplessis to become an Independent, recalled an instance
which occurred soon after he had agreed to defend Phillipe Hamel,
then a *Union Nationale* deputy, in an assault action:

> One night while we were talking about politics with friends,
> [Duplessis] turned to me: "Phillippe has given his case to you,
> hasn't he?" At the same moment he pulled a roll of banknotes
> from his pockets and extended them to me: "Here, take these
> for your costs." I responded forcefully assuring him that I was
> very honored to defend such a brave companion without
> charge. "But there are court costs," he explained. "Hamel has
> the means to pay and certainly would not want anyone else
> to assume the cost." Several days later, I met Duplessis at the
> barber shop in the Château Frontenac. He took me aside and
> smilingly confided: "You seemed upset the other night when I
> offered you money in front of the others, I understand you
> but now we are alone." He again offered me a number of
> banknotes of which I never found out the amount. "Please
> take them," he urged me, "if you want us to remain on good
> terms. . . ." (38)[5]

Duplessis ruled the province of Québec in a paternalistic style,
only seemingly directed by the principle that nothing, or as little
as possible, should change in the land of Québec. Anything new
had to immediately be brought within the controlled familiar. Perhaps because of this, perhaps because of political expediency or
perhaps arising from sincere belief, Duplessis articulated a strong
nationalist sentiment in Québec. Struggling with the Federal Government he forced a recognition of Québec's right to independent
taxation of individuals and corporations and diminished federal
taxation, all of which provided much of the financial impetus for
the formation of today's parallel state. Under his auspices Québec
gained an official flag—a white cross sectioning a blue background
into quarters, with a fleur-de-lis centered in each of its blue sec-
tions.[6] On the whole in his defense of the traditional values of
Québec against change from within or without, Duplessis ranks as
a shining example of that long line of Québec leaders whose goal
was survival, but only survival, at all cost.[7]

His resistance to outside influence was not solely directed against the English, whom, as Chaloult relates, he feared and respected because of their economic power and

> because he was a victim, without reason moreover and despite his apparent arrogance, of reflexes of inferiority . . . [and, of course] it is the Anglo-Saxon capitalists, who, traditionally among us, feed the campaign chest. . . . (1969:42)

For the French, however, Duplessis cared even less. He refused ever to visit France, and French visitors who passed his way were likely to be met with an insult and his favorite quote: "Nous sommes Français améliorés." Upon receiving Vincent Auriol, the President of the Republic, one day, he demanded, "How long have you been sitting in my office, Mr. Premier?" To which the startled guest responded: "I hardly know . . . possibly twenty minutes, I think." "Are you certain, Mr. Premier, that your government has not been overthrown in the meantime?" For once, faced with the icy return of this Gaul, Duplessis was insulted in kind: "Perhaps, Mr. Prime Minister, but they tell me that the contrary problem rages here: it does not change often enough" (Chaloult, 1969: 42–43; Laporte, 1960:47).

A question that has always plagued those who have attempted to delve into the machinations of Duplessis is that of his sincerity. In particular, was he really a nationalist or a man who only used nationalism for its certain electoral value, a value used to cloak an alliance with Anglo-American finance? Did he really intend to sell out the resources of the Province so easily to the English, or was he unaware or, perhaps, so awed by their supposed business expertise that he was unable to drive a bargain favorable to his province?[8] Was he a patriot or, as André Laurendeau has maintained, a "roi-nègre"?

In one instance, that of the nationalization of the Province's electrical resources, which had been liberally ceded by previous governments, Duplessis led the fight for nationalization throughout the 1936 elections only to toss the program aside after the elections. When Chaloult complained of his failure to carry his promises into action, Duplessis informed him: "You're not a child; at your age you must know that *a program is good before the elections and the elections are over*" (1969:67; emphasis his).

In other instances, and especially in the Asbestos strike of 1949, Duplessis showed himself strongly favorable for a nationalist to the cause of the American companies and opposed to that of the workers of Québec. When the workers struck demanding elimination of the asbestos dust from the air they breathed in the mines and a fifteen-cent-an-hour salary increase, the company fought back in the manner which it had always held in threat to maintain low wages: it hired "scabs" from the waiting reservoir of unemployed. When the workers protested, Duplessis sent provincial police to assure their replacements' safe passage. When the protest turned violent, Duplessis crushed it. Certain clergy, including the Archbishop of Montréal, Mgr. Charbonneau, rallied to the side of the workers, only to be labeled "Communsist" and, in Charbonneau's case, meet with exile for their pains.[9] Nevertheless, despite Duplessis' efforts, the workers gained at the end of their long strike the recognition of their unions, an augmentation of salary, and an agreement on the part of the company to improve their working conditions.

Hypocrite or no, at the time of his death at Québec's Ungava iron site, no real threat loomed to Duplessis on the political horizon. It was as if the whole province had been held in suspended animation for fifteen years with only a few, such as Trudeau and Laurendeau, willing to challenge his leadership. While it is doubtful that Duplessis ever had the slightest intention, urge, or motivation to "sell out" his people, his own personal fear of change coupled with his charisma and the saleability of populist-nationalist slogans, kept a man in power and a province from being born. Pierre Laporte, fittingly enough, captured Duplessis' forthright approach to progress and his paternalism in the following anecdote:

> A junior minister had prepared a working plan that covered several years. Proud of himself and full of enthusiasm, he went to Duplessis' office to outline his project. The Premier took the document and, without reading it, slipped it in a drawer and then said to the Minister:
>
> "Did I ask you to draft a plan? No. When I want a plan I'll ask for one."
>
> The saddest part of this story is the sequel. The Minister

ended his account of the incident: "And I never did anything else after that."

In one blow, Duplessis had house-broken his man. He became one of the contented slaves. (1960:73)

Small wonder that upon Duplessis' death the province of Québec erupted with the vigor of an adolescent rebellion, of a gasp for air, delayed a generation.

Trudeau and Lévesque

All the time and energy that we devote in proclaiming our national rights, in invoking our providential mission, in trumpeting our virtues, in crying over our transformations, in denouncing our enemies, and in declaring our independence, have never made one of our workers more skilled, one of our financiers richer, one of our doctors more progressive, one of our bishops more aware or one of our politicians less ignorant. Yet, with the exception of a few muleheads, there is probably not a French Canadian intellectual who has not spent at least four hours a week during the past year discussing separatism, this makes how many thousand times two hundred hours spent exclusively in twiddling our thumbs? For who can claim to have heard a single argument during all this time which was not already debated *ad nauseam* twenty years ago, forty years ago, sixty years ago? (Trudeau, 1967:176–177)

Strangely enough, the life of Joseph Philippe Pierre Yves Elliott Trudeau, the third French Canadian Prime Minister in the Canadian Confederation, has largely been spent opposing establishments. From his rebellious youth—spent mostly in exclusive schools from which his disregard for established rules occasionally resulted in his suspension, and later as a professional student and world traveler—until his entry into the Liberal Party and institutional politics in 1965, Trudeau's existence had always been that of a wealthy outsider, of a more sincere and less theatrical William F. Buckley of Québec's left. Born to relative wealth, which seemed to function more as a reservoir of security than a key to luxury, Trudeau entered law at *l'Université de Montréal* in 1940, later explaining:

I always loved justice and debating two sides of a question. I wanted to understand my rights so that I could fully profit

from them. I had no love for authority. Consequently, I
enjoyed contradicting men who claimed that I had no right to
do so. (Stuebing, *et al.*, 1969:25)

After completing his studies in 1943, he enrolled in a Harvard
graduate program in political economy "to learn how governments
function" (29). Finding Harvard at first a gateway to an understanding of Québec's backwardness, he soon lost interest, feeling
"I understood these subjects better than most of my professors"
(29), and left for a sojourn in Paris. Soon, tiring also of Paris, he
left to enroll in the London School of Economics, where he
studied under Harold Laski, secretary of the British Labor Party.
In 1948, as a man approaching twenty-nine who had not yet felt
pressed to find employment, he allotted himself a year and a half
to circle the world.[10] Rejected upon his return to Québec in a bid
to join the staff of a university in the province as a professor of
political theory, he entered public service in the office of the cabinet secretary, where he served until 1952. At this same period,
Duplessis' provincial police were engaged in a brutal struggle with
the Asbestos Miners. Trudeau offered his aid to the strikers and
soon addressed an assembly of more than five thousand miners.[11]

In 1950, the year following the strike, Trudeau, together with
Gérard Pelletier and several others, founded *Cité Libre,* a journal
which rallied the progresive-intellectual elite of Québec against
the reactionary dominance of Québec, symbolized by Maurice
Duplessis and his *Union Nationale.* Although the review's circulation never hovered much above one thousand, it became symbolic of the struggle of an emerging elite, owing its allegiance to
the industrial world, against the rural and clerical hierarchy
which still controlled the society.

Early in his leadership of Québec's left, however, Trudeau came
in conflict with an idea which was enjoying a rebirth of interest:
separatism. While all about him seemed to toy and many to bend
ever closer toward separatist doctrine, Trudeau, examining as he
did all "new" ideas with a jaundiced eye, found himself opposed
to an idea which was to form the very core of the province's left in
the 1960's.

In his staunch opposition to separatism, Trudeau has proven
the worth of his own self-analysis: "One need not look any

further for a consistent thread to my thought than that of opposing established ideas" (Trudeau, 1967:v). In countering the flow
of intellectual thought of his time, he proved the independence of
his thought beyond any serious doubt. In an article, "La Nouvelle
trahison des clercs," appearing in the April, 1962, issue of *Cité
Libre,* Trudeau took separatists to task as reactionaries. Taking as
his theorteical stance the argument that: "It is not the idea of a
nation which is backward but the idea that the nation must neces-
sarily be sovereign," he argued that the economic and political
realities of the modern world opposed the development of nation-
states and favored the formation of multinational units.[12]

Separatism, contrary to its modern image, Trudeau argues,
serves largely to prevent French Canadians from entering the real
struggle—that for economic and cultural expansion. "These men,"
Trudeau said, referring to Québec's separatists,

> have never ceased transmitting to our people what Pelletier
> aptly called "a state of siege mentality." But, as I have written,
> "the state of siege has been lifted a long time, the human cara-
> van has pushed a hundred leagues further, while we stew
> implacably in our juice not daring to cast a glimpse over the
> walls."
>
> . . . I find that several of those who used to think as I did have
> today become separatists. Because their social thought is
> leftist, because they work for the Laic school, because they are
> unionists, because their culture is open, they think that *their*
> nationalism is in the line of progress. They don't see that it is
> politically that they have become reactionaries. (175, 177)[13]

The struggles for equality in Canada have been so long and so
hard, Trudeau continued, largely because *Québécois* have always
reaped the benefits of their turning inward: backwardness. Under
these conditions can anyone really blame English Canadians for
not wanting to have the country's image carry any French traits?
"And why should they want to learn a language or participate in a
culture which we devote so much effort to degrade at all levels of
our educational system?" (176)

In brief, Trudeau concludes, all opportunities French Canadians
need can be gained within the Confederation of today. Separatism,
if achieved, will not liberate the energies of a people as so often

maintained, but merely doom them to a worse fate than they enjoy today.

As the threat of separatism grew in the early 1960s, especially with the ascending star of René Lévesque in the horizon, the Federal Liberals sought to induce the cream of Québec's federalists to come to Ottawa to counterbalance this threat. Finally, in 1965, their efforts met success with the recruitment of Trudeau, Jean Marchand, and Gérard Pelletier, labeled "the three wise men" by opposition leader John Diefenbaker. As Jean-Paul Desbiens wrote upon their decision to enter federal politics:

> With you three in Ottawa our options will become clearer. We are making the final test which will indicate whether or not Canada is viable. If you fail we will have no other option than to choose firmly the path of independence—without remorse or bad conscience. (Stuebing, et al., 1969:57)

Assigned at first to Prime Minister Pearson, Trudeau gained the post of Justice Minister in April, 1967. Despite, or perhaps because of, his image as a "swinger," aided by sporty dress, which once gained him a rebuke on the floor of the House of Commons from the opposition leader, and conspicuous escort of lovely women, Trudeau moved steadily toward the leadership of his party. On April 6, 1968, the congress of the Liberal Party of Canada elected him its leader, and on April 20, Pierre Elliot Trudeau became Prime Minister of Canada after only three years on the national scene. On June 25, the day of the national elections, the Liberals gained their first clear majority in fifteen years, and Trudeau was guaranteed a term as Prime Minister in his own right. Clearly all Canada sensed the need for a national politician of French Canadian extraction who could hold the nation together.

And of Trudeau's opposition within Québec? Vallières and radical separatists saw him from the beginning as a "traitor" to French Canada and later, with the advent of the October crisis, as a "fascist" ("Trudeau, un liberal?" Piotte asks, "mon cul"), as a man insensitive to the plight of the workers of his nation,[14] and even as a "fairy."[15] Frequently attacked outside of Québec for his excessive concern for French Canadians, he finds himself under attack within the province as a man who has "sold out" to English

Canada.[16] Trudeau can withstand the revolutionary separatists and probably his English Canadian opponents, but what of the new vigor of his old enemy separatism? What of René Lévesque?

René Lévesque, today leader of the *Parti Québécois,* is a man whose intelligence, rhetorical style, and proven administrative ability would make him a worthy opponent no matter what issue he espoused. As a man sponsoring separatism—an issue of great emotional appeal in today's Québec—he is worthy of all the fear federalists can muster. If there were ever a separatist to whom *québécois* could entrust their province, Lévesque is the man. If there were ever a man who could destroy confederation, Lévesque is the man. If Canada is to be severed, it will not be by revolutionary separatists but because the middle-class intellectual and business elite has cast its lot with workers under a new nationalist front, a front which, if it manages to come to fruition in this decade, will be the *Parti Québécois,* led by René Lévesque.

Lévesque is Gaspésian in origin, born in New Carlisle on the Baie des Chaleurs. He attended a Jesuit classical college in Gaspé, later continued his studies in Québec, and served in the Canadian Army in Korea. It was in his *Radio-Canada* program, *Point de Mire,* however, that his name became a household word in Québec. Chaloult remembers his program as being one in which "everyone watched to hear his commentaries on international politics and the events of the day" (1969:257), delivered in his familiar rapid speech and nervous chain-smoking style.

After the Radio-Canada strike, Jean Lesage, then newly elected head of the Liberal Party, asked him to stand election in the Liberals' attempt to defeat the post-Duplessis vestiges of the *Union Nationale.* Surprisingly, Lévesque accepted and was elected delegate to the National Assembly from Laurier in the June, 1960 elections, in which the Liberals gained fifty-one of the ninety-five Assembly seats. After his election, Lesage, possibly fulfilling a prior agreement not too willingly, tendered to Lévesque the portfolio of the ministry of Natural Resources, from which the latter led almost singlehandedly "la révolution tranquille," being personally responsible for most of the major reforms instituted by the Lesage government during its ensuing six years: the nationalization of the province's electrical companies, the creation of the *Société*

Générale de Financement and of the *Caisse de Dépots,* among others. As Chaloult remarks:

> He accomplished all that in spite of the silent hostility of the Prime Minister, who blocked him at every point ["lui mettait des bâtons dans les roues"] but had the intelligence to take credit for the reforms when they proved to be a success. Free, Lévesque would have achieved much more. (258)

Free he soon was. In the midst of the Liberal Party Congress of October, 1967, Lévesque left the party, and, opting for the sovereignty of Québec, formed the *Mouvement Souveraineté-Association,* whose goal was an independent Québec within a Canadian common market.[17] The following year, with the publication of *Option Québec,* Lévesque explained his reasons for rejecting the Canadian Confederation or any modification of it and opting for independence, and set forth his program for achieving a prosperous, independent Québec. Operating from the thesis:

> We are *Québécois.* What that means, first and above all, and in time of need entirely, is that we are attached to this sole corner of the world where we can be fully ourselves, this Québec that, we well know, is the only place where it is possible for us to be really at home, (1968:19)

Lévesque argues that nothing short of independence will suffice.

> Not being able to live as we are, conveniently, in our language, in our fashion, would have the same effect as if a member, not to say the heart, were wrenched from us. . . . This, once again, only the uprooted (*déracinés*)[18] are unable to understand. (1968:21)

There has never been anything natural in the union of Québec and English Canada, Lévesque argues. No ties of language, religion or culture bind the two peoples together. Of the gamut of human ties, only the economic interdependence of the two peoples looms large, he continues, so why not take the logical path and sever all ties except that one logical one. Why not cease wasting our energies in demanding our rights within an unnatural confederation, take them, and leave only that economic confederation which we both need? If we fail to take the logical course, Lévesque warns, we may well, both English and French Canadians, having our most precious potential, "disappear in the ample American bosom" (37).

As for French Canadians outside of Québec? Citing figures indicating the rapid assimilation of this group, Lévesque dismisses the argument that Québec must remain a part of Canada to protect them and adds that under the current Federal immigration policies Québécois may themselves soon join their fellow French Canadians in this respect. What to do? Cut our losses and make a unilingual state, free of the trap of bilingualism.

What of Québec's economy and standard of living? Low as they are, does not separation risk lowering them further still? Faced with the most torturous question of all for those contemplating separation, Lévesque responds, in effect quite simply, Anglo-Americans need our resources and will come for them—this time on *Québécois* terms. In the light of all this, must one still ask what to do? ". . . le Québec doit devenir au plus tôt un Etat souverain" (39).

In October, 1968, the *Mouvement Souveraineté-Association* became the *Parti Québécois.* The *Parti Québécois,* accepting Lévesque's premise that there were no modifications to be made within the confederation—only a break—established itself as a political party operating solely on the provincial level. In April, 1970, during Provincial elections held only a year and a half after its founding, the *Parti Québécois* gained 23.1 percent of the votes cast to the Liberals' 45.5 percent, the *Union Nationale's* 19.7 percent, and the *Ralliement Créditiste's* 11.2 percent—this despite the fact that the Liberal Party, panicking in the face of pre-election polls which showed the P.Q. with an even higher percentage of the votes, did all it possibly could, including in all probability staging the celebrated "coup de Brinks," to frighten voters away from the fledgling party.

What of Lévesque's possibilities for the future? Temporarily crippled by the October Crisis, it is quite possible that he gained support in the long run, as it became evident that management of possible *felquiste* student, intellectual, and perhaps even labor support was the real object in Trudeau's mind when he invoked the War Measures Act, rather than any real fear of insurrection.

In 1973 the *Parti Québécois* won 30 percent of Québec's vote and became the official opposition party to Robert Bourassa's Liberals. Although the concentration of its supporters in cities and the disproportionate representation of rural areas in the National Assembly kept its actual representation to six seats, its showing in its second electoral test gave clear evidence that the *Parti Québécois* enjoyed strong and committed support among a significant section of the Québec electorate. In the November 1976 election, the *Parti Québécois* gained 69 of the 110 seats, and the Liberals' share of Québec's electorate declined from 102 legislative seats to 28! As noted, Liberal Premier Robert Bourassa lost his seat in the 1976 landslide.

It can be noted that René Lévesque suggested in an article appearing in the July, 1976, issue of *Foreign Affairs* that:

> all in all, there is quite a serious possibility that an "independentist" government will soon be elected in Québec. At first sight, this looks like a dramatically rapid development, this burgeoning and flowering over a very few years of a political emancipation movement in a population which, until recently, was commonly referred to as quiet old Québec. But in fact, its success would mean, very simply, the normal healthy end result of a long and laborious national evolution. (1976:735)

In November 1976 the electorate was convinced that they could go beyond Trudeau's "Good government is a damned good substitute for national self-determination" (Trudeau, 1967: 161, 164); they want both "good government" and "self-determination." Lévesque is now in the process of convincing the people of Québec that the *Parti Québécois* plan for severing all formal ties save the economic one with the rest of Canada will best guarantee the *épanouissment* of the people of Québec.

QUEBEC IN CROSS-CULTURAL PERSPECTIVE 8

The Tie that Bounds: The Horizons Imposed by Language, Color, and Ethnicity

> A strange destiny, to be born and to die without having been alive. (Gilles Groulx, Québec cinematographer)

Perhaps the most profound effect of the use of language, ethnic and racial differences to form hierarchical organization within a society is their tendency to provide barriers to personal advancement, both as a result of discrimination and, as important, as a result of their influence in limiting personal perspective. The birth-ascribed nature of the more fixed hierarchical typing rendered upon the basis of ethnicity is such that individuals of relatively devalued groups within a society are faced with horizons imposed by an identity which carries with it a binding akin to a stigma.

The most striking example of the limitations upon personal perspective provided by devalued group identity is that of the caste system of India, in which much of an individual's life style, including virtually his entire economic and religious being, is acquired by birth. A man born into a potter cast remains a potter, an untouchable remains an untouchable, and a Brahmin, provided he does not commit some particularly polluting act resulting in expulsion from his caste, remains a Brahmin. As Berreman has noted:

... a person of shoemaker caste who becomes a school teacher
or politician, who is a vegetarian, who is orthodox in his pur-
suit of Hindu ideals, who has never touched a dead animal or
made a shoe, is still treated as a shoemaker in the caste hierarchy. He may be individually esteemed, but in the system he
is an untouchable; he is ritually polluted like every other shoemaker and he is treated accordingly. (1967:283)

The role of birth-ascribed hierarchies in limiting personal perspective has been described for the Japanese outcastes, the "eta"
or Burakumin, by DeVos and Wagatsuma. The despair of a lifetime
limited by stigma is most clearly brought to light in trauma-filled
attempts at passing by individuals and families and by ruminations
upon outcaste status by Burakumin authors and poets. One of
these, the Burakumin poet Maruoka Tadao, rela s his experience
as an outcaste in a particularly poignant light:

LET COME THE DAY TO SAY "ONCE IT WAS SO"

I heard whispering
Like the flow of wind from mouth to mouth
That under each armpit I am marked,
The size of an open hand.

Was it inherited from an ancient time?
My parents, so too I've heard
Were also bruised by nature's brand.

Yet of them no memory affords
Sight or feel of such a spot.

But in childhood I learned,
Through cruel heavy winks, how instinctively to hide.

What was it I so naively wrapped with rags,
And hidden, dragged, through dark months and years?

In these concealing rags, I had hid my heart,
When refound, it was sorely bruised
Shriveled red from stigma I sought to lose.

Without some fresh exposure, my songs would end in lies;
Tightly bound bruises but increase the inner plight.

Who marked my sides? For what unknown cause?
Why such a brand upon my very self and soul?
Even today, my ebbing thoughts,

So pale and cold, transparent as glass,
Hold me awake.
(Devos and Wagatsuma, 1967:239–240)

Studies of the effect upon American Negroes of racial hierarchy
in the United States are legion. Again and again, these analyses
turn toward the limiting effect of blackness in American society,
to the fact that blacks learn relatively early how limited is to be
their lot. Indeed, much of the role of the black mother and
woman in our society is oriented toward the cushioning—if not the
ensuring in the process—of black males to defeat. As Grier and
Cobbs have noted:

> Every mother, of whatever color and degree of proficiency,
> knows what the society in which she lives will require of her
> children. Her basic job is to prepare the child for this. Because
> of the institutionalization of barriers, the black mother knows
> even more surely what society requires of *her* children. What
> at first seemed a random pattern of mothering has gradually
> assumed a definite and deliberate, if unconscious, method of
> preparing a black boy for his subordinate place in the world.
> (1968:52)

The pervasiveness of the internalization of degradation and
felt lack of purity among blacks is illustrated most strikingly by
class distinctions made by blacks within their own milieu. Thus,
while any known Negro ancestry, however remote, immediately
places an individual within the lower-caste Negro population as far
as the society as a whole is concerned,[1] status within black society
is, *ceteris paribus,* determined by one's degree of lightness. The
effect of this association of "goodness" with "lightness" can be
seen in such black folk sayings as: "If you're light, you're right; if
you're brown, stick around; if you're black, get back." The following is an anecdote recently told me by a black acquaintance
concerning his first memory of discussing with his daughter what
color was to mean to her life:

> My little girl, who is as light as I am—my wife is the dark one—
> and I were driving through the Northwest (of Atlanta) when
> we came to a golf course. When she saw the ponds and creeks
> she asked if we could go in. I told her: "No, honey, that's not

for black people, it's only for white folks." "But daddy," she said, "*Momma's* black, you and I are white!"

In Québec, instances of realization of the limiting effects of French ethnicity upon one's life goals form a strong part of the psychic baggage one carries into life. This realization, especially for Montréal children, begins early. One *must* learn English or prepare for a life of inferior status. In time, one discovers that inferior status is virtually assured, regardless of one's command of the English language, as one learns that an English monolingual has more avenues to advancement than a French bilingual. Here, too, it is often one's mother who cushions her child to the realities imposed by his ethnicity. Often a child is told, as was Pierre Vallières, that he was born for "un petit pain" in preparation for his later understanding that he is a member of "un petit peuple" trapped in a *cul-de-sac* of the globe. As awareness of the scope of the world grows, the horizons of childhood, as limitless as thought, become ever more limited in relation to the scope of one's imaginings. As statistical information clearly indicates, the French Canadian's chances of advancement to the upper ranks of Québec society are disproportionately slim. Most individuals must settle for factory positions or the rural life and, in turn, condition their children for repetition of their cycle.

For individuals of the rural areas of Québec these limitations of personal horizons resulting from French ethnicity, although felt, do not seem to assume even remotely the level of affect felt by those of the urban middle classes, whose influence is greatly reduced in a society within, and at the bottom of, a larger society. As a result, those of the middle class imbued with strong appreciation for upward mobility find their ethnicity most clearly debilitating in their attempts to carve out an acceptable life. The workers of Québec, however much many would prefer French employers, will serve some master in any event. Faced with foremen acting as French buffers in most large English corporations and especially with the fact that there is no significant English competition for the working-class positions in Québec society, the working class of the province may well feel a residual of bitterness toward the English, but it is probably as much a class as an ethnic bitterness. The present and aspiring middle classes, on the other hand, find themselves in direct conflict with the English for many of the class-validating positions of the society. For them the struggle for expansion of personal horizons is stripped of class content and laden with ethnic feeling. It is this group, feeling cramped in its horizons and in close struggle with the English, which has been the driving force behind Québec's "Quiet Revolution" and press toward separatism.

Unlike the castes of India, the Burakumin of Japan and the blacks of the United States, French Canadians find themselves unified by a common language distinct from that spoken by the dominant group and clustered in a territory in which they are clearly in the majority. Dependent as they are, and are likely to remain, upon an English-dominated economy, as an ethnic group, they are offered an avenue of escape which is denied to the other, true caste, groupings. Middle-class *québécois,* feeling the pinch of ethnicity, can, as George DeVos has indicated in a personal communication: "mobilize [themselves] both psychologically and politically in terms of [their] separateness—rather than fighting lower status from within the system" and create a separate national state, or they can organize collectively on the basis of their ethnicity to "seize economic and political power in particular areas or through economic specialization" and make the system, or a significant portion of it, their own. On the one hand, they can, in effect, perform the feat so desired by many American blacks[2] of "casting off" the upper caste or ethnic group and gaining psychological, if not economic, *épanouissement* within a separate society, or, on the other, perhaps gain economic as well as political control of the presently constituted plural society of Québec.

In Québec, as elsewhere, however, inferior ethnic status is not without its compensatory benefits. Increased expressed interpersonal solidarity, gains in the expressive sphere in the process of reciprocal exploitation, and insulation against failure serve to provide some compensation for restricted horizons.

From the shared sense of uniqueness, of descent from the same few ancestors and of a sense of solidarity born from the proximity of a dominant people, *québécois,* and French Canadians as a whole, feel themselves knit closely as a group apart, as "nous autres." Much as blacks sense solidarity and express it in the generalized use of "brother" and "sister" as forms of address, *québécois* guard "tu" as a way of expressing a closeness to those who share their lot as French isolated in North America.

Much as blacks have made expressive gains from "rhythm" in bygone days and "soul" today, French Canadians attribute to themselves a *joie de vivre,* a loose enjoyment of life, a "knowing how to live," distancing themselves positively from the colorless English.

Chief among all compensatory gains acquired by members of a devalued ethnic group is the potential role of knowledge of one's ethnic status in explaining the inevitable failure of everyman. Failure which may well be the result of personal inadequacy may easily be rationalized away on the basis of ethnic inadequacy. Ethnicity thus may be gathered close as a protective cloak which permits an individual the luxury of feeling that he cannot *really* fail, that any failure is due not so much to personal qualities or to a self-fulfilling prophecy limiting one's efforts as it is to discrimination from an entrenched group, a group which must bear the collective burden of blame for the inadequacies of the people whom it oppresses.

Urbanization and Ethnic Identity in Today's World
The apparently worldwide phenomenon of increased emphasis upon ethnicity is a paradoxical one. On the one hand, industrialization and urbanization, with consequent increase in proximity among ethnic groups, appear to have heightened ethnic awareness among the world's urbanized populations, while on the other, these processes have made peoples of different ethnic backgrounds more dependent upon each other than ever before. Examples, such as the European Economic Community, of the continuing integration of peoples into economic and political union to achieve the large-scale markets necessary to efficient industrial operation, come readily to mind. At the same time, one finds increasing tension between ethnic populations in the market and elsewhere as certain groups, such as Italians in Germany and Switzerland or East Indians in Britain, have entered to perform the lesser tasks of the society vacated by the indigenous peoples in the process

of industrial advancement and have thereby acquired pejorative stereotypes. Undoubtedly, the phenomena of industrialization and urbanization, with such by-products as increased ease of communication and travel, in the twentieth century carry with them centripetal factors, tending to bring peoples closer together, as well as centrifugal forces, tending to highlight differences and drive them farther apart.

The very presence of massive numbers of individuals unknown to each other in urban situations may act to increase levels of ethnic awareness. Typical urban interaction demands daily contact with individuals only a portion of whose individuality is likely to be revealed. More often than not in interethnic secondary encounters in the city, it is the ethnicity of the partners in the relationship that stands paramount. Faced as one is with the need to classify vast numbers of individuals on the basis of limited criteria, it is no wonder that ethnicity often tends to loom large in multiethnic urban settings. In contrast, at home, with one's relatives, in one's close neighborhood contacts—in short, in one's primary reationships—interaction is not limited to a one-dimensional level but can reflect the panorama of individual personalities.[3]

The phenomenon of increased ethnic typing in cities—a situation which often leads one raised in a small-town setting to feel that urbanism promotes a wearing of one's ethnicity upon one's shirtsleeves—may even be seen in regions with the most severe ethnic distinctions: caste and race. In the United States, a division between North and South has often been made in terms of actual level of racial contact between blacks and whites. Thus, it is often said—I think correctly so—that intimate personal knowledge between individuals of the different racial groups is more widespread in the South. A black, it is said in conventional folk wisdom, "may get as close as he wants in the South as long as he doesn't go too far [occupationally]. In the North, he can go as far as he wants as long as he doesn't get too close." Again and again, American blacks have commented on what they perceive to be a greater concern with one's individuality in the South and a less equivocal attitude in defining the barriers of sexuality and commensality in the South than in the North. The North–South division recognized in these folk analyses is not, I feel, the most significant division at hand. Granting that there are subcultural differences in the areas which may, for example, tend to emphasize greater frankness in the southern portion of the United States, the relevant factor in race relations appears more to be degree of urbanization than geography. Essentially, blacks in the North are concentrated in urban settings which drew them from lives of marginal, sharecropper or rural labor existence in the South. Blackness in the North is an urban phenomenon, seen most particularly in sharply delineated sectors quite properly known as "ghettos." In the South, on the other hand, where urbanization is itself a rather limited and recent phenomenon—only a few cities such as Atlanta or Birmingham may be seen to bear a true resemblance to the northern cities where most blacks have congregated—black populations have remained largely rural or small-town. Thus, despite the rigid caste barrier noted by Warner (1936) and others, interaction between blacks and whites is often such that much more is known of a certain individual than that he is "black" or "white." The individual carries with him a whole cluster of identifying features—chief of which may well be race in most interracial encounters—which tends to blunt the expressive segregation of the North. Analogous phenomena hold for other ethnic groups of high resolution in the South. Thus, on the all-important religious level, Jews and Catholics are likely to be identified. They are by no means segregated, however, and are expected to (and do) interact more or less without ethnic reference. Even groups of separate linguistic backgrounds, such as the "Cajuns" of Louisiana and East Texas and non-Miami-area Cubans, tend to interact with blacks and whites to a degree apparently impossible within an urban framework.

Increased levels of psychic intensity of ethnicity with urbanization are quite clearly manifest in French Canada, where urbanization, especially on the order of that of Montréal, has meant a virtual severing of wide-scale interethnic contact, which might cause ethnicity to sink below consciousness. As Marcel Rioux has noted in discussing the development of class and ethnic consciousness in Québec, the traditional nationalism of pre-industrial Québec was that of only a limited portion of the population. "One has the impression," Dumont and Rocher wrote, "to find oneself in the presence of a *nationalisme de collège;* it is almost necessary to have completed one's secondary studies to understand its concepts" (quoted in Rioux, 1965:30). In the past, "the mass was not especially conscious of being French Canadian or even from Québec, but of such and such a village, of such and such a parish" (30). Today, however, true ethnic nationalism is very much on the rise and there has been a significant increase in the intensity of French identity, especially in urban areas.[4]

Urbanization in Québec has not only brought the two peoples in closer physical proximity and conflict but has done so in such a fashion that it is the ethnic difference which overwhelms all other factors in interaction. The very process of industrialization and urbanization which brought Canada's two great peoples *en masse* to each other's presence may well contain the forces which will eventually rip them apart.

The turning away of such masses of French Canadians from the Canadian unity in the past decade has, however, set in motion concern among much of the English population to understand and cope with French aspirations in order to avoid separation. Just as in the United States, where cries of "black power," the presence of black separatist groups, and ghetto riots created a climate of serious concern among American whites, the rise of separatism as an acceptable political alternative in Québec has given great concern to English Canadians and was a major factor in the selection of Pierre Trudeau as Prime Minister, the "parachuting" of French Canadians into upper-level positions of responsibility within the government, and the formation of a Royal Commission on Bilingualism and Biculturalism. Paradoxically, at a time when many have suggested that the use, and even the learning, of English may be losing ground among Québec's French population, many English Canadians are suddenly finding French a language worth knowing.

First and foremost, the rise of the intensity of French identity in Québec must be seen as a phenomenon of industrial succession. The rural life of Québec's past, with its surplus of human offspring, coupled with the province's natural resources, made it an attractive site for foreign investment. As capital entered the province and provided the magnetism of employment, a largely rural province urbanized virtually overnight. This urbanization, long delayed by the special isolation of *québécois,* initially was one of direct English management and French labor as the traditional occupational preferences of the French middle and upper classes rendered them unsuitable to the new economic order. In time, the natural forces of industrialization have created a class capable and *ready* to assume control of its economy and thus in direct conflict with the English incumbents of the province's most valuable positions. Not surprisingly under these circumstances, the rising middle, managerial class, in seeking to rend the barriers which it faces, has adopted a strong nationalist outlook. It is to its advantage to promote the French language and even, if necessary, the severance of federal union, to gain economic control. Long held back by a rural social order, this class has burst through and today holds sway over the political sphere of the province. As such, the future of Québec and of Canada is in its hands. Either the process of industrial succession will continue its natural course with the eventual assumption of control of the province's economy by French Canadians, or Québec's emergent managerial class will utilize its access to the province's political machinery to wrest control through separation. The heart is separatist and the expressive sphere is thus largely lost to English Canadian attempts to engender pan-Canadian pride. Only the instrumental sphere remains. If the feeling that English dominance of this arena is inextricably associated with Canadian unity is allowed to continue its growth, then Canada's days as one nation are in short number.

EPILOGUE:

AN ANTHROPOLOGIST IN MONTRÉAL

The discipline of anthropology has been traditionally limited to the study of relatively small primitive groups, many of which have been in the rapid lane to extinction. As such, the field has developed as a kind of verbal formaldehyde for the preservation of the record of human diversity, of alternate techniques for dealing with the problems of human existence. From the anthropologist's concern with the preservation and comprehension of the life-ways of alien peoples have emerged the two techniques central to anthropological perspective: participant-observation and holistic grasp of the culture at hand.

The technique of participant-observation, largely developed by Bronislaw Malinowski, consists of prolonged habitation with the people under study and, to as great a degree as possible, immersion in their activities. In attempting the difficult process of becoming a member of an alien group, the anthropologist is, of course, condemned to a greater or lesser degree of failure. Learning the language and customs as well as following the life routine of a people will not make him truly one of their number. Yet, even destined to remain estranged, the anthropologist, in becoming a participant, learns to glance long into the perspective of his chosen group. He learns, if chance and his work serve him well, to gain a conception of what it *feels like* to be a member of the society, to comprehend the affect underlying social relationships, and hopefully to translate them to his own people in such a fashion that some of his glimpses may be shared.

Perhaps secondary in the minds of many anthropologists, but as important an implicit aspect of their training as the more openly noted technique of participant-observation, is the tendency of anthropologists to approach societies as wholes. Long accustomed to dealing with small-scale societies and imbued with a sense that the group they have under study is in a sense their own—as no other may ever meet these people again with the intention of preserving their unique heritage—anthropologists have been especially conscious of a need to master all aspects of social intercourse, including such diverse and intertwined sectors as language, technology, economy, religion, and kinship. Enhancing still further this holistic perspective is the fact that the very discipline of anthropology is an amalgam of lingusitics, archaeology, physical anthropology, and ethnology. Indeed, until quite recently, anthropologists were trained as "jacks-of-all-trades" of the human condition. Expected to be capable of transcribing and analyzing alien languages and reconstructing history from fragments of material culture, as well as commenting on variations in physical adaptation, it was not unknown for doctoral candidates in cultural anthropology to be presented with a bag of bones tò age, race, and sex at their oral examinations by some elder concerned with the maintenance of the discipline's integrity.

Born of a holistic tradition of participant-observation forged in tribal and village societies, what becomes of the anthropologist in the city or in what have become known as "complex" societies? With his training specific to smaller units, can he find a role in an urban setting, and, if so, what is it?

With the current expansion of interest in urban problems, many anthropologists have chosen to enter urban studies emphasizing the participant-observation approach and have limited accordingly the scope of their studies to sectors of the city with whose individuals they have come in direct contact. This approach, which can best be seen as an attempt to analyze city life on a tribal level, is exemplified in such works as Elliot Liebow's (1961) excellent study of the life style of black street-corner men in Washington, D. C., *Tally's Corner;* by the sociologist William F. Whyte's (1943) study of an Italian slum in *Street Corner Society;* and by the emerging concern with social networks in the work of Mitchell (1969) and other social anthropologists. An even more profound extension of the participant-observation formula in city life may be seen in the work of Oscar Lewis (1961, 1965), who chose to concentrate upon individual and family perspectives of lives lived in urban poverty and, in so doing, entered the realm of biographical narrative. Excellent as many of these studies are, the vividness of their portrayals has relied almost totally upon a transplanting of the participant-observation technique to the city and has been gained at the cost of a loss of holistic perspective. Emphasis upon the tribe or the family has given us only a fragment, albeit an engrossing one, of the urban mosaic.

The sacrifice of holistic perspective in urban anthropological studies has not, however, been a total one. The anthropologist W. Lloyd Warner (1963), in his dissection of an American city in the early 1930s, brought with him the perspective of a man only recently returned from a sojourn among an Australian aboriginal people. As such, his approach to the study of the city combined an emphasis upon gleaning an understanding of the reality of social interaction from that held "out there" in the minds of the city's inhabitants with a concern for grasping the reality of the city as a whole. For him, the parameters of study were not limited by the rigors of participant-observation but were extended to include all he could find of relevance to the problem at hand.

Studies of urban and complex societies today included under the rubric "urban anthropology" need not be undertaken at sacrifice to either of the field's major tenets, but may be built firmly on both, recognizing the necessary modifications which present themselves as exigencies of urban work. Anthropologists, especially in dealing with literate urban populations, must extend the scope of their concerns beyond the level of oral utterance and develop some of the skills of the social historian and analyst of current affairs. Urban work requires taking full cognizance of written materials, including historical studies, census materials, newspapers, journals, novels, and polemical texts, as well as a realization that these sources are of as great an importance, if not more so, than information gained from the lips of an informant. Written sources, valuable in themselves as an introduction into the preoccupations and shared beliefs of a people, are indispensable in the formation of a holistic conception of a diversified society. Yet, it would be a mistake for an anthropologist to content himself with this level of urban research to the exclusion of the vivid cultural anchoring which can only be gained through participant-observation. The urban anthropologist, especially in working within a society with a long history of literacy, must take written materials into account yet still learn the language of the group and enter into the society as fully as possible in order to gain the added dimension of emotional understanding of the lives and interactions of its members.

Despite all concern with guarding the cornerstones of anthropological perspective, one fact yet remains which demands compromise: the very scale of a city, with its diverse peoples and lifeways almost precludes total comprehension. Obviously a concession to its immensity must be made. If this concession is not to be at the expense of methodology, then it must be a limitation of the scope of topical concern. Anthropologists, as all others approaching urban aggregations, must yield to the immensity of the world before them and reduce their focus to some degree. Thus, while one may not limit himself to the study of one urban tribe, he must limit himself to the scope of some particular concern, whether it be economic, religious, or social, which preoccupies the city's peoples.

For these reasons, I chose to attempt to analyze the situation of ethnic conflict in Canada, with concentration upon the peoples of Montréal and Québec, as it concerns the French, English, and immigrant populations of that nation. In seeking to grasp the situation, I engaged in field work from April, 1970 until August, 1971, relying heavily upon mastery of the French language, especially as spoken in Québec, participation in as many different social milieus as possible—taking advantage of the anonymity of the city which permits the assumption of various conflicting roles with the relative certainty that one will not meet with dissonant exposure in any of them—and study of the voluminous written material of a fully literate society undergoing an information explosion common to Western society in general. In short, I attempted to combine the problems and pleasures of participant-observation with those of holism, always returning to the matter at hand: that of the struggle of two peoples for hegemony in a corner of the American continent.

In attempting to cope with a topical problem permeating a nation, I found myself called both in my research and presentation from the traditional accumulation of data and field interviews common to anthropological research toward the kind of approach fostered by the "culture at a distance" school of Benedict (1946) in culture and personality writings a generation ago. Unlike previous studies of this genre, however, mine is best characterized as a "culture at a distance *up-close*" study of French Canadian ethnicity. As a traditional anthropologist would, I immersed myself in study of the language and in conversations and other interaction with the people under study. Unlike a traditional anthropologist, however, these "interviews" did not and could not form the bulk of my research. They were, in a sense, guiding posts, points of orientation upon which I was able to lean to construct an understanding of social processes from the immensity of the data at hand and, as such, served to provide a factual basis for a larger understanding.

Much of the first several months of my stay in Québec, from approximately April until August of 1970, were spent in studying the language, in orienting myself to Montréal, and in making a field survey of Québec, New Brunswick, Nova Scotia, and Prince Edward Island. From September until the end of December, 1970, I attended daily a school located in a small village some twenty miles south of Montréal which was divided almost equally between newly arrived immigrants to Québec from various nations who were undertaking French (and in some cases English) language studies, and *québécois* farmers who were attending winter school sessions emphasizing the learning of "proper" Québec French for the gaining of eighth grade equivalency certificates. During this period, in addition to improving my French, I gained a detailed understanding of the problems of immigrants to Québec as well as the traumas faced by a rurally oriented *joual* speaker in the urban Québec of today. Also during this period, and especially after the October Crisis, my evenings were generally spent in coffee houses and taverns with French Canadian friends in discussion of the dilemmas faced by Québec and by *québécois*. Much of the period from January until I left Montréal in August of 1971 was spent living in one of the poorer French areas of eastern Montréal, extending my network of contacts and immersing myself ever more deeply in problems of French ethnicity in lengthy discussions with French Canadians and in concentrated analysis of written sources. Since completing my fieldwork, I have returned to Montréal several times and have followed Canadian events with keen interest, even during periods in which I was engaged in teaching and research activities in Malaysia and Thailand.

In approaching my analysis of the sitaution of ethnic conflict in Canada, which I have chosen to refer to as a "crisis in *blanc* and white," I have made quite explicit use of racial metaphor with the constant understanding that the problem of ethnicity in Québec is *not* a racial one in the sense in which the term "race" is ordinarily used. The crisis in *blanc* and white is exactly that: a crisis born of the contact of two peoples of similar racial stock, speaking different languages and living within two virtually separate societies. Although much of Canada's French-English situation is quasi-racial, in terms of its dynamics, the situation is one of two peoples, *of two nations,* one heavily disadvantaged in relation to the other, residing within the same political entity.

Much of my concern in viewing the French presence in Canada has been with understanding patterns of personal behavior, of stances of action and attitudes, which permit French Canadians to cope with an ethnicity devalued in terms of the Canadian political entity as a whole. How have French Canadians dealt with the English presence, especially in recent decades in which this presence has invaded virtually every aspect of their lives? What avenues of action are today available and how can these be seen to relate to the traditional context of the society? What conceptual value does an urban-rural perspective have in understanding these mechanisms of coping? These are some of the questions which I have attempted to answer.

NOTES

Chapter 1, French Canada in Crisis

1. All translations of French texts are those of the author.

2. I use the term *Québécois* to refer exclusively to French Quebekers.

Chapter 2, La Nouvelle France

1. Voltaire's description of Canada as "a few acres of snow" appeared in a reference to the Seven Years' (French and Indian) War in *Candide:* "Vous savez que ces deux nations sont en guerre pour quelques arpents de neige vers le Canada, et qu'elles dépensent pour cette belle guerre beaucoup plus que tout le Canada ne vaut" (1934:81). "You know these two nations are at war for a few acres of snow in Canada and that they are spending much more for this fine war than all of Canada is worth."

2. Bracq informed his readers that: "The dominant aim of the French in North America, at the outset, was not material gain, but the welfare of the red men—to educate, to christianize, and to save them" (1927:18), while Desrosiers et Fournet referred to Cartier's erection of a cross and celebration of mass upon his arrival as an act which showed "by this that the ambition of France was less to acquire great countries than to spread the name and love of Jesus Christ" (1911:25).

3. Champlain, himself, possessed initially by a desire to find a Northwest passage to the East and later by a wish to establish a lasting French colony in America, was apparently not primarily motivated by this factor.

4. Until 1628, New France operated under the *édit* of Nantes, and Catholics and Protestants were treated as equals. After that period, Protestants were

not expressly forbidden to live in the colony but restricted to commercial occupations and that only on condition that they renounce all external observances of their religion (Salone, n.d.:44). When one considers thé severe persecution of the Huguenots in France at the time, the fact that many would have certainly wished to escape this by emigrating to New France and the fact that the colony itself was desperately in need of settlers, the decision to exclude Protestants was undoubtedly a fateful one.

5. The actual return was delayed until March 29, 1632, after Charles had received the unpaid dowry of his French wife (Salone, n.d.:36; Wade, 1968:14).

6. In 1660, the colony, with a population of approximately twenty-five hundred, had only ten thousand *arpents*, or approximately fifteen thousand acres, under cultivation. Of its three settlements, Québec, Trois-Rivières, and Montréal, Montréal was primarily a trading post, Trois-Rivières a fort, and only Québec, with its seventy houses, could truly be considered a town. Fully forty years after its initial settlement, the colony was not, in Groulx's considered opinion, viable (1960:48-49). The failure of the settlement to become economically self-sufficient was largely due to the countervailing trends at work in the appointment of a company intent on gaining profit in the fur trade to also colonize the land. The latter goal and that of the French government was undermined by the fact that settling the land required the hard work of clearing it of trees and protecting one's farmstead from Indians, while the trade of trapper promised an easier, more financially rewarding life. As Reid comments: "Small wonder that twenty years after the founding of Quebec the Hébert house was the only real homestead in Canada; that no more than six families of twenty-six persons could be described as permanent residents; that not until 1628 was the soil first broken by a plowshare drawn by oxen, and flour ground by even an impromptu hand-worked mill; under company direction only one and one-half acres had been cleared around the Habitation and all provisions had to be imported from France...." (1945: 30-31).

7. A notable exception was that represented by the *coureurs de bois*, or fur trappers, with whom the Church found itself locked in continual battle to prevent their lax Catholicism and debauchery from influencing missionized Indians and more settled colonists. This group, composed as it was of drop-outs from the life centered around Church, farm, and family which the Church attempted to promote, provoked early clerical leaders to a frenzy. In 1681, between one third and one half of the adult male population had opted for the forest life, spending most of its time away from the colony, inter-marrying with the Indians, and apparently even assimilating to various Indian groups. Talon, in an attempt to put an end to their sexual desertion, which he apparently reasoned cost the colony dearly in progeny and was also probably a prime reason for difficulty in controlling this group, ordered all eligible men to marry within fifteen days after the arrival of the boats carrying women to the colony or to lose the right to hunt and trade (Salone, n.d.:

256-257). Efforts to control the *coureurs de bois* still failing, various regulations were promulgated in an effort to correct the situation, including one prohibiting more than a twenty-four hour stay in the woods without permission under pain of death (267). Although the penalty was later reduced by Louis XIV, it provides a clear indication of how desperate was the loss of such a large segment of the population to Indian life styles. The rewards of Church, farm, and family, later to be revered by future generations as an idyllic life, coupled with threats of fine and imprisonment, were still unable to prevent the loss of massive numbers of colonists to the colony—a loss which was to produce the amalgam of French and Indian know as the *métis*.

8. The formation of the population into militia companies, unlike in France, where wars were fought by professional armies, was primarily made necessary by constant threat of Indian attack.

9. Even today rural dwellers often speak of the *rang* they are from as a primary referent of spatial identification.

10. Deffontaines remarks that: "The profusion of fences is typical of the French Canadian countryside: it is not so in English Canada. One sometimes wonders at this preoccupation with fencing, a sort of obsession, as it were, to encompass each domain" (1953:13).

Chapter 3, Maintaining a French Identity in the British Empire

1. This argument rang hollow, however, as British ships were shortly dispatched to France to bring brandy and wine to the colony for sale by *British* merchants.

2. Richardson, the leader of the opposition, wrote to a London correspondent that: "unhappily the Session commenced with a determined spirit of Party amongst the French members, for they had a private meeting, at which it was decided that an Englishman should on no account be elected speaker. We wished to conciliate and be moderate, and that the choice should fall on whoever might be best qualified to fill the Chair, from ability, habits of public business, and knowledge in both Languages, without distinction of Country. For this purpose three Grant, McGill and Jordan, were proposed, of which they might select one the most consonant to the general wish, but all was to no purpose, right or wrong, a Canadian must be the man, no matter however ill qualified; and the election fell on Mr. Panet, a Quebec lawyer, whose ideas and talents were never calculated for anything beyond the quibble routine and formality of a Court of Common Pleas, such as this Country has hitherto experienced (Kennedy 1930:212-213).

3. A project which was finally achieved in 1840 after the Rebellion.

4. Interestingly enough, none of the Rebellion's major leaders were executed, although twelve of the rank and file were put to death and sixty banished. Indeed, Papineau later returned to sit in the Canadian Parliament, and four of his followers became Prime Ministers of Québec.

5. Here Durham perceptively noted that: "The national hostility has not

assumed its permanent influence till of late years, nor has it exhibited itself everywhere at once. While it displayed itself long ago in the cities of Quebec and Montreal, where the leaders and masses of the rival races most speedily came into collision, the inhabitants of the eastern townships, who were removed from all personal contact with the French, and those of the district below Quebec, who experienced little interference from the English, continued to a very late period to entertain comparatively friendly feelings towards those of the opposite races" (24).

6. Riel was the leader of the *métis* ("half-breeds") of Manitoba, who in their dominance of the area's fur trade and their agricultural settlements on the *Rivière Rouge* were seen by the residents of Ontario immediately after Confederation to threaten a French encirclement. The area was forcibly annexed in 1870, and an uprising ensued which temporarily prohibited its incorporation. After persuasion by priests to surrender and compete for office, Riel surrendered and gained office, but was denied seating in Parliament and forced to flee to refuge in Québec from Ontario, which had announced a reward for his capture. After a second attempt to establish a *métis* state in 1885 to the west of Manitoba in Saskatchewan, Riel was captured and executed. His hanging exacerbated wounds of suspicion and today his name ranks with, if not above, the memory of the *patriotes* of 1837-38.

Chapter 4, Urbanization and Industrialization

1. ". . . it's a rough country, here. Why stay?"

2. The 1666 census of New France was the earliest expression of the modern census in which name, age, sex and other information was gathered for every individual in the colony. The concern of the French colonial authorities was such that after the conquest there was a hiatus of almost a century before as accurate and detailed information was recorded by British authorities.

3. Henripin's estimates were based upon the work of Mgr. Tanguay, who, in the latter nineteenth century, gathered approximately 1.2 million certificates of baptism, marriage, and burial, and reconstructed 120,000 families. Owing to the reliability of the Church records, his projections for the society as a whole are probably extremely accurate.

4. Henripin provides the following table reporting the number of infants of from 0-4 years of age reported for married women between the ages of fifteen and forty-four years in Ontario and Québec:

Year	Ontario	Québec	English Ontarians	French Québécois
1681	—	—	—	1.71
1734	—	—	—	1.45
1851	1.50	1.67		
1861	1.58	1.59		
1871	1.33	1.41		
1881	1.19	1.38		
1891	1.02	1.38		
1931	0.71	1.14	0.66	1.27
1941	0.60	0.90	0.57	1.05
1951	0.77	1.02	0.72	1.10

(Henripin, 1960:163)

Unfortunately, comparative information is lacking for the years 1760–1850, when all evidence, from Québec at least, seems to indicate that the differential between Québec French and Ontario English would have been greater.

5. While emigration to the United States drew from both English and French populations, immigration, consisting either of immigrants from the British Isles or immigrants from other European nations who later became absorbed into the English community, provided virtually no addition to the French populace.

As can be readily seen from the table, the population gains which the French wrought were neutralized by the effects of immigration and emigration. Only during brief periods of immigration decline due to war or depression was the trend temporarily reversed.

6. One of these areas, the *Cantons de l'Est* of Québec, knew a privileged status in which its English majority was granted permanent political over-representation. While its privileged status has continued to be a source of rancor among *québécois*, recent years have seen an influx of French Canadians and the elimination of English control in most of the area.

Although the very earliest settlers to this region south of the St. Lawrence plain were French, the English Loyalists who arrived at the end of the American Revolutionary War soon overwhelmed the few French in the area. From 1792 until 1812, most of the settlers were Loyalists and others from New England anxious to exercise their option to purchase twelve hundred acres, which they then assigned to the leader of the group of which they were a member. Subsequent English settlement, from 1814 until 1830, mainly consisted of settlers from Great Britain who had chosen to establish themselves in the Townships rather than with the mass of their number in Ontario. In 1833, the British-American Land Company was formed. Purchasing 1,324 square miles of crown land in townships at bargain rates, it became a major agent in retarding the French invasion of the region and in forcing French Canadians to turn to the factories of New England for a livelihood. Eventually, when the French gained the clear control of the area which they enjoy today, they gained it largely as a result of emigration by the English of the region to the urban centers of the United States and Upper Canada (Masters, 1967:130–159).

7. In an article entitled "Le Québec d'en-bas . . . ou la fin d'un beau rêvee en Nouvelle-Angleterre," which appeared in the Saturday supplement *Perspectives* of *La Presse*, the life of the ancestors of those who left "for a season" is analyzed in detail. To the author's dismay he found that the progeny of the four hundred thousand who left Québec during the last half of the nineteenth century under the pressure of the American English majority and the deep feelings of linguistic inadequacy (contained in such phrases as "sa langue que c'était du 'French Canuck,' c'est-à-dire quelque chose de bâtard . . ."), began to frequent English schools and have English friends. In asking directions in French of "un Pariseau, un Lessard ou un Bélanger" he was astounded to be answered in English or in a French which was a literal translation of English phrases. As a final note of faithlessness, the author cites Mlle. Diane Dupont, who told him (in French): "If I ever have children, they won't have French first names. I don't have many friends among the Franco-Americans. Why? I don't really enjoy seeing them, it doesn't do anything for me. The Americans have more to teach me. I like Québec. I was there last year, but I wouldn't want to live there" (Beaulieu, 1970:6).

8. Faucher and Lamontagne have suggested that New England, rather than Ontario factories, received the surplus migrants as: "The surplus population could not easily move toward Ontario because the absence of technical knowledge in iron works would have made it very difficult to find employment there. On the other hand, New England needed additional manpower, for its labour force was moving to the East-Central states" (1953:263).

9. Certainly Liebig's "law of the minimum," in which it was determined "that organisms may be controlled by the weakest link in the ecological requirement" (Odum, 1963:65) has direct reference to the end of the agricultural regime in Québec.

10. Of the ten major industrial employers of Québec, in 1969: Northern Electric (Canada), Alcan (Canada-USA), Dominion Textile (Canada), Canadian International Paper (USA), Domtar (Canada), Consolidated Bathurst (Canada), Noranda (Canada), Canadair (USA), Price (Canada-Great Britain), United Aircraft (USA), none are owned by French Canadians. Only at the eleventh rank does the first sign of *québécois* ownership surface with Bombardier Ltée.—the makers of "Ski-doo" (Parti Québécois, 1970:18).

11. When a French Canadian businessman does seek outside capital, he is often hampered by a general reluctance of French Canadians to invest in businesses, preferring instead to place their savings in government bonds and real estate.

12. I found, in purchasing items from French Canadian businessmen, that tactics which brought at the best only marginal returns among American and English Canadian businessmen often scored quite heavily, so that even a fair-traded motorcycle, for example, reaped accessory after accessory in dealings with a French Canadian dealer, while an English Canadian stipulated quite clearly conditions which fell far short. Another tactic which produced high

returns—as a mechanic's "throwing in" free parts and even an on-the-spot renegotiation and reduction of a television repair bill—was to begin interaction in English rather than French and at some point in the conversation (transactions often tended to be longer and more readily savored with French businessmen) change into French. Invariably, command of the situation shifted in my favor, and the outcome of transaction moved toward what seemed from my perspective to be my maximum benefit. In one instance, soon after my arrival in Montréal, involving the purchase of lumber, the several workers in the yard spoke continuously in *joual* among themselves while I, understanding but little of their conversation, spoke to one of them in English. Eventually, everything was readied for my departure except for sandpaper, which was nowhere to be found. When the worker spoke to his boss about it, indicating that he was going to give up his search for the paper, I quickly entered the conversation in French and explained that I really needed it. The owner, who was obviously very busy, left his desk and joined in the search. After finding the type I needed, he gave me a number of large sheets whose cost amounted to perhaps 10 percent of the total order and indicated: "C'est gratuit."

13. Bilodeau, *et al.*, (1971), in their *Histoire des Canadas*, refer to this period as "le début de toutes les industries dont le profit reposait sur la main-d'oeuvre à bon marché, le 'cheap labor,' et non sur l'exploitation des ressources naturelles. . . ." (455).

14. In the region of Lac Saint-Jean, the initial industrialization was carried out at the hands of French Canadian as well as English Canadian pulp and paper manufacturers. At the beginning of the twentieth century, however, the immense capital outlays needed for the hydroelectric development of the Saguenay forced an appeal to the American tobacco industrialist Duke, who later sold his interests to permit the Aluminum Company of Canada to build its major refinery making use of the inexpensive hydroelectric resources of the region (Bilodeau, *et al.*, 1971:534). Bergeron sees the flooding of the farmlands produced by this hydroelectric development as symbolic: "The *Canayens* saw the farmlands which they had cleared only with great pain and misery disappear under the effect of industrialization . . . [forcing] the *habitant* to become the employee of these same great companies which had come to steal his land and resources" (1970:186).

15. One outstanding exception is Hydro-Québec, the state-owned electric power corporation, which was created by the liberal party's nationalization of the English-owned electric industry of Québec (chiefly Shawinigan Water and Power) during René Lévesque's reign as Québec's Ministre des Ressources Naturelles.

16. This article, which emphasized the role of the French Canadian upper class as well as that of the English in exploitation of the province, is illustrated with an anemic-looking hen with caption "poule écoeurée" ("fed-up chicken").

17. The reign of Maurice Duplessis continued to favor industry despite

the fact that in his first election (1936) he campaigned with the slogan "Down with the trusts." His violent "anti-communist" campaigns, which were set off in full heat by strikes, his willingness to keep a stable of corrupt ministers, and his easy bargaining with the resources of the province—as his letting out of the Ungava iron deposits to Cleveland's Hanna Company—made his regime an industrial investor's dream. The provincial policy of active solicitation of foreign capital was also very much in evidence as Premier Robert Bourassa sought to fulfill his campaign promise to put "Québec au travail" by finding 100,000 new jobs by the end of 1971. His efforts to secure foreign capital carried him on a tour of European capitals and numerous trips to New York—including one in the midst of the October, 1970, crisis to attempt to reassure nervous investors. He fell far short of his goal of 100,000 and attributed this largely to the added caution of investors in the wake of the crisis and, by innuendo, to the growth of the separatist Parti Québécois.

18. However, the Catholic unions did not always avoid strikes at all cost, as in the 1937 Sorel Maritime Industries strike, the Louiseville textile strike which was broken up by the Provincial Police, and the famous Asbestos strike of 1949, which shocked both the clergy and the province with the spectre of the massive clubbings given the strikers by Duplessis' Provincial Police. From this moment, when it became clear that the "nationalist" government would tolerate no interference by its own workers with American investors—even when the industry in question involved a precious natural resource whose scarcity guaranteed investment capital in any case—Québec unions, though not as demanding as their American counterparts, were no longer docile partners of management (Trudeau, et al., 1956).

19. (Also see note 6, above.) The area known as the Eastern Townships, or les Cantons de l'Est, extends from the St. Lawrence lowlands to the American border and includes the following fifteen "protected" counties: Arthabaska, Bagot, Beauce, Brome, Compton, Dorchester, Drummond, Frontenac, Megantic, Mississquoi, Richmond, Shefford, Sherbrooke, Stanstead, and Wolfe. The region has an area of 9,120 square miles, approximately 77 percent of which is occupied. In 1961 its total population was about six hundred ten thousand (Masters, 1967:131).

20. The only active role which English-speaking individuals played in the community from the latter half of the nineteenth century on was that of outside entrepreneur entering the community to develop industries whose existence required the ready proximity of forests (tanneries, smelting furnaces, sawmills). As Hughes noted: "[although the investment and direction was often English] . . . the growth was always French. . . . It has, indeed, been the function of the English in Quebec to create points of activity to which the French population is rallied" (31; emphasis mine).

21. Other Drummondville industries producing for outside markets were: (1) a cotton goods company whose staff totaled 600 and which had home offices in Montréal and the U.S. The manager of the company was English Canadian with the corporation's only other English employees being its

technical advisor and two office clerks; (2) a silk-finishing company managed by an American, with its home office in the U.S. Of its 350 employees, there were a total of seven Americans, all in executive and supervisory positions; (3) a company manufacturing hosiery, which counted among its 300 employees seven English-speaking individuals, among whom five were Americans (executive, supervisory and maintenance people) and two were English Canadians (head dyer and assistant); (4) a silk weaving company managed by an Alsatian-American, employing 150 individuals, among whom the bookkeeper, practical millwright, and cloth inspector were English Canadian, the warping foreman, Polish-American, and the weaving foreman, New England French Canadian; (5) a lumber company employing 100 individuals, which, unlike all of the previously mentioned corporations, had its home office in Montréal rather than in the U.S. Its manager and secretary were English Canadian; (6) a company producing paper novelties having its home office in the U.S. and counting only its manager, designer, and several others among its non-French employees of a staff totaling 60; (7) a rubber heels manufacturer employing 50, managed by an English Canadian, and having its home office in Montréal; (8) a pencil company employing 40 with headquarters in the U.S. and its manager of Austrian-American stock; (9) a foundry employing 40 managed by a French Canadian with its headquarters in Drummondville; (10) a paper box manufacturer employing 30 managed by a French-Canadian with its home office in Drummondville. Of a total of 4,446 individuals, overwhelmingly French Canadian, employed in Drummondville, only 70 (1.6 percent) were employed in companies directed by members of the French ethnic group (Hughes: 48, 220).

22. The turnover rate among this staff was very low, which undoubtedly stymied French Canadians who hoped for advancement (52). Hughes notes that in any event: ". . . it is evident that French Canadians as a group do not enjoy that full confidence of industrial directors and executives which would admit them easily to the inner and higher circles of the fraternity—and fraternity it is—of men who run industry. This situation prevails throughout the province of Quebec. . . . The French Canadians of our community well know that no major executive of the local industries is 'one of our boys' who made good. A newspaper of the region once reported at length and with pride the appointment of a French assistant manager in an industry. Inquiry revealed that he would, at best, be rated as a departmental shop foreman. His appointment was one of a series of actions by which effective management of the plant was removed to company headquarters in another city. Yet that small appointment was news. It was as if someone had announced that the French Canadian could now hope for the higher positions in industry" (54). This pattern of exclusion of French from positions of major responsibility is clearly demonstrated in the mill in question, as the sole French Canadian member of the staff above foreman was the company physician, a man whom Hughes described as having "many other irons in the fire—a thriving medical practice, local property, family and political connections" (50), and whose appointment as physician to the labor force—he was not a personal physician

to the staff—was made primarily for diplomatic reasons.

23. Statements such as this were usually accompanied with the following stereotypes: " 'The French have to be told what to do and therefore cannot be trusted with jobs requiring initiative and the meeting of crises.' 'They are good routine workers but are inclined to take things easy if left to themselves.' 'They are so jealous of one another that they do not yield to the authority of one of their own number. " (55). While these same stereotypes still abound, even among French themselves, perhaps the most common argument against promotion of French Canadians today is that they are unwilling to accept relocation outside of Québec and thus forfeit the opportunity to gain the type of experience required by today's multi-national corporations. While this is certainly true to a marked degree, as few French Canadians feel at home even in other areas of Canada, the frequency and fervor with which this argument is offered as justification for non-promotion of French Canadians makes one wonder whether this is not just a rationalization born of a felt need to eschew the more obvious forms of ethnic discrimination of the past.

24. One of these was the sales manager for a large automobile agency owned by a French Canadian. His large number of French kin, his bilingualism, and his family's long background in the area stood him in good stead with his French customers, while the tendency of the English to trust their own in things mechanical granted him easy access to this market. The other instance was of an English assistant to the French manager of the town's local Woolworth's (72-73).

25. Foreign enterprises located in Québec account for 51.5 percent of the total exports of the province, and the province's English Canadian enterprises for 44 percent, while companies owned by French Canadians produce only 4.5 percent of the total exports of Québec (Rioux, 1969:124).

26. Blishen, in constructing an occupational class scale for Canada which combined income and number of years of education, found that the English, who represented 49 percent of the population at the 1951 census, were heavily over-represented in the upper classes and under-represented in the lower classes, while for the French, who numbered 29.5 percent of the population, the situation was reversed:

Socioprofessional Classes	Percent Total Population	Percent British	Percent French
Class 1	100	66.3	18.7
Class 2	100	54.0	26.2
Class 3	100	64.5	19.4
Class 4	100	59.6	22.8
Class 5	100	51.8	26.5
Class 6	100	42.2	36.8
Class 7	100	38.7	35.0
Average Percentage	100	49.0	29.5

(Blishen in Dofny and Rioux, 1962:313)

27. Thus, 205 of the directors of Montréal's banks are English, while only 44 are French; 106 English are found in the directorates of the city's Transport and Communications industries, compared with only 7 French. The English–French ratio for other important industries in the city: Iron and Steel, 90 English, 4 French; non-ferrous metals, 44 English, 3 French; non-metallic minerals, 27 English, 7 French; chemical products, 50 English, 1 French; pulp and paper, 83 English, 11 French (Dofny and Rioux, 1962: 315).

28. In the Foreign Service, only 17 percent of the staff at the upper levels were Francophones in 1965, when the "parachuting" of mission heads began, in which French Canadians were brought into the department and placed in leading posts by Orders-in-Council or through political appointments. Because of traditional low recruitment of Francophones, however, their proportion remains markedly low at other levels, and the Embassy and the various consulates of France were the only foreign missions where French was used to a significant extent (RRCBB, vol. III:145–146). As one trade union leader remarked of a "trip he took as a member of a labor delegation to a non-French, non-English country: our hosts 'knew they were welcoming French Canadians. They saw to it that wherever we went, we were greeted by someone who spoke French. And so, throughout the country, we could get along in French—*everywhere, that is, except at the Canadian Embassy*'" (Preliminary Report of the RRCBB:38–39).

Chapter 5, Crisis in Blanc and White

1. Reference to a bill introduced in the provincial assembly by the *l'Union Nationale* government of Jean-Jacques Bertrand in 1969, which sought to permit parents to choose which language their children would be educated in. The bill, which seemed to many *québécois* to be a prescription for hastening assimilation as immigrants were certain to take advantage of its passage by sending their children overwhelmingly to English schools, caused a major fervor in the province. Mass marches in the streets of Montréal and Québec, student strikes, and province-wide meetings of labor and businessmen were organized against the bill without effect. The Official Language Act of 1974, however, limited parental rights to educate their children in English to those children whose native language was English or who could pass an English proficiency exam before entering school.

2. The April 1 issue of *La Presse* brought a favorable response to Landry's letter from Gaston Gagnier, of Verdun, who described himself as "several times a grandfather." After praising Landry's courage for speaking up and noting that "it is reassuring to see that some students still exist who haven't lost their sense of reality," he adds that, while it would be unfortunate to see French disappear "after two centuries of survival, not to say stagnation," he, too, agrees that "in 50 years, and (perhaps) even before that, French will become a leisure art much as learning English or to play the piano and paint were in *la Belle époque*." Over the years, we've had our patriots, Gagnier continues, but what have all "ces beaux esprits" brought us: "le ghetto québécois."

3. It is worth noting here that, although the tenor of the letter is genuine, the signature "Yves Landry" may well be a *nom de plume,* as the author identifies himself with the same surname (of Norman-French and originally Scandinavian origin) as the author of a treatise on the same issue, . . . *et l'assimilation, pourquoi pas?,* Louis Landry (1969), who suggests that the only logical solution to Québec's problem is that which has always been dismissed as unthinkable—assimilation. Landry, who is married to an English Canadian, has moved from the drawing board to the bedroom and dedicated his book "à Marthe, ma souverainiste intime, Mère de mes six assimilés."

4. Rioux, referring to Miner (1939), notes that wider recognition of kinship almost certainly existed in the past, and concludes from his own study of the Acadian community of Chéticamp, Cape Breton Island, that it continues to exist in isolated and/or rural areas of French Canada today. In Chéticamp, he found that twenty surnames make up 90 percent of the parish population (such limited patronymic variety also being the rule for rural Québec), so that in order to identify an individual one has usually to name his father and grandfather. Thus: "Paul Chiasson would not be recognized by anybody unless he is called Paul-à-Timothée-à-Joseph. Sometimes the fourth generation has to be reached before the individual is properly identified. . . . When somebody phones, he should properly identify his party by saying, Placide-à-Paul-à-Lubin Aucoin. A local Acadian weekly, published in New Brunswick, prints a social column about Chéticamp, often omitting the genealogical ties of the individuals. The result is that practically nobody knows which individuals the newspaper is talking about" (382). One of Rioux's informants, who acted as a *défricheur de parenté* ("kinship clearer-upper") for his family, apparently orally possessed a kinship recognition vocabulary of some two thousand individuals, including members of his patrilineage back to 1785 and many secondary relatives, which was verified as far as possible through local parish records. Other *défricheurs* apparently possessed a similar capability, while Rioux estimates that the average individual knows about five hundred.

5. Indeed, a major factor limiting spatial mobility northward or westward among southern whites is undoubtedly the felt presence of a linguistic barrier between the two regions.

6. This similarity can, of course, be carried too far. Québec is not a region of North America "comme les autres"—its language is French, and thus its very structure, however anglicized many of its French Canadian critics at times claim it is, renders it quite different from English. As Gilles Constantineau, in another recent *Le Devoir* article, has shown, Québec is plagued by American television commercials "dubbed in" in French, often in too literal and thus faulty translations, as well as by French commercials which speak to another world in language which at best sounds stilted to Québec ears and at worst is incomprehensible (*Le Devoir,* 14 février 1972:6).

7. "Focus." *Point de Mire,* incidentally, was also the title of a program once presided over by René Lévesque on the French-language television network, *Radio-Canada.*

8. The Commission, in its preliminary report, indicated that "most young people [they had spoken with in a series of public meetings] felt that the

whole system should be abolished, once and for all, and that the province should separate from the rest of Canada."

9. The following chart was compiled by the Royal Commission on Bilingualism and Biculturalism, giving the average total income of Canada's non-agricultural labor force by ethnic origin and knowledge of the official languages. Note that one of the highest incomes of all is earned by the English monolingual Quebeker:

Canada

Ethnic Origin	Knowledge of Official Languages	Distribution (%)	Average Income
British	(Overall Average)	100.0	$4,852
	English only	93.2	4,758
	French only	0.3	2,783
	Both	6.5	6,284
French	(Overall Average)	100.0	3,880
	English only	6.4	4,017
	French only	36.5	3,097
	Both	57.1	4,350

Québec

Ethnic Origin	Knowledge of Official Languages	Distribution (%)	Average Income
British	(Overall Average)	100.0	$5,918
	English only	53.7	6,049
	French only	2.2	2,783
	Both	44.0	5,929
French	(Overall Average)	100.0	3,880
	English only	0.4	5,775
	French only	45.8	3,107
	Both	53.8	4,523

(After RRCBB, vol. 111:21)

Much of the wage increase noted among French who are bilingual may be the result of educational factors rather than bilingualism *per se*, as there is a strong association between level of education and bilingualism, at least in Montréal:

Percent of Males in the Labor Force who are Bilingual by Education

Ethnic Group	Years of School Completed				
	None	Elementary 1+ Years	H.S., 1-2 Years	H.S., 3-5 Years	University, 1+ Years
British	41	44	39	38	42
French	43	58	79	89	94
Other	19	35	53	52	61

(After Lieberson, 1970:140)

10. The criteria of use and proficiency are probably subordinated to number of years of "studying French" when the Montréal anglophone himself provides the answer to the census questions concerning his capacity to communicate in French, whereas French (bilinguals) tend to utilize the criterion of actual usage.

11. While his complaint that a knowledge of English is required in Montréal is by no means true, it has effectively served—or perhaps provided a rationale—to block his migration to the city.

12. By which I mean the degree of preoccupation with a given status or phenomenon. Thus, the psychic intensity of one's sense of mortality is increased during an earthquake, and American Blacks tend to evidence a greater psychic intensity of racial consciousness than do whites as racial categorization is seen to impinge constantly upon their lives.

13. Referring to previous promises made by the King government not to conscript men for overseas service.

14. The elimination of Québec English from this figure would yield a "no" vote among québécois of approximately 85 percent. Thus, 85 percent of québécois voted "no," while 80 percent of the population of the other provinces voted "yes."

15. I am quite aware that behavior which I have here attributed to a decrease in psychic intensity of French identity in rural areas may also be largely attributable to general rural-urban differences. However, in the city French interaction with a French stranger is much more likely to take place, often with the kind of informality characteristic among American Blacks, than with an English stranger. While the same is also true in non-urban areas, the shift is, in my opinion, more than can be accounted for by rural-urban differences. In fact, in the city, I became so habituated to identifying myself as an "anglais" that I initially missed the point of a comment one farmer made to another: "He is English, but he has lived in the United States." To him, the "Anglais/Français" divisions of the city were solely designations of nationality.

16. Regions are ordered according to approximate degree of urbanization, except in the case of the final category, which is a residual one.

17. Division of Montréal Island into Eastern and Western regions serves as a rough division of wealth and ethnicity. The Eastern section of the city itself is often referred to as "le ghetto français," while the wealthier English of the city are clustered in the West.

18. A proportionate representation in the legislature would have yielded twenty-five seats for the P.Q. Because of the heavy concentration of its votes in urban areas and disproportionate representation of rural areas of the province, its heavy vote yielded few seats.

19. He is referring here to the fact that French society is closed to English in general and not because of the fact that he is Jewish. French Canadians frequently evidence strong traits of anti-Semitism, and it is not unusual to hear the phrase "maudit juif" even among professionals.

20. Vallières, in remarking upon the importance of the milieu in which he

was raised, that of greater Montréal, upon his thought noted: "This book is not really the product of an individual but of a milieu. The milieu is that of contemporary Québec lived in Montréal and the metropolitan region. A *Gaspésien* would probably have written an entirely different book" (Vallières, 1968:22).

21. In guise of illustration, it is worth quoting from Desrosiers and Fournet's *La race française en Amérique,* a text designed for history courses taught in the schools of the province of Québec:

> Some say the French race should disappear in America. One even hears that it would benefit it to fashion its own death; and certain quarters are ready to vote her a first-class funeral. This is the Anglo-Saxon race which feels it should absorb the French race. Is it even necessary to mention this fact at this point? Many among us favor the absorption of one race to the detriment of the other. What good is it, they ask, to prolong a struggle whose eventual result can only be fatal for us? We lie down in the grave while our rights are being sacrificed without anything in return in Manitoba, in the western provinces and everywhere in our own province besides. . . .
>
> Are the pessimists right to throw up their arms and to hope no longer in divine Providence, which has provided us until this day with the miracle of conserving us and which desires to continue to do so if we can leave our stupor and prove that we are still capable of mounting a serious effort toward the future?
>
> These pages have for their goal the reawakening of energy and courage by showing in a simple exposé what is, at the present time, the vitality of the French race in America. . . . Its history forms one of the most beautiful pages that one can offer for the admiration of our contemporaries (Perrier in Desrosiers et Fournet, 1911:v–vii).

22. See DeVos and Wagatsuma (1967) for a detailed discussion of caste in Japan and in cross-cultural perspective.

23. The major form of extended black and white sexual relationships known in America—that between an upper-class southern white (in antebellum days, the slave owner) and his Negro mistress—seems to have virtually disappeared. Its appearance today is rare and usually confined to elderly, rural or small-town white males who continue to cling to the plantation system which continued to exist in all its essential social manifestations until the industrialization of the South in recent years. Such white male–Negro female relationships carried only a minimal sense of sexual pollution for the male and were, in fact, extolled in folklore. Negro male-white female encounters, on the other hand, have always been absolutely proscribed. Other than the obvious desire to maximize one's access to females while preventing competitors from doing the same, one cannot help but agree with Berreman (1967:316) that there is a sense that males can cleanse themselves of an external pollution in these encounters while for a female the pollution is much deeper.

24. The original French conveys the quality of her refusal better than can any translation: "elle refuse d' 'allumer le flambeau de l'hyménée aux cendres fumantes de (sa) malheureuse patrie" (40).

25. Of several literary treatments of the subject cited by Carisse, in only one, *le calvaire de Monique* (1953) ("The tribulation of Monique"), was a marriage actually consummated. The disaster precipitated by this decision to cross ethnic and religious lines in marriage has its ultimate proof when Monique's son, himself, marries an English Protestant. In another more recent novel, *le couteau sur la table* (1964), the French Canadian protagonist kills his English mistress when she leaves him to take advantage of the privileges of her class after having shared his bohemian existence (Carisse, 1969: 40). While poorly adjusted French–English couples come readily to my mind and of the only two incidents of incest brought to my attention in Québec both involved mixed marriages, it is difficult to be certain how aberrant couples involved in these marriages are. Ailene Aellen, in an unpublished master's thesis, "Second Generation Effects of Mixed French–English Marriages," has suggested that the children, at least, produced by these marriages are not maladjusted. "The mixed English–French Canadian," she concludes, "does not feel that the world is a disorganized and chaotic place, and apparently considers it quite natural to express his loyalty toward both ethnic groups. . . . He is not [even] more cosmopolitan than his ethnic fellows in spite of his ethnic background" (1967:106).

26. The term "British" belies the level of "English" endogamy, as many of those classified as Dutch, German, or of other ethnic origins meet the folk criteria for, and consider themselves, "English."

27. In Québec, the differential is 1.6 percent, with 96.4 percent of French males and 94.8 percent of French women marrying endogamously (RRCBB, vol. IV:294).

28. This by no means exhausts the possible explanations, as matters of sexual preference and intraethnic boredom may enter as well as concern for future offspring (see discussion of assimilation below.)

29. One dentist explained to me that although he, himself, refused requests to remove entire sets of teeth, a girl who chose not to find another dentist still found it possible to thwart him by refusing fillings and having each tooth pulled out independently as it became abscessed. Eventually, in one case he related to me, he was forced to decide between continued tooth-by-tooth extraction and removal of all teeth, some salvageable, in order to insert a proper dental plate. He yielded to reality and chose the professionally unappealing alternative of complete extraction.

30. It should be noted, however, that the tension of being almost passable within the larger society, but not quite, may be more frustrating than clearly bearing an outcaste stigma.

31. Even police officers making *une descente* ("a raid") give their orders in the "tu" form: "Montre-moé tes papiers, pis vide tes poches." ("Show me your identification then empty your pockets.")

32. Usage of the term is adopted from Braroe (1965).

33. "Esoteric" stereotypes are stereotypes held by members of a group concerning themselves, while "exoteric" stereotypes are those held by members of a group toward another group (Jansen, 1959). The combination and importance of the concepts esoteric-exoteric with that of reciprocal exploitation can be seen in the matching exoteric (white) and esoteric (black) stereotypes of black sexual superiority and intellectual inferiority. In accepting the positive former premise, blacks find a degree of compensation for the latter negative premise, which is inevitably coupled with it.

34. The French, of course, view themselves as superior lovers, and one of the most valuable goals of a French Canadian male is to convince an attractive "anglaise" of the validity of this stereotype. Although English partners have some value in sexual matters, their performance is constantly belittled.

In a recent movie, *Après-Ski*, set in the Laurentian mountains north of Montréal, the French ski instructors who star hop from bed to bed dispensing pleasure generally, but most of all to an American woman on vacation with her husband. Her husband, portrayed, as always, as a Texan, is called away suddenly on business, permitting his wife to seek enjoyment among French males. His sudden return surprises his wife *in flagrante*, and her lover barely manages to escape discovery. Fool and cuckold that he is, he shows no awareness of anything out of the ordinary. Instead, at the moment he enters the room, he unzips his pants and says: "Honey, I'm back."

Intercourse with French females is minimized and, indeed, the most delectable of them spurns the repeated efforts of the various instructors to gain intimacy, as she prefers girls. In a long, protracted segment which seems to be the focal point of the film (which, incidentally, was the talk of Montréal), she and another nude woman engage in a slow motion pillow fight to the tune of a popular song.

Another "put-down" of English sexual adequacy can be seen in the following joke told me by a French Canadian, which also contains an interesting esoteric perspective:

> A group of loggers had been in the woods north of La Tuque for months without seeing a woman. When the chance came to join a group going into town for the weekend to buy some stores and have a couple of nights on the town, Jacques leapt at the opportunity. Once in town, they all checked into separate hotel rooms to bathe before hitting the taverns. To his great surprise, Jacques found a naked woman lying in his bed waiting for him and immediately crawled under the covers to join her. When the others came to get him, he told them he didn't feel like going out. Only with great effort and with threats to leave him behind were the others able to separate him from his room when it came time to leave. Several days later, a couple of Québec provincial policemen pulled up to the camp asking for Jacques. The foreman got him. Confused, he responded to their questions: "Were you at the Provincial Hotel on the night of February 23?" "Yes." "In room

206?" "I think so. Why?" "Did you notice the dead woman in your bed?" "Dead! I thought she was English!"

Interestingly enough, as perhaps indicated in the discussion of endogamy mentioned above, the image of the virile Frenchman is not without its detractors. As one Yugoslav with several French Canadian girlfriends told me: "These guys take their girls out for years and never touch them. I take them home the first night and screw them."

35. Again and again one hears comments such as a whispered one I overheard from the sole English teller in a Montréal bank: "Let them take over. I'd like them to try it on their own for a while and really mess things up. Then they'd come back to us asking us to get them out of their mess."

36. While the French have turned necessity into a psychic victory, the English have, of course, learned to guard themselves, oftentimes by responding haughtily in English as if to say: "*I* only speak English." Indeed, especially among English of the lower classes, the phrase, "I don't speak French" seems frequently to be uttered with a sense of pride.

37. Her sister had recently married an American, which apparently had not resulted in a rupture with her parents, as the groom's parents had visited them for several days, managing as best they could in a small town where virtually no one, including of course their daughter-in-law's parents, spoke English.

38. Her presence was an important factor, in that he knew her well and was obviously interested in impressing her with his bilinguality, a quality she lacked.

39. See *joual* below (Class divisions within French Canadian society.)

40. Mitchell Sharp, a member of the Federal cabinet, has met a similar response in his efforts to learn French. At a publication party for a book titled *Les incommunicants* given by Léo Leblanc, a Québec representative in Louisiana, James Demongeot, a Louisiana millionaire supporter of French causes, spoke of an encounter with Mr. Sharp. He had, Demongeot said, travelled several times around the world without ever meeting anyone who spoke French worse than he. "But I found him," he said, "when I encountered Mr. Sharp, your minister, and I couldn't keep myself from telling him: *Sir, you speak French so badly that it gives me pleasure to hear it. If I had complexes, I've just lost them.*" The individual who recounted this tale for *Point de Mire* did so because "it proves . . . that French for an anglophone, in particular 'our' anglophones, seems to be an insurmountable language." (Borduas in *Point de Mire*, 30 oct. 1971:4; emphasis his).

41. A joke going the rounds during the crisis asked: "Sais-tu qu'ils ont trouvé Cross?" to which one naturally responded, "Non, où?" and received in return, "Au derrière de Laporte." ("Have you heard they've found Cross?" "No, where?" "Behind the door (*la porte*)"/"In Laporte's ass."). This joke was surely the joke of the moment, despite the fact that Laporte was generally a popular figure and had, in fact, been one of the initial figures in "*la révolution tranquille*" in his publication of a deadly accurate and humorous

biography of Maurice Duplessis, *Le vrai visage de Duplessis* (1960). See discussion in Chapter 7.

42. One conversation on *the* issues I was having in the town of Mount-Royal, an upper middle-class suburb adjacent to Montréal proper, was interrupted with a passion, at a point in which I mentioned that French Canadians feel uncomfortable outside of Québec because it's their home, with a very intense: "But it's our home, too!" Of course, it had not occurred to me that the *québécois* feeling truly at home precluded that.

43. This charge refers—in addition to the prime minister's ethnicity—to a feeling of many English that cabinet and other governmental posts have been packed with French Canadians and that the English provinces, in general, and the western provinces, in particular, have been neglected in favor of Québec.

44. The title, *"The Impertinences of Brother Anonymous,"* was chosen because Desbiens, then a teaching brother and later editor of *La Presse*, chose to preserve his identity to avoid the "ennuis" which he knew publication under his own name would bring. In this effort he was unsuccessful, and when his identity was discovered he was transferred to Rome to continue his studies.

45. *Joual:* a term coined by André Laurendeau, former editor of *Le Devoir*, to refer to the French spoken by most *québécois*. The term itself refers to a "mispronunciation" of *cheval* ("horse") and serves as a summary encapsulation of the dialect. Desbiens referred to it as "a boneless language: the consonants are barely pronounced, a little like the languages spoken (I imagine from the records I've heard) by the dancers of Hawaii: oula-oula-alao-alao. One says: 'Chu pas apable,' rather than: *je ne suis pas capable;* or, 'l'coach m'enweille cri les mit du gôleur,' in lieu of le moniteur m'envoie chercher les gants du gardien ["the coach sent me to look for the goal-keeper's gloves"; note the usage of English: 'coach,' 'les mit,' and 'gôleur'], etc. . . . Notice that I haven't been able to transcribe *joual* phonetically. *Joual* doesn't lend itself to a written form, as it is a decomposition, and no one can fix a decomposition except Edgar Allen Poe" (1960:24). The division of spoken French in Québec into three separate categories in itself raises some doubt as to the validity of the division, as Dundes (1968) has remarked upon the sway which tripartite categories hold over our thoughts, tending to impose themselves naturally upon continuous phenomena.

46. One wishing social mobility will seek to speak as "international" a French as possible within the limits imposed by a desire not to be *too* French and thus be almost excluded from any level of Québec society. A *québécoise* of my acquaintance, born in Québec but married to a Frenchman, speaks such a clearly accented international French that she is referred to in the rural setting where she lives as "la française." Although her husband loathes the language of his neighbors and becomes quite angry if she slips into it, she does so from time to time "to bring us closer together."

47. The fact that I am an American probably provided me with easier access into the realm of linguistic inadequacy than that likely to be gained by

most English Canadians. French Canadians generally realize that they are held in higher regard by most Americans—as "French," a completely respectable identity—than by their own English-speaking countrymen. Frequently, I was told by *québécois* that they preferred Americans to English Canadians, as they were considered to be less aloof, less unfriendly. The major factor favoring preference of Americans, however, (if this is in fact the case) is probably the fact that, except in rather limited areas of the United States, French Canadians are not associated with unfavorable stereotypes.

48. His use of *joual* seemed to have been partially motivated by some of the same reasons which caused President Johnson to seemingly relish the reputation he gained for crassness among Washington's "Kennedy intellectuals."

49. As Desbiens remarks, "I flatter myself to think that I speak a correct French; not elegant, but correct nevertheless. This fact doesn't seem to bother my students in their speaking *joual*. I make no impression on them. . . . To make myself understood I frequently have to have recourse to one of their *joual* expressions. We literally speak two different languages and I'm the only one who speaks both. . . .

"What can we do? The entire French Canadian society is giving up. . . . We are a servile race. We had our backs broken two hundred years ago, and it shows.

"Signs of this are everywhere: the government, through various organizations, offers night courses. Those most frequently enrolled in are the English courses. You can never learn enough English. Everyone wants to learn English. There is no concern with organizing French courses. *Entre jouaux, le joual suffit* ["Between *joual* speakers, *joual* works fine"]. . . . What's important is heaven, not French. One can be saved in *joual*" (27).

50. One of the major criticisms of Desbien's book was: "What will the English think?" As Rolan Girard editorialized in *Le Travailleur* (Worcester, Mass.): "Just at the moment where the old myth of 'French Canadian patois' began to lose its hold on Anglo-Saxon thought, our French Canadian cousins have found a completely picturesque replacement for him: *joual* speech. To speak or not speak *joual*, this is the new subject of debate among French Canadian dilettantes. Little matter what the impression one makes in Toronto, New York, or Paris, provided that one can prove that the language of *québécois* is not French but really *joual*. . . . On the other side of the forty-fifth parallel, they practice a fourth theological virtue: denigration" (Desbiens, 1960:31-32).

Chapter 6, Can an Acceptable Identity be Forged?

1. Arès's calculations are based upon those of immigrant stock in Montréal who speak either English or French as their maternal language. There is a great deal of evidence to suggest that even a higher proportion of more recent immigrants have opted for English. The total number of those of immigrant stock, including recent immigrants, knowing only English of the two major

languages, in contrast to those knowing only French, is in the English favor 4½ : 1.

2. The "ravanche des berceaux" has turned against French Canadians. Whereas in 1951 their birth rate was 23 percent higher than that for all Canadians, in 1965 it was 5 percent *below* the general Canadian birth rate, and all the available evidence suggests the discrepancy is increasing (Rioux, 1971: 188).

3. At federal government funded but provincially administered (at Québec's insistence) language schools for immigrants, the *Centres d'Orientation et Formation des Immigrants* (C.O.F.I.), immigrants are required to follow French courses first and then, if deemed necessary, they *may* be permitted to take English courses. This is done on the assumption that if French becomes the first useful language of communication within their new environment its use will persist. It is also hoped that the students will tire of the courses—which last twenty weeks for each language—and minimal living allowance, and seek employment in French before entering the English courses. In many cases, students sit through French courses *very* reluctantly, openly demonstrating their lack of interest in French by seeking out English-speakers, carrying English dictionaries, and reading, as best they can, English newspapers. Virtually everyone is waiting for the English courses (which are only infrequently taught by English Canadians and seem to be taught at a lower level of competence than the French courses), a fact which both instructor and student are well aware of, adding to the burden of the French instructor.

4. I have witnessed numerous encounters of this nature, including those between immigrants and their French Canadian girlfriends. Frequently, relationships between French women and immigrants will be entered into in English as a result of lack of primary interest on the immigrant's part in French (the language in which he will have some competence at first meeting will, in any case, usually be English), the fact that the *québécoise*, herself, wishes to improve her English, and that vis-à-vis the immigrant she is, *herself*, the bearer of the prized language. In interacting with these couples, I usually spoke French. In one case, in a wholly French nightclub, at a table which, with the exception of a Czech immigrant and myself, was wholly French, the immigrant responded to my speaking French with: "What do you want to speak French for now? *They* can speak English."

5. This is a conclusion which cannot be readily dismissed as a product of paranoia as it has firm factual grounding. It is well known that separation is an "unthinkable" option in the eyes of the federal government and, in particular, in those of Pierre Trudeau, despite the fact that the *Parti Québécois,* an openly separatist party, currently enjoys the largest support of any among French Quebekers. From this premise, a memory of the government's immediate and severe response to the October, 1971 crisis, and a realization that many, perhaps a majority, of immigrants, counselled at Canadian Immigration Bureaus abroad before arriving in Montréal are not aware of the importance of the French presence in the city (several have told me they were

shocked to discover French in Canada, as they had thought it was wholly an English country—apparently dual-language translations of official documents make no impression on those who read neither language), it is reasonable tp assume that if the diminishing of the proportionate importance of the French in Québec is not an intended result of immigration, it is at least not a by-product unacceptable to the Federal government.

6. Despite a provision requiring the teaching of French in English schools, the effect of this bill, far from promoting the cause of French, had opposite results. Under its conditions, most immigrants are free to opt for English, and English continue in virtually all instances to choose English as the language in which to educate their children, while French parents have themselves been offered the chance to choose whether or not their children will attend English schools. In one small town of approximately one thousand people southwest of Montréal (Howick), whose population is divided evenly between French and English, approximately fifty French-speaking children are reported to be currently attending English schools, while no English children attend French schools (Raboy, Marc: *Montreal Star*, May 12, 1970:3) before the 1974 enactment of Québec's Official Language Act removed the option for French parents to send their children to English schools.

7. Figures in parentheses are those of the RRCB, vol. I, 1967:33.

8. In Québec, for the province as a whole, a greater percentage of those whose ethnic origin is English speak French as their maternal language (9.4 percent) than those of French origin who today speak English as their maternal language (1.6 percent) (RRCBB, vol. I:32). Calculations of language retention, based as they are upon census response to the inquiry: "To what ethnic or cultural group did you or your ancestor (on the male side) belong on coming to this continent?" fail to take into consideration the fact that many of the marriages resulting in the assimilation of the progeny of Québec English males may have occurred in the distant past, especially during the waves of English immigration after the conquest, and that French gain from intermarriage in Québec, which presumably resulted from more frequent marriage of bilingual offspring with the major ethnic group of the province, may have declined in recent years.

9. Numerous examples of situational passing, or understressing of French ethnicity, have come to my attention in other areas of Canada. In one instance, in a small Ontario town in the St. Lawrence Valley, a young college student of my acquaintance who attended an English school impressed me as English until I met his father, whose accented English immediately alerted me to speak French. At the moment I began to speak French, indicating at the least a very sympathetic attitude, the student seemed quite pleased and joined in. In another instance, a young professional woman from Manitoba whom I met at an English party in Montréal only indicated her Frenchness when forced to through a conversation initiated in French by a woman who wore her identity on the cuff and took great relish in engaging in a cross-room conversation in French in the midst of her respectful English colleagues

—all slightly embarrassed by their lack of comprehension. The girl, herself, who dated regularly an English Canadian, confessed that having been raised in Manitoba, even with its important French minority, she was ashamed of being French. The act of coming to Montréal, itself appeared to have been a means of testing out her ethnicity on more friendly ground.

10. The woman, who lived in a building in which I had an apartment, apparently felt that I was Jesus Christ. At first, I thought her prolonged conversations with me in the hallway on the subject were merely a result of a pleasing fantasy on her part, but in time, with her repeated talk of Christ's return, my "aura," my hands, and her requests for me to attend her church services, I began to doubt her ability to discriminate between the two of us.

One day I heard her in a hushed conversation in French with an individual who was apparently a bill collector, and decided to ask her in French in she was a *canadienne-française*. When I did, she told me that her family was French and invited me into her apartment to look through her old family albums containing pictures of her father and her brother, a Catholic priest. Upon seeing his photograph, I asked her what he thought of her conversion to Protestantism. He did not know, she explained, as relations with her family had been broken off years before. At this point she began a long, rambling discussion of the horrors of promiscuity and that the only real salvation was belief in our Lord, Jesus Christ, without answering—at least any more directly than she was able—the question.

The other instance of prolonged situational passing in Montréal, that of the manager of a rooming house in a mixed French-English area, was very curious indeed. Upon meeting him the day of my arrival in Montréal, I rented a room in the house. To my knowledge, and to all external evidence, he was English. At the very moment of my arrival, even, his Englishness seemed validated by the fact that our conversation was interrupted by two young French Canadians who were going to visit a girl in the house. As they mounted the stairs, he demanded: "Where are you going?" to which they responded, "Seize!" "Where?" he asked. Seemingly puzzled, they responded "Sixteen." As he showed us our room he began to complain about the maid service. His maid, French naturally, hadn't come to work that day, a fact whose repetition was accompanied by a commentary on the unreliability of the French. In the meanwhile, he would have to do the cleaning in the building.

During the several days of my stay, I frequently encountered him mopping or vacuuming. Each time, as if he had forgotten I had already been told, he repeated his tale of problems with his French maid. In time, I became convinced that there was, in fact, no maid and his denial served to elevate him from the status of maintenance man to owner (I had also begun to doubt his ownership of the building). Late one night, I descended the basement stairs to remove some luggage from my car parked in the rear of the building, when I passed his office and noticed that his radio was tuned to a French station. Poking my head in the door, I asked him if he was working late in my uncertain French. Shocked, he responded to me in an accent which I already recognized clearly—that of the native *québécois.*

11. Other decisions possibly resulting in assimilation, such as a decision by French parents to send children to English schools, are most frequently attempts to give the child full access to both worlds and will be discussed under *Integration* (below).

12. Carisse found that the English sector dominated in the family in the following areas (ranging from 61 percent to 10 percent in decreasing degree of dominance over French: magazines read, association in which membership was held, television watched, newspapers read, language spoken to spouse. language spoken to boys, language spoken to girls, dominant language of general usage. The French sector was dominant in the following areas (ranging from 54 percent to 2 percent in decreasing degree of dominance over English): residential location, social connections with relatives, worship, school attended, visits to friends. While French residential location dominates over English by 54 percentage points, French choice of school dominates by only 12 percent, suggesting that the presence of an English spouse exerts strong pressure to transcend locality in this regard (1969:43).

Within the Canadian forces, which are heavily dominated by English language and ethos, French personnel tend to marry English females in a proportion significantly greater than in the population as a whole. Of the Armed Forces married sample gathered for the Royal Commission on Bilingualism and Biculturalism, 49.4 percent of the French personnel were married to French-speaking wives, while 41.1 percent had English-speaking spouses. Marriages of English personnel, on the other hand, were with English spouses in 93.5 percent of the cases and with French in only 3.2 percent. The Commission's report suggests that: ". . . many Francophones have, possibly rather early in their careers, chosen to adapt, integrate, and even assimilate to the English-language milieu offered them by the Forces" (RRCBB, vol. III: 325–26).

13. Of all Québec marriages entered into by French females, 1.91 percent are with spouses who are neither English nor French, while this is true for only 0.98 percent of marriages of French males (RRCBB, IV:285). For Montréal (1962), the discrepancy is even more marked, the percentages being 6.4 and 2.6 for females and males, respectively (1969:40).

14. Examples of this can be found on almost any public conveyance entering or leaving Montréal. One vivid example: a French woman in her thirties was boarding a bus for the United States after visiting relatives in Montréal. As she took leave of her relatives in French, she directed her children on the bus in a heavily accented English. During the return trip, she conversed with her children—both of whom spoke accentless English—only in English.

15. An interesting sixth possibility has been suggested by Rodrique Tremblay (1970) in *Indépendance et marché commun Québec–Etats-unis,* that Québec seek to resolve the problems which French ethnicity in Canada have produced by separating from Canada and entering a common market

relationship with the United States. While his intention in advocating this position is not assimilation but improvement of the economic condition of *québécois*, a strengthening of bonds between Québec and the U.S. could only heighten pressures toward assimilation. Interestingly enough, the results of a poll taken by *l'Institut Canadien de l'opinion* indicates that 69 percent of *québécois* are favorable to a common market arrangement with the U.S., whereas only 18 percent are opposed (13 percent offered no opinion). In Ontario, on the other hand, only 51 percent favored such an arrangement, 32 percent were opposed, and 17 percent expressed no opinion (Tremblay, 1970:85).

16. For more detailed discussion of Trudeau and his role, see Chapter 7, "The Minority Politician: Pragmatist or Roi-Nègre?"

17. Jean-Charles Harvey, in *Pourquoi je suis antiséparatiste*, takes much the same tack as Trudeau, arguing that it is not federalism which has endangered French survival in North America—as, in Québec at least, the French are in control of their schools and other "instruments of culture"—but their position as an island in the midst of English-speaking peoples. The rewards of separatism might be momentarily gratifying psychologically, but they are unlikely to be economically so. In his chapter "Nationalism or Jingoism of the Weak," he offers the following example of what he views as a tendency of French Canadians to affix blame for all imagined slights on the English: "The other day, for example, a young restaurant waitress, to whom I had given a dollar bill—a bilingual bill—gave me a knowing smile and pointed out the inscription 'UN DOLLAR' with her finger! See, she said, how they treat us. It's still English [the bills had recently been made bilingual in response to French demands]. It should read *UNE PIASSE* [Piasse is the common pronunciation of *piastre* in Québec]! I can't get over it coming from such a pretty mouth, such a French lesson worth easily *CENT PIASSES*. I tried to tell her how "dollar" was called "dollar" on all the world's continents, even in France, one designated it as such and that a *piastre* had never had the value of our present currency, but she continued to smile with a pensive air! 'How can anyone be so ignorant and so unpatriotic!' I was talking with a separatist."

18. Again and again the commissioners of the Royal Commission on Bilingualism were faced with the question: "Why do you want to make us speak French here in X. . . ?" To which the chairman invariably responded that in all probability large parts of Canada would remain unilingual and that in any case "the commission has never intended that the idea was to make all Canadians become bilingual." The response to this clarification? Invariably it was: "In that case, what is the point of your inquiry?" (RRCBB, Preliminary Report:27).

19. Evidence that many English Canadians still hold this view is ubiquitous. A recent poem appearing in *Montréal-Matin*, and originating from United Press International's Toronto Bureau, of Charlotte Whitton, described as "the former mayoress," illustrates a commonly held English Canadian

attitude: "An ulcer in the duodenum handicaps a man. A little bilingualism tears a nation apart. This is why I am and I will always remain unilingual." As the editor of *Montréal-Matin* rhetorically questioned: "This poem can be printed without comment, can't it? (11 mai 1970:3).

20. *Point de Mire's* discussion of the recommendations of the Duhamel commission to make Québec bilingual was headlined "speak white or else ... " and appeared in an issue in which the journal's cover simply read: "Speak White Now" (14 mai 1971).

21. While true separatism precludes a Federal union with the rest of Canada, it does not dismiss the possibility of a common market relationship.

22. Jean-Paul Desbiens echoes the sentiment that English Canadians are not exactly "world-beaters" in indicating that he couldn't care less what English Canadians think about discussion of the quality of French in Québec: "... first prize, one week in Toronto; second prize, two weeks in Toronto; third prize, three weeks in Toronto" (1960:32).

23. The nature of the effect of Duplessis' death can also be seen in the fact that in Pierre Vigeant's major *Le Devoir* editorial for February 11, 1958, he stated that "the cheques printed by the government represent our only major grievance." When the currency was finally made bilingual in 1962, the action was greeted by a terse *Le Devoir* editorial headed: "IT'S TOO LITTLE AND TOO LATE" (Myers, 1964:1, 55).

Two other instances of rebellion prior to Duplessis' death are worth noting despite the fact that their incidence is more indicative of attempts to maintain group identity than to create an open society. One of these was Quebec's squelching of Federal attempts to gather ethnic data for the 1961 census under categories which would, for the first time, include the category "Canadian" alongside those of "French," "English" and the various other national groups. Since French Canadians frequently, and more so at that time than today, thought of themselves as the only "real" Canadians, there was a genuine fear that the "Canadian" response might hide the true French strength in Canada.

Another illustrative incident concerns something incredible to imagine in today's Québec: the *Société St.-Jean Baptiste*, today in the forefront of efforts to eliminate English as an official language in Québec, joined with its English counterparts to make plans for celebrating the two hundredth anniversary of the English victory on the Plains of Abraham with the theme "two centuries of progressive cooperation." Marcel Chaput, later author of *Pourquoi je suis séparatist*, felt constrained to respond to *Le Devoir* in a letter headed *Race de Vaincus*:

> It appears that great rejoicings are in preparation at Quebec ... the battlefield will be heavily decorated with red ensigns and the gaiety of our brave *Québécois* will be generously alimented with the music of "Rule Britannia" and "God Save the Queen." And what, pray tell, are

the circumstances which will cause such a celebration? None other than that it is the bicentennial of the battle on the Plains of Abraham. I have never read news which made me feel so saddened. . . . Next September 13, the anniversary of this sadly glorious battle, the *French* and *English* national associations of Québec will fraternize warmly on the Plains to mark (read carefully): the battle which led to the end of the French Regime and saw Canada pass into the hands of England. All as if there were something for us French Canadians to rejoice over. France is beaten. Long live England. . . .

Mr. Director, there is something here which gives us cause for despair. When the so-called national elite does not see anything odious or absurd in a commemoration that associates on the same level conquerers and conquered, not to say butchers and sacrificed, then that people deserves the epithet vanquished race. To try after two hundred years to stifle in his breast the bitterness of a military defeat, is Christian, but to invite his compatriots to climb over the coffins of their glorious dead so as to better kiss the conqueror's boots is against nature" (Marcel Chaput, *Le Devoir,* 8 juin 1959:4)

24. The life and personality of Duplessis is discussed in more detail in Chapter 7, "The Minority Politician: Pragmatist or Roi-Nègre?"

25. In a later *Le Devoir* editorial, Gerard Filion offered several counter-arguments: the chief negotiator of the Corporation was a French Canadian, the local management was wholly French Canadian, and a number of Québec representatives to Parliament were as vindictive toward the strikers as were any English Canadians.

26. While the final measure is offered for its biting effect, there are, in fact, numerous French professors from countries other than Québec and France, including many from Black African nations, today teaching in "International French" in the schools of Québec.

In December 1972, Chaput founded the *Parti républicain du Québec,* which, while today defunct, was the first provincial party dedicated to gaining Québec's independence. In 1972, a photograph of Chaput appeared in *Le Devoir* over the caption "Le Ghandi d'Amérique," heading a call for a "Pétition publique de l'Atlantique au Pacifique" to form a new political party, Le Parti Canadien-Français. The party is intended to operate on an exclusively federal basis to avoid conflict with the *Parti Québécois* and has as its objectives: "(1) To unite all French-speaking members of the Canadian Confederation in a single common front in Ottawa; (2) To make Québec recognized as the national state of the French Canadian people having the right, as do all free peoples of the earth, to self-determination, equality, and national independence" (*Le Devoir,* 20 mars 1972:5).

27. The P.Q. has prepared a number of studies on various aspects of Québec independence as *La souveraineté et l'économie* (1970) and *La solution: Le programme du Parti Québécois* (1970), all of which are designed to present in convincing detail and assurance the reasonableness of the separatist

solution. The essential program calls for an autonomous Québec within a Canadian common market, if possible. If the federal government should be unwilling to negotiate such an economic relationship, then Québec would be forced, under the *Parti Québécois* program, to sever all ties.

28. One radical separatist informant opposed to the long-term goals of the Parti Québécois argued that separatism must not be construed as anti-English, or even nationalist, but only as the most efficient means of casting off English colonialism.

29. The action of the FLQ cell headed by the Rose brothers in "executing" Pierre Laporte placed the FLQ in a position difficult to explain as accident. With the population of Québec stunned in the days after Laporte's "execution" or "murder," depending upon one's perspective, I came upon a revolutionary separatist acquaintance who was quite angry and indignant over the fact that Trudeau had thwarted the FLQ's demands. Trudeau's behavior, he argued, demonstrated beyond a shadow of a doubt his lack of concern for life. In fact, this revolutionary separatist argued: "Trudeau killed Laporte!"

30. Schoeter's imprisonment resulted in his disillusionment with the FLQ. In 1967, on the condition he leave Canada, he gained his release and left for Belgium with the intention of continuing his studies at l'Université de Louvain. Due to the Flemish-Walloon conflict, the Belgian government decided not to risk his presence and denied him permission to remain. He is currently reputed to be working clandestinely in Belgium after having traveled throughout Europe and meeting Swiss rejection in an attempt to gain political asylum. His wife filed for divorce two weeks after his capture (Morf, 1970:20–22).

31. This ends "Le troisième vague" for Morf, who is less willing to credit terrorist action to the FLQ without substantial proof (i.e. convictions) than is Pelletier, who credits to the third wave actions occurring for a full year after the capture of Schirm's group. There can, however, be little doubt that these attacks properly belong to the FLQ, as virtually all of them were claimed by the organ *La Cognée.*

32. Bail guaranteed for one of those involved was signed by "François Marcelo." According to a court handwriting expert, the signature had been written by Pierre Vallières (Morf, 1970:80).

33. "My father was loved by his camarades (at the shop). But at home he was a beaten man. He wasn't alone in his lot. Many of his friends had been defeated by their wives. But, unlike my father, they reacted violently, 'le soir de la paye,' getting drunk, beating their wife and throwing the entire family out of the house. The next day, though, they would go to confession and become gentle, silent husbands again" (108). The "payday" drunk is widespread in Québec. On payday the taverns of the province, wholly male bastions in which it is illegal for a woman to enter, are filled with boasting, intoxicated males. Frequently, a woman will make a furtive forage into the tavern to attempt to bring her husband home before too much of his check

is spent. Invariably, she is met with derision, and a husband who treats her cavalierly to retain status with his companions until, having tarried too long on alien soil, she slinks toward the door. Referring to this scene and the great consumption of beer at home in the province, one *québécoise* suggested to me that the fleur-de-lis on the province's flag should be replaced with beer bottles.

34. La rue Saint-Jacques holds a special place of infamy for many *québécois* as it is considered to be the seat of English domination.

35. Wages paid by French Canadian firms are as a rule quite below the level paid by English firms—justification for the need to accept a lower salary in French firms being offered by the supposed necessity to do so to maintain the French concern's existence in the face of English competition and in the fact that *québécois* represent a captive work force in oversupply.

36. "Ouvrons les frontières, ce peuple muert d'asphyxie."

37. Vallières, along with Charles Gagnon, Me. Robert Lemieux, Michel Chartrand, and Jacques Larue-Langlois, was charged with taking part in an illegal and seditious conspiracy aiming to overthrow the government of the province of Québec and brought to trial in February, 1971. The indictment arising from the War Measures Act was declared unconstitutional by the judge hearing the case and Vallières was released.

38. Editor of *Le Devoir*.

39. Vallières's reappraisal of the situation threw remaining FLQ cells into confusion. In a communiqué, the "cellule Perrault," referring to him as "the uncontested leader of our struggle," asked "will someone take up Vallières's mantle in the armed agitation? If future events are favorable to it, we will respond to the call of this new chief" (*Le Devoir*, 18 decembre 1971:7).

40. Undoubtedly a major factor in Vallières's decision was the fact that Montréal's mayor, Jean Drapeau, seeking election in the midst of the October crisis, used tactics of confusion between the FLQ and the major opposition to his Parti Civique, FRAP (Front d'action politique), composed largely of liberal separatist elements, to sweep the entire slate of city council candidates and assume unopposed control of the city. At one point, Jean Marchand, a federal cabinet member, in an interview with a Vancouver television station, accused FRAP "of being a cover for the FLQ." Although he later apologized, claiming unconvincingly that his imperfect knowledge of the English language had caused him to err, the damage was done and the fear inspired by the fact that a high-ranking federal official, presumably with inside knowledge, had associated FRAP with the FLQ assured its crushing defeat.

41. The five hundred thousand dollar ransom was to be "une taxe volontaire," recalling Jean Drapeau's usage of the term to cover a municipal lottery which proved so profitable that it was taken over by the province in the massive *Loto-Québec*, *Mini-Loto*, and *Super-Loto* lotteries. It was to be delivered in nine armored Brinks trucks to Dorval International Airport, the trucks recalling the celebrated "coup de Brinks" preceding the April, 1970 election, in which securities were transferred from the province on the eve of

the election, spelling out clearly what would happen to the province's economy if the *Parti Québécois* was victorious. The "Gars de Lapalme" are a group of independently contracted postal drivers who lost their positions when the government consolidated its operations and eliminated private contracting in the sector. After negotiations and prolonged picketing, the government agreed to hire the workers in federal service but not to recognize their right to retain their union. This was rejected by the Lapalme drivers, who several years later continue to picket the capital and demand a settlement on their terms: employment with the Federal government and retention of their union. Their fame was enhanced by vocal revindications (including pointed stickers placed in the inside chute of many post office boxes in the city: "Pensez des gars de Lapalme," i.e., "Are you certain you want to be so near a post box with this matter unresolved?") and their provocation of Trudeau, to the point where he allegedly rolled down the window of his official limousine to respond to the screams of picketing Lapalme drivers with: "Mangez d'la merde!" (or, variously, it is said with the earthier "marde").

42. Sources for the chronology of the events of October are: Jean-Marc Piotte, *Jour après Jour* in *Québec Occupé;* Jean-Claude Trait, *FLQ 70: Offensive d'automne; La Presse; Le Devoir;* and personal notes.

43. Reference to Jean Drapeau's restaurant, "le Vaisseau d'Or."

44. During Expo-67, panels were placed in certain strategic areas of heavy tourist travel, seemingly to hide certain slums from tourists.

45. At this time, Bourassa himself was virtually unguarded. Only after Laporte's kidnapping was a detachment of the Sûreté du Québec sent to his residence.

46. At this point I received a phone call from a French Canadian friend: "Did you hear Drapeau's speech? Wasn't it incredible? . . . The man *is* a fascist!"

Deprived of the benefit of a terrorist "opposition" and plagued by opposition to the exorbitant cost of the 1976 Montréal Olympics—whose cost many felt was deliberately misrepresented to gain initial support—Drapeau was only able to gain 55 percent of the vote in the 1974 elections.

47. Jean Drapeau had earlier stated that: "The growing terrorism in Québec has pushed certain citizens of good faith to envisage the formation of a provisory government which might have been a band of revolutionaries."

48. "The night before, we had hesitated as to whether or not to kidnap the U.S. consul or the commercial representative from Great Britain. We chose the commercial representative. We hoped that the kidnapping of a British diplomat would crystallize the positions of the two communities of Montréal, meaning the French and English Canadians" (from "90 minutes en compagnie des ravisseurs de James Cross," *Choc.* No 9, decembre 1970: quoted in Pelletier, 1971:94).

49. Lemieux, son of an English mother and a French father, was brought up in the western and English Montréal suburb of Notre-Dame-de-Grâce (or "NDG" as it is always referred to), attended law school at McGill, joined a

major Montréal law firm, and then began to represent legal aid and political cases. It was through this latter activity that he became involved with the FLQ and established an identity as a revolutionary separatist.

50. The leader of the *Créditistes*, Réal Caouette, in a speech delivered before the Chamber of Commons in Ottawa on October 19, offered his opinion: "I am certain that the heads of the FLQ are aware of all that is going on, including the hiding place of their bandits, and maintain that these chiefs must immediately be brought before a firing squad and told to tell all concerning the acts, organization, and even the existence of the FLQ, which seeks to destroy the free society in which we live. They must be forced to inform against their murderers and bandits under threat of losing ten of their numbers for each of the assassinations that they commit" (quoted in Pelletier, 1971:18).

51. "Pantoufle," literally "slipper," is best translated here as "armchair." Pelletier's preponderant concern in the crisis "was the existence in Québec of a great number of conscious or unconscious *felquiste* sympathizers as well as *the sum total of facts and presumptions which rendered plausible the possibility of an 'insurrection,' meaning grave civil disorders, in particular in Montréal.*" (Pelletier, 1971:127; emphasis his).

52. René Lévesque announced, "Québec no longer has a government." Michel Chartrand, commenting after his release from custody, referred to the War Measures Act as "the most extraordinary terroristic undertaking that anyone has ever heard of in Québec or in Canada" (*La Presse*, 29 avril 1971:F1).

53. A poll taken March 5-11 by students at l'Université Laval showed that time had somewhat diminished support for the government. At that time, 35.1 percent of the respondents wholly agreed with the federal government's October actions, 30.9 percent partially agreed, 22.5 percent completely disagreed, while 11.5 percent either were noncommittal or did not respond (Bellavance et Gilbert, 1971:47). Interestingly enough, a breakdown of the felt threat of the FLQ to the social order indicates that it was considered to be potentially much more severe among French Canadians and "others" than among English Canadians in Québec:

Is the FLQ a Threat?	Ethnic Group			
	French	English	Others	Total
Yes	26.6%	6.9%	26.9%	22.4%
No	73.1%	87.5%	53.8%	73.6%
Neither	3.3%	5.6%	19.3%	4.0%

54. The appeal of English education was once again demonstrated in a 1972 survey conducted by the Montréal Catholic School Commission, which showed that almost 50 percent of those surveyed in English schools spoke Italian as their native language. Equally significant, 11.5 percent of students

whose native language was French were attending English-language schools, while only one percent of those who spoke English as their native language attended French schools. With the passage of Bill 22 and its restrictiơns upon parents' rights to educate their children in the language of their choice, reports circulated of immigrant children attending special English schools to prepare them for the English exams which they must pass in order to avoid being assigned to French schools.

Chapter 7, The Minority Politician

1. Later in his "first great English speech," Laurier sought to relieve the mounting French-English division over the affair by suggesting that Riel was best seen as a madman and "a religious and political monomaniac" rather than a hero of a people who, nevertheless, had gained the right to a hearing through their martyrdom (Wade, 1968:420).

2. Bourassa was one of Louis-Joseph Papineau's grandsons and himself *seigneur* of Montebello on the Ottawa River.

3. *Joual* for "toi, tais-toi!" ("You, hush up!")

4. Laporte records the explanation of one Minister who began to speak and then just as suddenly sat down: "The battery in my hearing aid fell to the floor. I could no longer hear what Mr. Duplessis was saying" (1960:62).

5. At this point of rejection, Duplessis changed, for the first time, to the more distant "vous" form.

6. At first Duplessis opposed this flag, feeling that it smacked too much of separation. Only when he was convinced that separation was not involved, and besides an important 10 to 20 percent of the population favored independence, did he yield and adopt it as his own.

7. At times, Duplessis' behavior, especially in the matter of religion, caricatured the traditional values of the province. Not only did he profess his devoutness, constantly attending religious services and speaking with clergy—although he felt free to blaspheme the Church and attack many of its leaders as either "communists" oʀ on a more personal basis—but reportedly in his earlier days was prone to wake those of his ministers and political friends who had spent Tuesday night with him (he was a bachelor) talking politics into the late hours of the morning and lead them dreary-eyed from little or no sleep to early Wednesday Mass.

8. It must be noted that Duplessis himself cared little for money, its only use being that, knowing the weaknesses of others, he was able to use the money-diverting powers of his office to gain allegiance from them. It is quite likely that Anglo-American investors played upon his greatest weakness—flattery—and succeeded in gaining access to the province's resources much as others gained access to its coffers.

9. Mgr. Charbonneau, declaring: "The working class is a victim of a conspiracy which is trying to crush it, and when there is a conspiracy to crush the working class, it is the duty of the Church to intervene" (Voisine,

1971:79), ordered collections taken for the strikers at churches throughout the province. Duplessis quickly dispatched two cabinet members to Rome. "Shortly after their return to Quebec and reportedly after receiving a midnight visit from officers of the Provincial Police, the Archbishop submitted his resignation to the Pope, 'for reasons of health,' and climbed on a plane for Victoria, B.C." (Chapin, 1955:66–67).

10. Trudeau later journeyed to the Soviet Union in 1952, with a group of economists and businessmen, and was for a time denied entrance into the U.S. as a result of this trip. In 1960, he journeyed to Communist China, later co-authoring with Jacques Hébert, *Deux Innocents en Chine Rouge*, recounting their experiences.

11. Jean-Paul Geoffrey, then strike director of the *Confédération des travailleurs catholiques du Canada*, recalled that: "he wore a long reddish beard and looked like the 'hippies' do today. . . . He had some interesting things to say (to the strikers) and said them simply. They called him Saint-Joseph because of his beard" (43). Jacques Hébert remembers that: "It was really something to see this young man speaking to 5,000 miners. It was very moving. I remember that he discussed democracy, justice, and liberty in a fashion that they understood. He spoke their language" (43–44).

12. He takes exception to Marcel Chaput's bandwagon approach to Québec's independence—that scores of countries have found independence since World War II, Why not Québec?—by noting that if one examines the nations which have gained independence in the past several decades one finds again and again that these are multi-ethnic nations. In this sense, it is Canada, he argues, which is well ahead of its time, *not* Québec separatists.

13. Needless to say, separatists have taken issue with Trudeau's argument that they are not in the line of progress. One of these, Pierre Vadeboncoeur, having known Trudeau, Pelletier, and Marchand personally, defends them against charges of treason: "I knew them (Pelletier and Marchand) very well, although less intimately than Trudeau. I don't like to see people cast aspersions on their character because they have a right to their honor, which is real" (1970:53), but feels that all three, and especially Trudeau, are stubbornly, if sincerely, in error. Trudeau can only see, Vadeboncoeur argues, the new Québec nationalism as "a transposition of the old myth . . . [an idea] very superficial and even erroneous" (24). "Trudeau, as if in a dreamworld, continues to curse at the old fox Duplessis. He seems to still believe, as did Duplessis, that cunning country-slicker, in a Québec free of our old establishment (unless Duplessis was only making fun of it). But here he is twenty years behind in comparison with Maurice, who was himself at least a quarter of a century behind the times. All this leaves us way behind, unless one has decided, as have *Québécois*, to do away once and for all with all this rural business" (52).

14. Vallières, for example, took the judge to task in a recent trial for having said he would like to be as great a Canadian as Pierre Trudeau! "As

for me, I would be ashamed to love Pierre Elliot Trudeau, who shows more concern for the monkeys of Borneo than for the workers of Lapalme, who he had told to eat shit ("marde") (*Le Procès des cinq;* 1971:76).

15. Frequently before his marriage, Trudeau was referred to as "une tapette." Several months after his marriage, an item appeared in *Pointe de Mire* alleging that after examining Mrs. Trudeau for signs of pregnancy and discovering none, a physician was approached by the Prime Minister: "You told my wife that she isn't pregnant? That can't be! we have done everything that one needs to do. . . ." "Alas, Monsieur Elliott, that is the way it is." "But it's impossible. How can you explain it?" "It's very simple. Do you have a Montréal telephone book with you? Good, very well, take it, open it to page 624. Now read line 24 in the second column, and you will have your answer" (*Point de Mire,* 14 mai 1971:11). The answer? The name "Fourlas," which, when pronounced, is identical to "fourre-la," "screw her."

16. He also came under some attack before his marriage for supposed excessive concern with the dating of beautiful women to the detriment of the nation's concerns. He became sensitive enough to heckling on the order of "Hustle wheat, not women!" that at one point he struck a heckler in the face.

17. Lévesque's decision came as no great surprise to most and certainly not to Pierre Trudeau, who had often met with him at the Westmount home of Pelletier during Lévesque's tenure as Minister of Natural Resources. "Often these meetings ended in violent arguments between Lévesque and Trudeau, who carried on a lively, yet amicable, intellectual combat . . . [among the subjects upon which they disagreed was that of nationalization of the electric companies, of which] Pelletier remembers that Trudeau had some reservations concerning the nationalization. He was of the opinion that it 'was not a pressing matter' " (Stuebing, *et al.,* 1969:50–51).

18. The term déraciné, while translated literally "uprooted," is frequently used in a pejorative sense similar to "assimilated."

Chapter 8, Québec in Cross-Cultural Perspective

1. The playwright Tennessee Williams, who is openly homosexual, is reputed to have emptied an exclusive New Orleans restaurant, not because of sexual habits particularly repugnant in that area of the nation, but by jokingly referring to himself as an "octoroon" in conversation with a companion.

2. Much of the recent black revitalization movement in the United States may be seen as an effort by blacks to define themselves in ethnic, rather than caste, terms.

3. This increase in ethnic awareness is often of a selective nature. Thus certain groups, such as the Algerians of Paris or the French of Canada, are singled out for special pejorative treatment, while other groups, such as the Yugoslavs of Paris or the Dutch of Canada, are more readily accepted.

4. Rioux himself, from numerous interviews with Québec young people on the threshold of adulthood, is also convinced "that ethnic or national consciousness is much more alive than that of class consciousness, that ethnic consciousness is more developed in Montréal than *en province,* that it is much more a middle-class than a worker or peasant phenomenon" (31).

REFERENCES

Adams, Howard
   1968   *The Education of Canadians, 1800-1867: The Roots of Separatism.* Montréal: Harvest House.

Aellen, Ailene Carol
   1967   *Second Generation Effects of Mixed French-English Marriages.* Master's Thesis. Montréal: McGill University.

Angers, Francois-Albert
   1971   *Les droits du français du Québec.* Montréal: Editions du Jour.

Association Québécoise des Professeurs de Français
   1970   *Le livre noire de l'impossibilité (presque totale) d'enseigner le français au Québec.* Montréal: Editions du Jour.

Barbeau, Raymond
   1965   *Le Québec bientôt unilingue?* Montreal: Les Editions de l'Homme.

Barthe, Ulric
   1890   *Wilfred Laurier on the Platform: 1871-1890.* Québec: Turcotte & Menard.

Beaulieu, Michel
   1972   "L'Amérique en français de France." *Le Devoir,* 14 février, 1972:10.

Benedict, Ruth
   1946   *The Chrysanthemum and the Sword: Patterns of Japanese Culture.* Boston: Houghton Mifflin.

Bergeron, Léandre
   1970   *Petit manuel d'histoire du Québec.* Montréal: Editions Québécoises.

Bellavance, Michel, et Marcel Gilbert
1971   *L'opinion publique et la crise d'octobre.* Montréal: Editions du Jour.

Berreman, Gerald D.
1967   "Structure and Function of Caste Systems; Concomitants of Caste Organization." In DeVos and Wagatsuma, *Japan's Invisible Race.* Berkeley: University of California Press.

Bilodeau, Rosario, *et al.*
1971   *Histoire des Canadas.* Montréal: HMH.

Bouchette, Errol
1901   *Emparons-nous de l'industrie.* Ottawa.

Bracq, Jean-Charles
1927   *L'Evolution du Canada français.* Paris et Montréal: Pion et Beauchemin.

Braroe, Niels Winther
1965   "Reciprocal Exploitation in an Indian-White Community." *Southwestern Journal of Anthropology,* 21:166–178.

Brochu, Michel
1962   *Le Défi du Nouveau-Québec.* Montréal: Editions du Jour.

Brunet, Michel
1953   "Premières réactions des vaincus de 1760 devant leurs vainqueurs." *Revue d'histoire d'Amérique française* VI, 4:506–516.
1954   *Canadians et Canadiens.* Montréal: Fides.
1958   *La Présence anglaise et les Canadiens.* Montréal: Beauchemin.

Carisse, Colette
1969   "Orientations culturelles dans les mariages entre Canadiens français et Canadiens anglais." *Sociologie et Sociétiés,* 1, 1:39–52.

Chaloult, René
1969   *Mémoires politiques.* Montréal: Editions du Jour.

Chapais, Thomas
1921   *Cours d'histoire du Canada,* (Vol. II: 1791–1814; Vol. III: 1815–1833). Québec: Libraire Garneau.

Chapin, Miriam
1955   *Québec Now.* New York: Oxford University Press.

Chaput, Marcel
1961   *Pourquoi je suis séparatiste.* Montréal: Editions du Jour.

Charney, Ann
1973   "The Transformation of a 'White Nigger.' " *Maclean's,* May, 1973: 36–58.

Chartrand, Michel, *et al.*
   1971   *Le procès des cinq.* Montréal: Les Editions Libération.

Cloutier, Eugene
   1967   *Le Canada sans passeport: Regard libre sur un pays en quête de sa realite* (2 vols.). Montréal: HMH.

Comité de documentation du Parti Québécois
   1970   *Le Souveraineté et l'économie.* Montréal: Les Editions du Jour.

Commission d'Etude sur les Laics et l'Eglise
   1971   *Croyants du Canada français—1.* Montréal: Fides.

Cook, Ramsey
   1966   *Canada and the French–Canadian Question.* Toronto: Macmillan.

Craig, Gerald M., ed.
   1963   *Lord Durham's Report.* Toronto: McClelland and Stewart.

Deffontaines, Pierre
   1953   "The *rang*-pattern of Rural Settlement in French Canada." In Rioux and Martin, eds., *French Canadian Society* (1964). Toronto: McClelland and Stewart.

Desbiens, Jean Paul
   1960   *Les insolences du Frère Untel.* Montréal: Les Éditions de l'Homme.

Desrosiers et Fournet
   1911   *La race française en Amérique.*

DeVos, George, and Hiroshi Wagatsuma
   1967   *Japan's Invisible Race: Caste in Culture and Personality.* Berkeley: University of California Press.

Dofny, J. and Marcel Rioux
   1962   "Social Class in French Canada." In Rioux and Martin, eds., *French Canadian Society.* Toronto: McClelland and Stewart.

Dumont, Fernand et Jean-Charles Falardeau
   1964   *Littérature et société Canadiennes-françaises.* Québec: Les Presses de L'Université Laval.

Dundes, Alan
   1968   "The Number Three in American Culture." In Alan Dundes, *Every Man His Way.* Englewood Cliffs: Prentice-Hall.

Durocher, René, et Paul-André Linteau
   1970   *Histoire du Québec: bibliographie sélective (1867-1970).* Trois-Rivières: les éditions du boréal express.

Eccles, W. J.
   1968   *Canadian Society During the French Regime.* Montréal: Harvest House.

Falardeau, Jean-Charles
n.d.   "The Seventeenth-Century Parish in French Canada." In Rioux and Martin, eds., *French Canadian Society* (1964). Toronto: McClelland and Stewart.

Faucher, Albert, and Maurice Lamontagne
1953   "History of Industrial Development." In Rioux and Martin, eds., *French Canadian Society* (1964). Toronto: McClelland and Stewart.

Ferland, Jean-Baptiste
1861   *Cours d'histoire du Canada.* Montréal.

Fortin, Gérald
1971   *La fin d'un règne.* Montréal: HMH.

Frégault, Guy
1968   *Le XVIIIe siècle canadien.* Montréal. HMH.

Frégault, Guy, and Marcel Trudel
1963   *Histoire du Canada par les textes.* Montréal: Fides.

Garigue, Philippe
1956   "French-Canadian Kinship and Urban Life." In Rioux and Martin, eds., *French Canadian Society* (1964). Toronto: McClelland and Stewart.

Grier, William H., and Price M. Cobbs
1968   *Black Rage.* New York: Bantam.

Groulx, Lionel
1956   *L'appel de la race.* Montréal: Fides.
1960   *Histoire du Canada français.* Montréal: Fides.

Harvey, Jean-Charles
1962   *Pourquoi je suis antiséparatiste.* Montréal: Les Editions de l'Homme.

Harvey, Vincent, O. P., *et al.*
1961   *L'église et le Québec.* Montréal: Editions du Jour.

Hébert, Jacques
1963   *J'accuse les assassine de Coffin.* Montréal: Editions du Jour.

Hémon, Louis
1924   *Maria Chapdelaine.* Montréal: Fides.

Henripin, Jacques
1954   *La population canadienne an début du XVIIIe siècle.* Paris: Publications de l'Institut National d'Etudes Demographiques.
1957   "From Acceptance of Nature to Control: The Demography of the French Canadians Since the Seventeenth Century." *The Canadian Journal of Economics and Political Science* 23(1):10–19.

1960   "Aspects démographiques." In Wade, ed., *Canadian dualism/La dualité canadienne*. Toronto: University of Toronto Press.

Hughes, Everett C.
1943   *French Canada in Transition*. Chicago: University of Chicago Press.

Jansen, William H.
1959   "The Esoteric-Exoteric Factor in Folklore." In Alan Dundes, *The Study of Folklore*. Englewood Cliffs: Prentice-Hall.

Johnson, Daniel
1965   *Egalité ou indépendance*. Montréal: Les Editions de l'Homme.

Kennedy, W. P. M.
1930   *Statutes, Treaties, and Documents of the Canadian Constitution*, second edition. Toronto: Oxford University Press.

Keyfitz, Nathan
1960   "Some Demographic aspects of French-English Relations in Canada." In Wade, ed., *Canadian Dualism/La dualité Canadienne*. Toronto: University of Toronto Press.

Lacoste, Yvon
1966   *Une étude des statistiques des marriages inter-ethniques de Montréal pour les années 1951 et 1962*. Unpublished master's thesis. Montréal: Université de Montréal.

Lanctôt, Gustave
1941   *Les Canadians français et leurs voisins du sud*. Montréal: Editions Bernard Valiquette.

Landry, Louis
1969   *... et l'assimilation pourquoi pas?* Ottawa: Les Presses Libres.

Laporte, Pierre
1960   *The True Face of Duplessis*. Montréal: Harvest House.

Laurendeau, André
1962   *La crise de la conscription*. Montréal: Editions du Jour.
1970   *Ces choses qui nous arrivent*. Montréal: HMH.

Laurin, Camille
1970   *Ma traversée du Québec*. Montréal: Editions du Jour.

Lazure, Jacques
1970   *La jeunesse du Québec en révolution*. Montréal: Les Presses de l'Université du Québec.

LeBlanc, Emery
1963   *Les Acadiens: La tentative de génocide d'un peuple*. Montréal: Les Editions de l'Homme.

Lessard, Marc-André, et Jean-Paul Montminy
1967   *L'urbanization de la société canadienne-française*. Québec: Les Presses de l'Université Laval.

Lévesque, René
   1968   Option Québec. Montréal: Les Editions de l'Homme.
   1970   Présentation. In La solution: le programme du Parti Québécois.
          Montréal: Editions du Jour.
   1976   "For an Independent Québec." Foreign Affairs 54(4):734-744.

Lewis, Oscar
   1961   The Children of Sanchez. New York: Random House.
   1965   La Vida. New York: Random House.

Lieberson, Stanley
   1970   Language and Ethnic Relations in Canada. Toronto: John Wiley
          and Sons.

Liebow, Elliot
   1967   Tally's Corner: A Study of Negro Streetcorner Men. Boston:
          Little, Brown and Company.

Maheu, Pierre
   1964   "En guise d'introduction." In Montréal, la ville des autres. Parti
          Pris, numéro spécial, 2, 4:10-20.

Mailhiot, Bernard
   1963   "La psychologie des relations inter-ethniques à Montréal." In Con-
          tributions a l'étude des sciences de l'homme. Montréal.

Masters, D. C.
   1967   "The English Communities in Winnipeg and in the Eastern Town-
          ships." In Wade, ed., Regionalism in the Canadian Community
          (1867-1967). Toronto: University of Toronto Press.

Melançon, Jacques
   1956   "Retard de croissance de l'entreprise canadien-français." Actualité
          économique 31:503-522.

Miner, Horace
   1939   St. Denis: A French-Canadian Parish. Chicago: University of Chi-
          cago Press.

Mitchell, J. Clyde
   1969   Social Networks in Urban Situations. Manchester: Manchester
          University Press.

Morf, Gustave
   1970   Le terrorisme québécois. Montréal: Les Editions de l'Homme.

Murrow, Casey
   1968   Henri Bourassa and French-Canadian Nationalism. Montréal:
          Harvest House.

Myers, Hugh
   1964   The Quebec revolution. Montréal: Harvest House.

Naud, Leonce
    1972 "Ottawa prépare-t-il un autre Labrador dans le Nouveau-Québec?"
          Le Devoir, 11 février 1972:5.

Odum, Eugene P.
    1963 *Ecology*. New York: Holt, Rinehart, and Winston.

Papineau, Louis-Joseph
    1827 *Addresse à tous les électeurs du Bas-Canada*. Montréal: Réédition
          Québec (1968).
    1839 *Histoire de l'insurrection du Canada en réfutation du rapport de
          Lord Durham*. Montréal: Réédition Québec.

Parti Québécois
    1970 *La solution*. Montréal: Editions du Jour.

Pelletier, Gérard
    1971 *La crise d'octobre*. Montréal: Editions du Jour.

Piotte, Jean-Marc
    1971 "Jour après jour." In Piotte, *et al.*, eds., *Québec Occupé*. Montréal:
          Parti Pris.

Porter, John
    1967 *Canadian Social Structure: A Statistical Profile*. Toronto: McClel-
          land and Stewart.

Proulx, L'Abbé Louis
    1837 *Défense du mandement de Mgr. l'évêque de Montréal*. Montréal:
          Réédition Québec (1968).

Rameau, E.
    1859 *Les français en Amérique*. Paris: A. Jouby.

Reid, Allana
    1945 *The Importance of the Town of Québec (1608-1703)*. Unpub-
          lished master's thesis. Montréal: McGill University.

Report of the Gendron Commission (Report of the Commission of Inquiry
on the Position of the French Language and on Language Rights in Québec)
    1972 *Book I: The Language of Work*. Québec: L'Editeur Officiel de
          Québec.
    1972 *Book II: Language Rights*. Québec: L'Editeur Officiel de Québec.
    1972 *Book III: The Ethnic Groups*. Québec: L'Editeur Officiel de
          Québec.

Richard, Jean-Jules
    1971 *Le feu dans l'amiante*. Montréal: Réédition Québec.

Rioux, Marcel
    1959 "Kinship Recognition and Urbanization in French Canada." In
          Rioux and Martin, eds., *French Canadian Society*. Toronto: Mc-
          Clelland and Stewart (1964).

Rioux, Marcel (cont'd.)
    1965   "Conscience Ethnique et conscience de classe au Québec." *Recherches Sociographiques*, 6, 1:23–32.
    1969   *La question du Québec*. Paris: Seghers.

Ross, Aileen D.
    1941   *The French and English Social Elite of Montréal*. Unpublished master's thesis. Chicago: University of Chicago.

Royal Commission on Bilingualism and Biculturalism
    1965   *A Preliminary Report*. Ottawa: Queen's Printer.
    1967   *General Introduction: The Official Languages* (Vol. 1). Ottawa: The Queen's Printer.
    1968   *Education* (vol. 2). Ottawa: The Queen's Printer.
    1969   *The Work World: Socio-Economic Status* (part one), *The Federal Government* (part two), (vol. 3). Ottawa: The Queen's Printer.
    1969   *The Cultural Contribution of the Other Ethnic Groups* (vol. 4). Ottawa: The Queen's Printer.
    1970   *The Federal Capital* (vol. 5). Ottawa: The Queen's Printer.
    1970   *Voluntary Associations* (vol. 6). Ottawa: The Queen's Printer.

Rumilly, Robert
    1940   *Histoire de la province de Québec*, vol. 1. Montréal: Fides (1971).

Ryan, Claude, ed.
    1971   *La Québec qui se fait*. Montréal: Editions HMH.

Salone, Emile
    n.d.   *Le colonization de la Nouvelle France*. Paris: Librarie Orientale et Américaine.

Savoie, Claude
    1963   *Le véritable histoire du F.L.Q.* Montréal: Editions du Jour.

Sloan, Thomas
    1965   *Une révolution tranquille?* M. Van Schendel., trans. Montréal: Editions HMH.

Smiley, Donald V.
    1963   *The Rowell-Sirois Report*, Book 1. Toronto: McClelland and Stewart.

Smith, Bernard
    1970   *Le coup d'état du 29 avril*. Montréal: Editions Actualité.

Stuebing, Douglas, *et al.*
    1969   *Trudeau, l'homme de demain*. Hélène Gagnon, trans. Montréal: HMH.

Taylor, Norman W.
    1964   "The French-Canadian Industrial Entrepreneur and his Social Environment." In Rioux and Martin, eds., *French Canadian Society*. Toronto: McClelland and Stewart.

Thwaites, Reuben G., ed.
    1905   *New Voyages to North-America by the Baron de Lahoutan* (orig. 1703). Chicago: A. C. McClurg & Co.

Trait, Jean-Claude
1970 *FLQ 70: Offensive d'automne.* Montréal: Les Editions de l'Homme.

Tremblay, Roderique
1970 *Indépendance et marché commun Québec-Etats-Unis.* Montréal: Editions du Jour.

Trudeau, Pierre Elliot
1956 "La province de Québec au moment de la grève." In P. E. Trudeau, ed., *Le grève de l'amiante.* Montréal.
1967 *Le fédéralisme et la société canadienne-française.* Montréal: HMH.

Trudeau, Pierre Elliot, *et al.*
1956 *La grève de l'amiante.* Montréal.

Turenne, Augustin
1962 *Petit dictionnaire du "joual" au français.* Montréal: Les Editions de l'Homme.

Turi, Guiseppe
1971 *Une culture appelée québécoise.* Montréal: Les Editions de l'Homme.

Vadeboncoeur, Pierre
1970 *La dernière heure et la première.* Montréal: Parti Pris.

Vallières, Pierre
1968 *Nègres blancs d'Amérique: Autobiographie précoçe d'un "terroriste" québécois.* Montréal: Parti Pris.

Voisine, Nive
1971 *Histoire de l'Eglise catholique qu Québec (1608-1970).* Montréal: Fides.

Voltaire
1934 *Candide.* George Havens, ed. New York: Holt, Rinehart and Winston.

Wade, Mason
1964 *The French-Canadian Outlook.* Toronto: McClelland and Stewart.
1968 *The French Canadians, 1760-1967* (2 vols.). Toronto: Macmillan.

Wagley, Charles, and Marvin Harris
1958 "The French Canadians." In *Minorities in the New World.* New York: Columbia University Press.

Warner, W. Lloyd
1936 "American Caste and Class." *American Journal of Sociology* 42:234-37.

Warner, W. Lloyd, *et al.*
1963 *Yankee City.* New Haven: Yale University Press.

Whyte, William F.
1943 *Street Corner Society.* Chicago: University of Chicago Press.

INDEX